THE EDITOR AND THE REPUBLIC

THE EDITOR AND
THE REPUBLIC

Papers and
Addresses of
William Watts Ball

Edited by
ANTHONY HARRIGAN

Chapel Hill

THE UNIVERSITY OF NORTH CAROLINA PRESS

CONTENTS

INTRODUCTION

WILLIAM WATTS BALL said, "If I have a principle in this calling, it is that the personality of the newspaperman should be suppressed, the ego be exorcised." This is the principle, and being a man who believed in the supreme importance of principle, he abided by it during his sixty-two years in the newspaper profession. The suppression of personality was his approach throughout a long and significant career. It was the manner of the man—elevation of principle and not of any personal quality.

Yet for Americans at large, students of our history and political development, this reluctance to advertise himself was unfortunate. William Watts Ball was a great editor in the old tradition. He was a believer in the verities of the old Republic as it was in the days before 1860 when corruption in government was not prevalent. He was bred out of the tradition of Robert Y. Hayne and John C. Calhoun, the tradition of devotion to the states and to the Republic.

In this day of Gallup-poll studies of reading tastes and the application of assembly-line methods to publishing operations the editors of American dailies lack the influence and force their predecessors enjoyed. What is happening is that newspapers are coming out of the pre-corporate, pre-managerial era and cost accountants, personnel managers, promotion experts and specialists in entertainment merchandise are impinging on the domain of editors, the strong individuals who once imposed their personalities on their newspapers and *were* their newspapers in the mind of the public.

This is not to say that newspapers where the owners resist streamlining which is accomplished at the expense of integrity and social responsibility do not exist, for such papers as are in the hands of family dynasties often manifest a resistance to managerial reorganization on Big Business lines. That there is an irreplaceable handicraft element in the process of publishing a newspaper is recognized by enlightened owners. Nevertheless the pressure exerted against the owners is very strong inasmuch as managers tend to deplore editorial controversy which may result in lowered circulation. Another black mark for the editorial page, in the eyes of the business office, is the fact that the editorial page is not directly revenue producing. Consequently one finds managerial opposition (I specifically exclude owners) to the role of an editor as the bold and enlightened instrument of the publisher's will. And, therefore, many editors today never contaminate their minds with radical ideas—ideas that go to the root of things, that is—though the ideas be radically conservative as were those of William Watts Ball.

Ball until the time of his death October 14, 1952, wrote incisively, boldly. His writing was unafraid. He wrote on subjects taboo in the American press and continually delivered himself of unpopular opinions. He was the gadfly of the press in his native state of South Carolina, and more than one demagog suffered from the power of his editorials. That he was known and respected among editors and editorialists of courage, among historians of the South such as Margaret Coit and Gerald W. Johnson, and by men of affairs such as Bernard Baruch is not surprising. Nevertheless, he was for the most part unknown to the intelligent men and women in the great states of the Republic. These readers hunger for strong thinking. Little but meaningless prattle and "canned" opinion is found in too many newspapers. Strong voices are not often heard in this land. Strong voices are few and far between because of organized pressure groups. Yet, as William Watts Ball said, "A newspaper, be it the *Thunderer* in a great city or a mousey country weekly, is a person, a voice, and must tell the truth, speaking it audibly, even as John Smith must and does if he is an honest man. If he, the editor, be required to write that which he does not believe, he should resign. No man should hire himself to lie for another."

It is deplorable that in the Republic, wherein thousands of meaningless and trivial tomes reach the shelves of the booksellers, the publication of these papers and addresses has not been accomplished prior to this occasion. True, Ball's personal recollections of South Carolina's surrender to democracy have been made available in book form. But none of this powerful thinker's political and social essays is to be had.

It is likely that these papers and addresses will give rise to irritation on the part of a certain class of readers. It is inevitable. A writer who thinks in a bold fashion cannot cater to the likes and dislikes of the moment. Not everyone can be pleased when one's intention is to utter truths. And our own day is a heel-to-toe, fantastically cautious epoch. It fears excess, is terrified of zeal, and dreads that it will be dubbed out-of-step in the illusory march of history. This generation, this epoch, this Republic—is in dire need of a stirring. It is William Watts Ball's writing that can stir Americans who live complacently with the liberal orthodoxy. His work speaks eloquently of the role of the editor in relation to the fate of the Republic.

II

The characteristic bent of his mind was acquired, William Watts Ball said, from his ancestry and from the old South Carolina College. He was born in Laurens, in upcountry South Carolina, December 9, 1868, eight years before the carpetbagger rule of South Carolina came to an end. His father, Beaufort Watts Ball, whom he called "the Colonel," onetime slaveowner and Confederate officer, was a prominent lawyer, a figure in politics, and a friend of the leading South Carolinians of the day. Hence young William Watts Ball was acquainted with leaders from his earliest youth. His mother, Eliza Watts Ball, was a woman of powerful intellect and practical instincts. The Balls and the Wattses were descended from the people who had come down into the Carolinas from Virginia (the Balls from Culpepper) in the years before the Revolution when the tobacco lands were declining in fertility. The first Ball immigrant was styled "Gentleman" according to the custom of the old Dominion. He owned one slave in 1800 and worked with his hands.

William Watts Ball has made explicit that his people laid no claim to aristocracy. They were landowners, slaveowners. In the interior of South Carolina, in the upcountry, the gradations between the "one-horse farmer" and the wealthy landlord were, in

Mr. Ball's phrase, "gentle and many." "If," he observed, "we said we were Bourbons, it was a derisive answer to the demagogues who plied the term to us, their political opponents, first."

The future editor was raised by a father and kinsmen, former Confederate soldiers, who were in their prime when he was in his boyhood and young manhood. They were educated men, tested men. He described this time as having the atmosphere of the historic South Carolina where standards existed—high standards of honesty, intellectual as well as moral. His father had graduated from the South Carolina College in 1851. A powerful tradition operated upon William Watts Ball from the first day he saw the light in that big frame house set in a grove of oaks near the old upcountry town of Laurens.

III

William Watts Ball inherited his code. Fortunately, to the precepts given at home within the circle of his kin was added an excellent education at the old South Carolina College. He entered this institution in the graduating class of 1887, the year that it reopened as a liberal arts college. In those days it was a great school. The professors were men of real intellectual distinction and strong character. The college was still independent; the trustees were not interfered with in the performance of their duties. He said that in college he was always more or less a rebel; he was, always, "against the government." He was, he asserted, not with the law-abiding crowd that always held up the hands of the executive. In the college one of the strong influences on him was that of the Reverend J. W. Alexander, professor of moral philosophy. He was a straight-out thinker and told his students, impressed upon them, the necessity of holding firm to their convictions. He instructed his students in the importance of intellectual courage. He taught the boys to think for themselves. The professor whom William Watts Ball knew best of all was R. Means Davis, a friend of his father, who was the professor of history and political science. The textbook employed in this professor's courses was John Stuart Mill's *Political Economy*. That volume had a great influence on the future editor. He asserted that it got into his system. Another of Ball's texts, one employed by the Reverend Doctor Alexander, was Herbert Spencer's *Data of Ethics*.

IV

Following his graduation at the age of eighteen and a half, he taught school for four months at Johnston near Edgefield, South Carolina. Later, in 1888, he did postgraduate work at the South Carolina College, paying his expenses by teaching in the public schools. He hoped to obtain both the M. A. and the law degree. However, he was forced to discontinue his plan of working toward the two degrees at the same time. Hence there was nothing for the young man to do but study law, which he did. In May, 1890, he was admitted to the practice of law in the state. Then his father managed to find the money to send him to John B. Minor's famous summer law school at the University of Virginia.

During that summer of study William Watts Ball was offered the Laurens *Advertiser*, a weekly newspaper. He decided to purchase the newspaper, paying $1,500 for the property. It was his belief that he could practice law and edit a newspaper at the same time. Had he entered the profession of law in a serious way he might well have achieved a high place. His cousin Richard C. Watts came to be Chief Justice of South Carolina.

Three and a half years after he first commenced to wrestle with the problems of a country weekly he moved to the city of Columbia, capital of South Carolina, where he edited the Columbia *Journal*. This newspaper did not prove to be a financial success, and Ball and his business associate discontinued publication, paying subscribers for the unpublished part of their subscriptions. He also was engaged in free lance work, sending news stories to the New York *World*, the New York *Herald*, several Chicago newspapers, one Philadelphia newspaper, and newspapers in a number of other cities. The news gathering associations were not completely formed at this time, and newspaper men in communities across the country wired in stories to the leading newspapers. Ball was earning a good living from this free lance newspaper work when he was called, at the age of twenty-six, to the editorship of the recently established Charleston *Evening Post*. He continued as editor of this newspaper until it was in a sound and solvent state. His next move, in February, 1897, was to the Greenville *News* where he served as editor. In June, 1898, he returned to Laurens and practiced law for a time, appearing in court on a number of occasions. Indeed this was a time of decision, as both law and journalism loomed as possible careers.

In 1898 he spent three or four months in Philadelphia where he served on the news staff of the Philadelphia *Press*. This proved to be a splendid postgraduate education in newspaper work. In 1899 he applied for a position as city editor of the Jacksonville *Times-Union and Citizen* and secured it. It is interesting to note that he served in this position during the great Jacksonville fire of 1901 that obliterated 456 acres of the old Florida city.

In 1902 William Watts Ball returned to Laurens because of his father's illness. Then in 1903, when Narciso G. Gonzales, editor of *The State*, was assassinated, Ball offered his assistance to that paper in the emergency. Ambrose Elliott Gonzales, brother of the deceased editor, asked Ball to handle the trial of the assassin, who was James H. Tillman, lieutenant-governor of South Carolina. Ball wrote that never in South Carolina was there such a gang of scoundrels and ruffians assembled as gathered at the trial of Tillman. At this trial Ball did such a magnificent job of reporting that his reputation in the state was established. However, he said that the reporting he did was abysmal, inasmuch as he acted as prosecuting officer in his stories to the newspaper. After the trial (Tillman was acquitted) Ball received offers from *The State* and the *News and Courier*, the two leading newspapers in South Carolina. After six months on *The State* (in 1904) as news editor, he removed to Charleston where he served as assistant editor of the *News and Courier* until 1909. Ball considered Ambrose Gonzales the greatest man for whom he ever worked, or with whom he was associated. He termed him his patron, if not his patron saint. In 1909 Gonzales offered him the position of managing editor on *The State*. He accepted. In 1913 President Wilson named W. E. Gonzales, editor of *The State*, United States Minister to Cuba. Ball, who was serving as managing editor, was appointed editor. He served as editor of *The State* for ten years, until Gonzales returned from abroad and resumed control of the family property. In the same year that Gonzales took up the editorial duties, William Watts Ball, without solicitation, was elected to the chair of journalism at the University of South Carolina. He served as the first Dean of Journalism. He remained at the University from 1923 to 1927, at which time he was offered the editorship of the *News and Courier*.

Ball was in his fifty-ninth year when he came in June, 1927, to the *News and Courier*, but despite this he served longer than any previous editor.

v

Thus at the age of fifty-nine William Watts Ball entered upon a remarkably productive and influential period as an editor. The excellence of his work in Columbia was matched by his brilliant service as editor of the *News and Courier* in the historic city of Charleston. As one South Carolina newspaper said when he was named editor:

"Dr. W. W. Ball has accepted the editorship of the *News and Courier*. No wooer and wooed in a matrimonial alliance, ever matched up any better. The traditions of the one and the training of the other will always keep the couple out of the divorce courts."

The *News and Courier* (the *Courier* had been established in 1803 and, hence, was the oldest daily in the South) had been purchased by The Evening Post Company in 1926. At the time of Ball's coming to Charleston in 1927 the publisher was Robert Manigault, son of the Arthur Manigault who had insured the solvency of the *Evening Post* in 1895 when Ball was editor. With the *News and Courier*, as with *The State*, Ball asserted that he was singularly fortunate. In fact, he affirmed that he had a completely free hand under the management of the Manigault and Gonzales families.

The question of the degree of freedom he enjoyed as editor came into sharp focus in 1940 when Ball's opposition to the Santee-Cooper power project in South Carolina resulted, a number of local politicians alleged, in the removal from the city of certain federal offices. A delegation from the Charleston Retail Merchants Association called on the publisher and demanded that he take action regarding Ball's policies. The publisher referred the delegation to Ball, saying that he had nothing to do with editorial decisions and that it was a matter properly within the realm of the editor. In short, the publisher, Robert Manigault, gave full support to his editor. Ball gave the delegation a polite hearing, and then proceeded in the execution of his editorial policy. He wrote in the editorial columns his own view of the situation at hand. "Is it expected and demanded that a newspaper calling itself honest should stand by in silence, lest some of its friends suffer loss by not sharing in extravagant and wasteful spending of public money by genial politicians? . . . If the editor of the *News and Courier* is an obstacle to Charleston, a thorn in its flesh, he is prepared at a moment's notice, to remove himself. He is not prepared to move from his opinion." It is this bold and honest policy that caused the *News and Courier*, under William Watts Ball's editorial direction, in the words of the Birmingham, Alabama, *Age-Herald*, to be " . . . read, marked, learned and inwardly digested by discerning scribblers in countless sanctums."

It is impossible to think of Ball's career as editor of the *News and Courier* without measuring his opposition to the political, economic, and social revolution which has taken place in the United States under the name of the New Deal and that of the Fair Deal. From almost the very beginning of Roosevelt's administration, Ball was in opposition to those Rooseveltian policies that he regarded as inimical to our republican form of government and the traditions of personal resourcefulness that he considered the foundation of society on this side of the Atlantic—the traditions that constitute our heritage as a people.

He was an advocate of states' rights. But, so are some persons whose motives are neither noble nor just. William Watts Ball was an American conservative because his first passion was political liberty and because he did not hold with various democratic dogmas which cancel out the importance of the states. His states' rights views and attendant ideas had a philosophical, a historical basis. They did not stem from the desire to exploit any race, monopolize any industry, or give an unwarranted special privilege to any class. He understood full well that not all the covetous individuals are on the leftist side. He said that there "always has been the struggle, the battle, between the conservatives, the defenders of John Doe's freedom, and the money-getters, the greedy, the covetous. That is the world battle this day."

Day in and day out, year in and year out, for many decades William Watts Ball hammered out the structure of his political philosophy, a conservative philosophy. Ball's position was clear and simple. He dreaded kakistocracy—rule by the worst class; change for the sake of change; a superstitious attitude towards the paraphernalia of the democratic process; the lack of respect for ancestral wisdom; the bundle of impudent materialist claims which pass for human rights in our time; Utopian fancies of economic reorganization; the lust for absolute equality; dependence upon professional politicians who thrive on flattery of the base and ignorant. His fundamental principles were love of liberty; jealousy of Federal encroachment on the rights of the states; a dread of the unfit and irresponsible participating in political decisions; a faith in property as the foundation of liberty.

An extremely valuable product of his career is *The State That Forgot*. This book is the definitive chronicle of his own early life. It is a splendid portrait of a troubled era that evoked the best in the old aristocracy (the term means rule by the best and as here used has none of the flavor of snobbery) of both Low-Country and Up-Country South Carolina. In this book is a deeply pessimistic view of the future of South Carolina and, by implication, the future of the Republic.

Throughout his career as an editor Ball fought the demagogues, the uncouth, the gallus-snapping leaders of the desperately ignorant, and the smooth city demagogues and rascally politicians who often bore fine old names and who mouthed high-sounding phrases but who were as evil and as dangerous to the body politic as their rougher brethren. *The State That Forgot* gained for William Watts Ball a measure of the national recognition that he deserved and that he, unlike some less talented editors and writers, never sought. Henry Steele Commager, the historian, in reviewing *The State That Forgot*, wrote: "Mr. Ball has witnessed the complete degradation of the democratic dogma. ... The editor of the conservative Charleston *News and Courier*, he is at once one of the most distinguished and most intelligent citizens of a state less deficient in such citizens than the *American Mercury* would have us believe."

VI

This introduction, however, is not the place to give the full story of William Watts Ball's crusading career as an editor. That is part and parcel of a biography. The record itself is to be found in the files of the *News and Courier* and *The State*, in the thousands of columns of editorial matter he prepared for publication.

Ball was an intense and active editorial worker, and his writing stood out from the writings of his editorial associates. The manner of expression was as distinctive as the man himself. From the first he was known as a paragrapher. Several years ago a New Zealand newspaper correspondent interviewed Ball. Upon returning to his native land he wrote that "He (Ball) has been reared on the classics and spoke with the incisiveness and vigour of other and more robust days." Or, as one South Carolinian aptly described the situation: "Dr. Ball warns against calling his name, instead of the *News and Courier*, when referring to the editorial columns. It is a difficult process to do it. He never takes a vacation that we do not discover it, without being told. He is what they call a *sui generis*."

The principal characteristic of his long career as an editor of a daily newspaper was his sense of duty to the public, to the thinking element, that is—for the majority of men, in his view, do not think, never have. His basic policy as an editor, his personal belief, can be found in an article he wrote in the Laurens *Advertiser* on January 21, 1903, following the assassination of Narciso G. Gonzales by "a friend of the people": "Mr. Gonzales believed in 'personal journalism.' His creed called upon him to denounce meanness, vice and wrong, not in abstract, but in the persons of the doers. In discussing public men he thought of them as public figures. Who they were or what counted nothing with him, it was their relationship to his policy and that policy was simply a high conception of the public good of his people. . . . His discernment of sham and fraud and trickery and dishonor was keen and so for the 12 years of *The State's* life he has stood guard and earned the hate and inspired the fear of the vile in South Carolina. . . . If a bad man comes to the surface and honor and safety of the state is imperiled, what guardian, what protection have the great people who make the state unless it be an unterrified press?"

If one substitutes the name of William Watts Ball for that of Gonzales it is as true. And inasmuch as he believed in an unterrified press, he was not terrorized by the niceties and conventions of the American newspaper profession that often, nearly always in our epoch, forbid discussion of the faults of the press, its failures, its weaknesses. Ball realized (he did so long ago) that a considerable number of newspapers are in the thralldom of the business management. It is not that the newspapers grant special favors to advertisers in the form of retouching or slanting of news. The fault is that editors have been pressured into allowing their pages to become overloaded with junk, with syndicated nonsense, gossip, recipes, claptrap medical advice. The cutting edge of many newspapers has been blunted. William Watts Ball asserted that many editors edit by the device of columnists, thereby avoiding responsibility for views set forth in their papers.

At the root of the trouble with American newspapers is the enormous financial interest in a modern publishing organization. This was his opinion. Newspapers are great properties involving millions of dollars. Rare is the individual in our time who is able to establish a newspaper with his own means. And it is a fact that corporations guided by managerial boards do not, cannot, have the singleness of mind and the integrity of belief of an individual owner. However, Ball believed that with changes in modes of printing, with a lessening of basic costs, will come a renewal of independence, a return to the freedom of the early days. But, so it should be acknowledged—Ball said of today's conditions that never in his recollection had the American press been so stifled as at the present. As for the newspaper chains, he knew full well that they wear their chains.

This bold thinking, bold expression in the fight for true freedom of the press was only a part of his struggle in the cause of individualism, the cause he considered the major struggle in the world today. He asked: "Is man an individual or a particle in the mass?" He answered: "If a man can be jelled, massed, then the Russians are right. But, in my opinion, men are individuals, each a little god." He added, though, that "Each man should worship and give praise to a Supreme Being." It was William Watts Ball's belief that if each man be an asserting voice he will find that voice through the press.

VII

Ball said of himself that he was a man of irregular habits. However, one suspects that the truth is that he was first and last a writer and hence the physical environment was not a matter of prime concern to him. Towards the end of his days his office in the modernistic *News and Courier* building was a quarter peculiarly his own. There was a high-backed plantation-type writing desk. Ordinarily, it was littered with old newspapers, magazines, clippings from journals, galley proofs, and pieces of editorial copy in one or another stage of composition. His workroom in the eighteenth-century house in which he resided on Water Street one block distant from High Battery was a jumble of books (everything from an early edition of Edmund Burke's *Works* to *Southern Politics In State And Nation* by V. O. Key, Jr.), old filing cabinets, scrap books with the record of his newspaper career in the nineties, letters and notes from friends and fellow newspapermen, and one of the finest collections of rare Caroliniana in any private library. And all these books and papers were in the hopeless but productive disarray characteristic of a writer's private realm.

It was the custom of Ball to write at his office in the morning. In the evening he would retire to his workroom to type a short piece of editorial copy or to make an entry in the diary he kept from 1916 on.

Ball was attired in the manner of a gentleman of his generation. It was his custom to wear suits of a dark gray color and a short black bow tie. That he was as distinctive in appearance as he was in manner of expression is not a case of overstatement. He was of middle height and solid framed. Visitors to his office at the *News and Courier* usually went away with the image of him at his desk, leaning back in a swivel chair, cold pipe in his right hand, while he told one of his superb, involved stories of South Carolina. His features were extraordinarily active and mobile. It was a habit of his to close his eyes while he searched his memory for a word or the precise phrasing employed by a political acquaintance of many years gone by, speaking in a slow and reminiscent manner, rubbing his hand down across the hair at the back of his head, and, suddenly, leaning forward in his chair to pronounce with power and vigor his conviction regarding the subject under discussion—his eyes burning a hole into the skull of his questioner. The expressions that crossed his features were varied. Sternness and the ruthlessness of conviction alternated with gentleness and great good humor. There was in his entire manner as a person, intense concentration, remarkable individuality. Positive as were his views and strict his political philosophy, in his personal relations Ball manifested the greatest warmth and courtesy. To his staffers he was a beloved chief who never had a pompous or dictatorial moment.

For many a year Ball was a legend in South Carolina and among editors throughout the South. There are innumerable stories of "Billy" Ball, stories of his amazing memory in recollecting some happening of Reconstruction days; of his salty remarks concerning what he dubbed "The Office Holding Industry"; of the several boxes of matches he used in vain attempts to light his pipe between sentences; of his willingness to print in the "Letters to the Editor" column of the *News and Courier* the most derogatory remarks concerning his ideas, his style, his person. These stories are mentioned because the stories told about a man are, in their way, as revealing as the facts set down in an accurate manner.

VIII

The manner of man William Watts Ball was and the nature of his ideas on public questions for many years past were not such as would bring him prominently into the view of the country at large. The harvest of publicity, the glittering edifice of a national reputation is in the majority of cases the property of those who own or manage vast publishing organizations (size in a newspaper is not indicative of virtue) or those editors who are in the vanguard of the national administration.

This is all by way of explaining the prevailing state of ignorance, on the part of the public, concerning one of the most independent newspapermen and political writers in the United States.

William Watts Ball was called a reactionary. A writer for the *Nation* dubbed him that "irascible and autocratic editor." One reconstructed South Carolina newspaper said in the course of an editorial, "At Charleston, S. C., where Dr. Ball and chronic dyspepsia run together to form the *News and Courier*...." These charges were hurled at him many times. But his critics and those who hated him for his frankness and brilliance (he was not beloved of any set of politicians) do not seem to realize that he was proud to be in reaction against the evil and ruinous policies of the recent decades.

In this far from candid age in which we live there are few editors who will admit to conservatism. This was not so in the case of William Watts Ball. He was noted as much for his candor as his probity. He was not ashamed to admit that he did not subscribe to the popular orthodoxy. He was critical of the press and its pretense of being the "voice of the people," its boast of complete independence. He was the arch-opponent, in South Carolina, of the liberal theories of the national administration. He was straightout in his belief in political conservatism. Consequently he did not harvest a crop of the canned and prefabricated, the engineered publicity that is the lot of public figures in our day.

In his long career Ball managed to speak unpleasant truths regarding many an influential group in the State and the Republic. Though a onetime owner of shares in cotton mills, he recorded in his diary that he approved of the mill hands organizing into unions. Known as a determined opponent of the integration of the races, he recognized that the Negroes in South Carolina have often received no more than a farmer's mule—fodder and shelter. He did not let the Johnny-come-lately states' rights advocates forget that they were faithful lackeys of the national administration in the days when it was politically profitable to be a Roosevelt servitor.

His was a career that did not win him the praise of politicians nor the homage of the newspaper and magazine industry in this day wherein the press is an outlet for organizational publicity. Organized capital, organized labor and organized office-holding did not manifest any great love for this man who held to independence and acknowledged no master in Washington, Wall Street, or the headquarters of the labor unions. Nor was he a slave to Party. He was a gold Democrat who participated in the Palmer-Buckner "bolt."

As the editor of a Southern newspaper commented when Ball retired as editor of the *News and Courier* in 1951, "Those who have read Mr. Ball's pithy, pungent editorials have always had the highest regard for his independence of thought. He is a journalist of the old school who writes what he thinks, and the reader knows instinctively that he takes dictation from no other source except his own conscience."

Therefore, as one of the few truly independent editorialists of recent times, it is important that his views regarding the American Republic be available in permanent form. This Republic is moving toward a great crisis, and the writings of William Watts Ball will assist in enabling us to see far and clear. The papers and addresses presented in this volume are not drawn from the editorial columns of newspapers. They are documents he prepared on special occasions. They indicate the scope and range, as well as the force and individual quality of the thought of William Watts Ball. This book presents him in a more formal fashion as an American thinker, a thinker who related his activities as an editor to the living traditions of the old Republic as ordained and shaped by our forebears in this land.

It is a high honor to share in the ingathering of the papers and addresses of the late William Watts Ball, to assist in the task of bringing his ideas and individual viewpoint before a new audience. In this great conservative's writing is the key to a sound understanding of the American place in history—our history, past, present, and future.

ANTHONY HARRIGAN

Charleston, South Carolina
February 1, 1954

THE EDITOR AND THE REPUBLIC

THE INDUSTRIAL REVOLUTION IN SOUTH CAROLINA

(1911)

"The Industrial Revolution in South Carolina" was published during William Watts Ball's term of service as managing editor of *The State*, Columbia, S.C. It was prepared for delivery before the South Carolina Press Association meeting in the summer of 1910 and is reprinted with permission from *The Sewanee Review* (April, 1911), Vol. XIX, No. 2, 129-37.

IF the Southern states have been, by comparison with their northern sisters, backward in the industries, if their people have not amassed money rapidly and in huge quantities, and if after more than a century and a third of life as a part of the American republic they are dependent upon other sections in large measure for capital to develop their natural resources, it is at least to be said that they have been singularly free from class conflicts. In the American states commonly called rich and prosperous in a sense not yet applicable to those of the South—where, undoubtedly, African slavery was an insuperable obstacle to general industrial advance so long as it lasted—clashes between laborers and capitalists have been frequent and bloody. In the "white" states, where the wage-earners have been and are numerous and widely separated from the relatively small number of wealthy employers, industrial jealousies and contentions have been and are incessant and often violent, and apparently they grow in number and in menace. In the South, the white people are racially homogeneous to a degree; in spite of some inevitable social differences, there is much that is common to all Southern white men, and their poverty, the misfortunes they have suffered and the dangers that they have had to face have welded them together and saved them from the cruel dissensions usually incident to material progress under competitive conditions. Shall this immunity continue? As the sun of a new day rises to unfold the clear prospect of a splendid prosperity, is it possible that it may be enjoyed without the attending miseries of class divisions that so often have made prosperity unreal elsewhere? With strikes of weekly or daily occurrence in one or another part of the North to admonish the people of the dangers of what we carelessly call "prosperity," can they do nothing to ward them off, or must they actually run to meet them and beckon them to enter? Is it not possible for the South to furnish the world with the spectacle of prosperity that is not wholly selfish and unequal as between man and man? Surely, such questions seem worthy for men to ponder even if any other than the replies suggested by unhappy human experience appear quixotic, and that is my excuse for casually reviewing the industrial and political changes that have taken place in South Carolina during the last twenty-five years and which substantially have been paralleled in most of the Southern states. Moreover, I make bold to hint at ways by which the evils of a wealth into which the South is about to come may be shunned, in the hope that at least they will not be dismissed as visionary by those who take thought of the future of their country.

Not since 1884, the year before Captain Benjamin Ryan Tillman unbosomed himself at Bennettsville, has the political temperature been so low in South Carolina. In that year the stagnation of despair was the characteristic. In 1910 the political sea is becalmed, the people having embarked on another sea. Earnestly, diligently, joyously, they are busy—making money. They have no time for politics; they do not seek help from politicians. They do not need it.

In 1884 half a mill increase in the tax levy maddened the people. They were poor. Many of them could not make buckle and tongue meet, no matter how they sweated and strove, and, with the price of cotton going down and the price of money at the bank staying up, they began to grope blindly and strike blindly in all directions. The condition was not peculiar to South Carolina; it marked all the agricultural states. And so, when a politician offered any remedy, they snatched hungrily at it. They were in no temper to weigh accusations and explanations and examine them under the microscope. Anything that was labeled legislative medicine they swallowed without a grimace and then smacked their lips. In state after state whoever ran about crying a nostrum was hailed gladly and paid handsomely from the only moneys that the people had—the scant supply in the public treasury, the "rascal counters wrung from the hard hands" by the tax-gatherer.

But we had no real political revolution in this or any other American commonwealth. We had a change of officials, tagged somewhat differently, but they were men of the same race, the same station in life, with the same stakes in the community and the same fundamental habits and motives as their predecessors. Consequently, no constitutional change followed; in a few years the flurry passed and the people took up again their accustomed modes of thinking and doing. Though the division of the people was sharp and accompanied with cruel laceration, it was not deep —it was only skin deep. The tough ligaments that held them together could not be sundered by "declamatory flourishes."

The movement that for the time turned things topsy-turvy in the early nineties—and this I would especially insist upon—was not a laboring man's movement. It was agrarian. It was the uprising, in the main, of the disheartened but landowning farmer— not of his wage-earning tenant or hired man. The landowner was so poor and distressed that he was a capitalist—that his business was one of buying labor at the lowest price and selling the product of labor at the highest possible price.

That the farmer tills his land with his own hands does not change his nature as capitalist if he owns the land, but in those days he was so poor, so weary of hand and sick of spirit that he imagined himself in precisely the same plight as the hired man, who had nothing save labor to sell. Wages being low, the latter had everything to gain and nothing to lose by alliance with the landlord, and so the political blending of white landlord and white laboring man was complete. Yet the laboring element in the population, exclusive of the landowning laborers, was small compared with what it is now: when lands are low-priced they are easily acquired and easily held. Besides, the mill operative population was small and the cities and towns were small—with relatively small numbers of non-owners of homes. The agriculturists were told and believed that "town men"—lawyers, merchants, and bankers—were their oppressors, and most of them believed it; but of course, everybody knows better now. The latter groups were poor, too—just as many of them, proportionately, as of the farmers, were reduced to bankruptcy—and from the same causes. Depression in agriculture brought poverty and woe to members of every calling in the South, because agriculture was almost the sole basis of Southern wealth. In retrospect, the artificiality of the differences of the nineties is plain, and because they were mere "sound and fury signifying nothing" they did not permanently divide the people. The crimination and recrimination might be ever so blatant and offensive—the ruling political classes of white men were one at heart, though they were unaware of it and denied it to themselves, and they could not array themselves in hostile camps. In spite of contrived antagonisms of fanciful warp and woof, they clung together, not only by reason of racial unity and the Negro menace, but by reason of the absence of a true economic difference. A solid body cannot be split by the bursting of percussion caps on the surface.

So soon as the "times got better," the price of cotton going up, the old quarrel was forgotten, and in ninety-nine out of one hundred instances, perhaps, the politicians who fattened while it festered were kicked into submissive obscurity by the voters. But the truth that I stress is that there was one preponderant class, the landowning farmers: all others, professional and business men and laborers, were dependent upon and bound up with them and were so small in numbers, power, and influence as to be almost negligible in the electorate; certainly they were not important enough to be separately considered, though a seeming separation was temporarily forced.

Briefly, let us examine the new and changed picture. Instead of a dozen small scattered cotton-mill villages, we have now more than a hundred in this state, some of them large, peopled by many thousand white voters, scarcely any of whom are homeowners and all of them wage-earners—men who have only labor to sell. Without statistics at hand as to the number or increase in white farm laborers, conditions point unmistakably either to the rapid growth of such a class or else the complete abandonment of the farms to Negro labor directed by landlords and overseers. Twenty years ago the man who had a thousand dollars or was able to borrow it, could purchase a productive farm of one hundred acres, as improvements went in those days, in a desirable neighborhood. Now, the one thousand dollars will purchase only ten to twenty acres. Formerly, any able-bodied and industrious young man could become a landlord without heroic exertions. Owners were eager to sell land on any terms. If money was scarce, land was so cheap and abundant that a young man who promised well could buy it, whether or not he had a dollar of capital.

The small farmer suffered less, comparatively, from the depression than the great landlord; his little farm gave him a home; he worked with his own hands, and Negro labor was so plentiful and cheap that, if a skilled manager, he could produce cotton at some profit, no matter how low the price. He lived scantily, he endured hardships, and even in the nineties (of course I am speaking now of the exceptionally thrifty and industrious) he saved money. When the price of cotton began to bound up in 1902, he had gained a start, he had an invaluable education in frugality, he knew how to save. Thus, some thousands of men who had no capital twenty years ago are become well-to-do landowners—they are especially numerous in the Piedmont district.

The farmer boy of to-day is afraid to start on twenty acres; he cannot buy a $5,000 or $10,000 farm of one hundred or one hundred and fifty acres and he is reduced to the alternatives of leaving the farm, of working on the farm for wages, or of going to a remote district far from schools and railroads where lands are still cheap. The landlord, whether he have one hundred acres or two thousand, is contented and prosperous. With cotton bringing twelve cents or more a pound, he is almost sure to make ends meet, and, as a rule, he saves money rapidly—with which he buys more land.

The wealthy farmer, reaping a profit of $5,000 a year, reaches out to a region where the lands are cheap and buys another ten acres. Having plenty of capital, he improves and develops his added possessions. In a word, we have in the South a quickly growing wealthy landlord class. In some sections, notably in eastern South Carolina, the princely estates of ante-bellum times, which engendered and nourished a beautiful culture, the glory of the "old South," are being reproduced on an even more splendid scale. A generation must pass before this regime of planting wealth will be in full flower again, but the signs are that cotton and all farm products will continue indefinitely to command high prices, and that seems to insure its permanence. The natural and inevitable result of high-priced land, if uncorrected, would be more landless men.

Twenty years ago the Southern cities of 10,000 and 20,000 inhabitants had 2,000 and 5,000—notably Florence, Sumter, Spartanburg, and Greenville in South Carolina. Scores of new towns have sprung into prominence and some important new towns have come into being. The bulk of this new urban population is composed of skilled and unskilled laboring men who have only labor to sell—who wish to sell labor high and buy goods cheap.

Now I come to the central thought of this paper: we are in the midst of an industrial revolution; instead of a dominating landowning class, we have two classes of people, landowners and other capitalists (the owners of stores, mills, and shops), and a white wage-earning class, and the latter is swelling immensely in numbers and political potency. Though I have no figures, which I should have, descriptive of the new condition, one has but to look about him to be convinced of the essential truth of my assertion. It is too early to say that the white laborers on the farms (exclusive of landowning laborers) will reach numerical importance, but the drift is in that direction. That the town and village laboring class is large and growing, is the present fact.

Some loose commentator has said that a political revolution is due in South Carolina at the end of thirty-year periods, speaking roundly. If we reckon 1890 as such an event—and this I deny—

another is to be expected in 1920—and this I do not prophesy—
but it is reasonable to prophesy that when next there shall be a
cleavage in the body politic in South Carolina, it will be on the
lines of capital and labor—the landowners forming the center of
the capitalistic array and the wage-earners of every sort uniting
in opposition.

In 1885 there was, as I have said, the stagnation of despair in
politics, to be followed by the commotion among the landowners
five years later. In 1910 we have the same stagnation on the part
of the landowners, but from an opposite cause. The farmers are
not and cannot be aroused to acute political activity, because
they are contented; but, if there be no outward unrest on the
part of wage-earners now, that is no reason why it may not show
itself at any moment. The cost of living to the laborers is heightened as the farmer's prosperity is heightened, at least that is the
rule for the moment; as the farmer's happiness intensifies, the
struggle becomes sharper and more painful for the consumer of
the farmer's products. On this it is as well not to dwell; the hint
should be clear enough; almost everybody knows something of
the evil that a talented agitator, trammeled with no scruples and
with a genius for harangue can do when in a democracy he
sniffs office and power, not to mention graft; but I make a short
excursion to touch a single aspect of this next upheaval that I
have shaped in speculation.

Positively and fully I avow a belief that the race sympathy is
so strong among the whites that serious and permanent division
with appeal to the Negro as an incident cannot take place, at
least within this century or the next, on industrial or other
grounds. This I assert as a personal belief, to forestall misinterpre-
tation, but there can be no harm in frankly contrasting the conditions of 1890 with this next political rending. The people being
essentially of one class in 1890, the differences being of distorted
and picturesque exaggeration and on the surface, there was never
an actual peril of appeal to the Negro vote. Unconsciously, the
factions felt the shallowness of their bickering and the great
sound, healthy, white body politic held firmly together, though
there may have been skin abrasions that smarted. Besides, the

people of the South were but fourteen years in front of the dumb agony of actual Negro denomination. There was but one class of white people in 1890.

With two classes of white people, the danger of coalition by one or the other with a third class apart and aloof (that third class being the Negroes), is trebled. This is almost mathematically true—it flows from the multiplication of points of contact. Two of these classes will have in common one of the strongest motives, if not the strongest, known to the human heart—the motive to get the most bread and meat for a day's work. In 1890 nearly all the white people had the common motive of giving the laborers, most of whom were Negroes, the least bread and meat for a day's work—they were eager to buy labor cheap and sell products high. Obviously, the conclusion emerges that if any conscienceless demagogue should arise to attempt the destruction of white unity, the way would be clearer for his knavishness than it has been heretofore. In the end he would fail, but he might precipitate some years of uneasiness accompanied with pains and wrenchings to the commonwealth.

Finally, I come to the conclusion that in furthering the industrial development of South Carolina, it is the duty of the press and public alike to address themselves vigorously and diligently to the prevention of the unhappy political division which I have ventured to outline as a looming danger. And this consummation is to be effected by developing the man as the industrial unit. To my mind, a community of 1,000 heads of families owning their own homes is superior in every desirable way to another having 10,000 heads of families of whom 1,000 own homes. The ownership of a home is the sheet-anchor of good citizenship. Increase of town population is a boon, first of all to the real estate holder who has land to sell, and then to the merchant, hotel keeper, and every other capitalist, including the farmer who supplies the town market; but to the wage-earner, who has only labor to sell and its price to buy with, it may be, it usually is, the reverse. Arguing from this premise, the first step should be to encourage, to stimulate, to enable so far as possible, the wage-earner to become a capitalist; that is, to stake himself in the community by buying a home.

Illustratively, it is infinitely more important to help employees in the cotton mills, by educating them, by inducing the formation of building and loan associations and savings banks, and by drilling them to the uses of these facilities to acquire homes, than it is to induce the building of another cotton mill. I might give a score of illustrations, but the point is not hard to discern—that the problem is to strip the laboring man's task of every hampering and hindering difficulty and to strengthen him morally through the schools and by other means, so that the number of men who have something besides their hands shall be steadily and rapidly increased. That, above all other agencies, will fortify the commonwealth against the devilment of the demagogue.

It is a common practice to rail with more or less coherence and a good deal of meaningless fine frenzy about "trusts," but the monster trust is the land trust. When the land prices have mounted so high that the poor cannot own farms and the broad acres are in the hands of the few, as in most of the old countries, the chances of the average man to better his condition shrink to a pitiable thinness. That is why immigrants come to America. The task, then, and it is one of the chief tasks confronting the state, is to make the landless South Carolinian a landlord; and the way to do this is to educate him to be an expert farmer, so that he may earn a comfortable livelihood on ten, fifteen, or twenty-five acres—such a farm as any strong young man may hope to purchase and pay for. In Holland, in France, and other countries, a body of land containing twenty-five acres is a farm of more than respectable size, and there is no reason why South Carolina should not have thousands and tens of thousands of farms of this description.

When the man has been industrially developed so that he shall share as he ought to share in the resources of the state, the germs of political evil in him are eradicated. If there be approaching in the distance the flames of a political revolution started by the ignition of the laboring man's discontent, the wise policy is to start a counter flame to meet it, check it, and overcome it, by helping to convert him into a small capitalist, into a homeowner in the town or a landowning farmer in the country.

THE FREEDOM OF THE PRESS IN SOUTH CAROLINA AND ITS LIMITATIONS

(1913)

"The Freedom of the Press in South Carolina and Its Limitations" was prepared by William Watts Ball for delivery before the South Carolina Press Association. In his absence it was read June 27, 1913, before the convention at the Isle of Palms, S. C., by John S. Reynolds, of the staff of *The State*. It is reprinted with permission of the *News and Courier*, of Charleston, S.C.

TO discuss the freedom of the press is to discuss freedom itself, at least in modern times. Liberty and press liberty are correlative terms. The one implies the other. They are inseparable. The press is necessarily free if the people are free. While the press will be and always is a little freer than the rest of mankind, while the press is the far-flung skirmish line of advancing fighters for liberty, it can not be too far in front. It will always be held back as the people are held back; it can do no more than a company of pioneers blazing paths. The company must be and is composed of bold and bright-eyed spirits, not afraid to look ahead, but always it is held in leash by the powers in the rear. In a word, the press is sensitively responsive to the prevailing opinion of the people. It sucks its life from the people's good will, and the newspaper that gallops too far ahead cuts itself off from its commissary and starves. Later the marching battalions may come upon its fading footprints, and they may have some value as guides. The over-daring newspaper's sacrifice may not have been wholly in vain, but this newspaper is exceptional; the press as such must serve only as a company of pioneers armed with picks and lanterns.

I

The press since the invention of printing has been the convenient instrument for broadcasting truth. Before the invention

of type the truth was disseminated by the written word and before that by the spoken word. To attempt to suppress the truth
now is no less futile and no less stupid than it was in the day of
Balaam, when, Balaam failing to speak the truth as he was bidden,
the Almighty put it into the mouth of an ass to rebuke him.

The freedom of the press is the boast of English-speaking people. Like other boasts, it is relative in its truth, a little more than
half-true, perhaps, but so far from being wholly true as the people are from being wholly free.

When the king is supreme the press is his creature, with here
and there one of the component creatures asserting a degree of
rebellion, pointing a little way toward freedom in front of the
King, and at right angles to his path, the audacious editor paying
the cost of his indulgence in liberty with his head or a prison
term.

When the mob rules the press is its creature, or, if it resists, it
is mobbed. When money rules, through banks, railroads and
other corporations, the press is again its creature and the editor
indulging an instinctive appetite for freedom, as some of the tribe
always do, is put to death by a hunger lock-out.

II

The English press had its origin in songs and ballads celebrat-
ing public events, and then in "intelligencers" or letter-writers
employed by statesmen and rulers to keep them informed of
affairs by correspondence. This was in the sixteenth century.
Then came the "news books" of the seventeenth century, issued
at irregular intervals. These were followed by the pamphlets,
called "diurnals," and after a few years they came to be issued at
regular intervals, under the same name, thus taking on the defining characteristics of the modern newspaper. The issuance of
news-books was at first subject to the license of the Crown and
the appearance of diurnals at stated intervals of time began in
1641, when the people rebelled against the Crown. The license
privilege was abolished promptly, together with the Court of
Star Chamber; but when Cromwell became the political boss
naturally all the diurnals were suppressed in order that the boss'

organ, conducted by one Henry Walker, might have the monopoly of printed expression. The first of the English editors, or the man who is so regarded and who preceded Walker by a few years in the direction of what he called "the perfect diurnal," was Samuel Pecke, who is described as "a tall, gaunt, hook-nosed fellow," and was known as "the bald-headed buzzard." These early editors of the diurnals appear to have been a rather common and scurrilous lot—and naturally enough. They were not free. They were the puppets of great men. They were iron-mongers, tinkers, or other craftsmen, with an itch for writing, who turned editor and through fear of the jail of hunger for rather scant fleshpots were duly subservient to their patrons. John Dillingham, in his *Parliamentary Scout*, was the first writer of "leaders" (1645), and it may be of interest to remark here that in these early times the editors were for the most part Presbyterians. Of Henry Walker, Cromwell's press agent, the first editor to print advertisements in his newspaper, by the way, Sir Francis Worthy, in his "Welcome to Hell," wrote:

"To Henry Walker, I bear much affection.
He's red-haired, of Iscariot's right complexion."

III

It should be said for the fellows, however, that they seem to have accepted their frequent prison sentences with philosophy, if not complacency. One of them, Benjamin Harris, fled to Boston on the ascension of James II and set up, December 25, 1690, the first American newspaper, which in due time was suppressed on account of a revolting attack on Louis XIV, of France. The Crown licensing of newspapers ended finally in 1695 and in the first years of the eighteenth century the tripod began to attract men of talent, such as Jonathan Swift, Bolingbroke and Daniel Defoe. Until about 1712 the power of the press rapidly enhanced, but at that time a law was passed requiring that newspapers be printed on stamped paper. Taxation, of course, proved far more chilling to newspaper expansion than persecution and it was not until 1855 that the stamp tax was repealed. In the latter half of the eighteenth century the freedom of the press was fought out in the English Courts. Thomas Erskine, who became Lord Chancellor, was its eminent forensic champion, and John Wilkes and John Horn Tooke were writers about whom the battles raged.

The Crown and the Government were forever resentful of criticism, and their remedy and only remedy for the expression of printed opinion was the jail. The right to print reports of debates in Parliament was only won after long and painful effort.

In spite of the Stamp Act, newspapers multiplied and evasions of the tax by cheap publications were numerous. Upon its repeal, a great crop of low-priced journals instantly came into being.

IV

This imperfect sketch of the development of the English press will serve to illustrate the irrepressible conflict between officialdom, or government, and the newspapers. The press in England was always just a little freer than the people were and a little less enslaved than they were, the difference in favor of the press being the disposition of the newspaper writer to think and speak a little ahead of the main body. Not until comparatively recent years has the newspaper press exerted an influence of predominant significance. The novels of Charles Dickens and Benjamin D'Israeli were reforming and corrective influences seventy-five years ago incomparably greater than the newspapers. Dickens directed the attention of the people of England to the workhouse, debtors' prison and Chancery Court abuses, and the newspaper press was content to play second fiddle to satirists of his transcendant ability. Nowadays we have a far larger school of problem story writers, but most of the substantial results in the improvement of social conditions are accomplished by the newspaper reporters and caricaturists working under the direction of editors unafraid.

The pertinent question is, how free is the press in the United States and, especially in South Carolina? The Federal and State constitutions, almost without exception, say solemnly that the press is and shall be free, and that its rights and privileges shall never be abridged—a saying to be taken with more or less salt, according to time, place and circumstance.

V

The principle that the newspaper shall be accountable in damages for injury to the reputation of an individual has never been and never will be protested by an intelligent newspaper. Even though the publication be without malice, it is fair and right that a newspaper recompense a merchant if it publish him falsely to be a bankrupt. When a railroad train runs into an open switch and a passenger's leg is broken, the presumption is that some one connected with the railroad, the president of the company, the board of directors, the engineer, the conductor, or the brakeman, has been at fault. The railroad company pays the passenger the damage as assessed by the jury, and ought to pay it. In the same way, when the news editor of a newspaper allows to be printed a dispatch of a correspondent that "Jas" Smith, of Brownsville, has been indicted for larceny, and it transpires later that the correspondent wrote with his pencil "Jos" Smith, the newspaper ought to pay damages if it be proved by a reputable man in the same community named "Jas" Smith that he has been damaged by the publication. The risk of falling into such error is one that the publisher must accept, his safety depending on the accuracy of his remote correspondent, the telegram sender and receiver, his news editor, printers and proofreaders, just as the railroad company must rely on the accuracy and fidelity of its hundreds of employees. The factor of human frailty enters into every business and industry.

VI

Let us suppose, however, that upon the occurrence of a railroad accident, a passenger whose leg has been broken lies silent in a ditch at night, refusing to ask assistance of the skilled surgeon sent to the scene by the railroad company for the purpose of rendering aid to the injured. Suppose, and it is not an impossible supposition, that the ignoble wretch reasons that he will obtain larger damages in case his broken limb be not set promptly, than otherwise, and suppose that his concealment of his injury from

the railroad company until after action be brought by his lawyers
be proved, would that conduct be approved by the legislature
and courts of South Carolina? Obviously, it would not be. The
passenger's self injury, inflicted in a negative way, would doubtless cause the jury to bring in a verdict of nominal damages.

It is a curious and singular fact, meantime, that this commonwealth, boasting in its constitution of its protection of the press,
positively encourages, through its legislators, a course of conduct
exactly parallel with that of the railroad passenger who conceals
his injury in order that it may be aggravated and that his claim
for damages may be magnified. This association has for a number
of years urged upon South Carolina legislatures the passage of an
act requiring that a person injured by a publication in a newspaper shall, before bringing action in the courts, call the attention
of the publisher to it, and so permit him to print an apology or
explanation and to plead the latter publication in mitigation of
damages. The act has not been passed. Such an error as that in the
"Jas" Smith and "Jos" Smith illustration may creep into a newspaper, "Jas" Smith may suffer silently in his community for a
year and 364 days and then enter suit. The suit may be the newspaper's first knowledge of the error. In all these weeks and
months, the newspaper has been denied the poor privilege of
exerting its influence to repair the damage unwittingly done and
it is denied the further privilege of submitting to the court and
jury that "Jas" Smith did not give it the opportunity to extend
first aid to the injured. Such relation of the newspaper to the
aggrieved party is probably unique in the law of torts and its
obtrusive and outstanding injustice seems not to have dawned
upon the consciousness of South Carolina statesmen.

Casually it may be observed that whether applied to newspapers or other concerns, the law of torts is even more archaic
than most branches of the law and evidences of disposition on the
part of lawyers to cure its defects are small.

VII

The law of criminal libel is without any of that basis in reason
that justifies compensation in damages for private injuries. The

maxim of the common law is "The greater the truth the greater the libel" and its theory is that a criminal libel should be punished because it "tends to cause a breach of the peace." Pompously as this theory has been defended and extolled by the masters of the common law, it is not even consistent with that system. It can not be reconciled with that other and sounder maxim that "Words do not justify a blow." Certainly if the application, face to face, of a vile epithet does not excuse instant and violent retaliation, it is absurd to say that the distant application of an epithet in cold print should be impliedly admitted as provocation for physical assault. The law of criminal libel, as Thomas Cooper, of South Carolina, pointed out in his treatise eighty-three years ago, is a survival of the tyrannous procedure of the Court of Star Chamber. Kings and governments have clung to it as a convenient instrument for gagging the press upon occasion. In South Carolina it was robbed of its sinister vitality by the constitution of 1895, which sets forth that proof of the truth of an alleged libelous charge shall in no case be prohibited. That, by the way, is the sole statutory advance that the freedom of the press has made in this commonwealth since it became a commonwealth and, though in late years, criminal libel prosecutions have been rare, it is of no minor importance. It is not unlikely that we shall have recurrences of appeal to criminal libel law in the future. I would like to give credit to whom it is due for the change made by the constitution of 1895, but my inquiries have not discovered the name of its author. Probably our constitutional convention followed the example set by some other state, when it extirpated a part of the law so dangerous and so contradictory to that press freedom which all our state constitutions have pretended to perpetuate.

VIII

Reverting to my thesis that the press is a little freer than the people, I remark that the people of South Carolina are far from free. The chains of ignorance hang heavy on them. In a population of 1,515,000 by the census of 1910, 835,000 are Negroes.

While socially and politically the presence of this race in majority is perhaps the ruling factor in our progress, or want of it, it must for the present be ignored. Suffice it that there is little or no mutual interest of a practical nature between the South Carolina press of today and this great mass of humanity, occupying the same territory that the 679,000 whites occupy. For the purposes of our discussion the Negroes would as well inhabit their native African jungles.

Of the 679,000 whites one in each ten is unable to read or write his name. Another one in ten can barely read or write his name and is, therefore, no more a reader of newspapers than is a babe born blind. Thus, one-fifth of our white population are cut off from newspapers as though they lived under a Russian despot.

As compared with Great Britain, Switzerland, France, Germany and such American states as Wisconsin and Massachusetts, the great mass of our people struggle in the march of civilization. I attribute no fault to them. I am one of them, and it is my misfortune as it is theirs, that South Carolina labors under a tremendous handicap, as compared with the populous white states. Great regions of our state are thinly settled and undeveloped. The physical advantages of good highways, school houses, churches, telephones, railroads and telegraph lines are supplied to them with difficulty. In other parts of the state about 150,000 whites, failing to compete with the Negro on the farms, on account of the latter's low and often depraved standard of living, have been driven to flee to manufacturing towns as cities of refuge, and there they have segregated themselves. In the mills the labor is long, dreary and deadening to individual and family aspiration, the mill village life swiftly engenders a discouraging class consciousness and the separation of the white people into groups is accelerated. The general result is that an immense part of our minority of white people is not a reading people. At a guess I should say that not more than one-half of the 162,000 white male adults of voting age in this state, according to the last census, are readers of daily newspapers and that one-third either read no newspaper or read one so little that its effect upon them is negligible.

IX

In monstrous contradiction to this condition we have in South Carolina what is perhaps the nearest approach to universal manhood suffrage that is to be found in any civilized state, if we regard only our white population. Our primary is our real and only election where the popular will is tested. In this election it is well-nigh impossible to prevent any male participating who has a white skin and appears to be 21 years old. Whatever safety the state has rests solely in the innate honesty of the white people. Our primary elections are conducted on the honor system, and I refrain from debating whether or not that system continues satisfactory. Had the reform bills in England in 1832 been accompanied with a grant of universal suffrage to the people of England, I suppose that England's constitution would not have survived half a dozen years. We are engaged in South Carolina in a political experiment that deserves to command world-wide attention for its magnificent audacity and I fear that we are for the most part naively ignorant that it is in progress.

But what has this to do with the freedom of the press? I answer that we have a state ruled by two widely separated classes, a repetition of D'Israeli's *Two Nations*. The one the printed word appeals to; the other is swayed by the spoken word from the lips of the haranguer in campaign years. If that haranguer be a demagogue, if he be bound by no scruples and if he have sympathy with and understanding of the passions of the non-reading people, his task of inflaming them is simple and easy. To array them against the press requires little effort. For them the "Fourth Estate" does not exist, except as an ally of the reading class whom they have been taught to distrust. If ten per cent of the informed and reading people be politically vicious, they may exert a tremendous influence on the ignorant. It is easier to inflame than to allay, to ignite than to quench. There is always latent discontent in the less fortunate element of any population and there always are knaves to incite it to activity for their selfish ends.

x

A consequence of this condition is that the press of South Carolina has been elevated into a political issue *per se*. The haranguers point to it as a menace. They do not forbear by implication to threaten its existence. They introduce measures to expropriate its material possessions, and they describe it as violent, mendacious and tyrannical. This indictment has been so dinned that many reading people fancy that the newspapers of South Carolina are rabid in their manners of expression, when the plain truth is that, by comparison with the newspapers of the average Northern state, their utterances are mild and restrained. Some ten years ago a railroad wreck in New York occurred and the most conservative newspaper of that city, one that is honest and bold, but that speaks peculiarly to the "high-browed" wealthy, printed in an editorial article a tabulated list of the millionaire directors and officers of the railroad company and said in terse Anglo-Saxon, "These men are murderers." I know of no parallel to that editorial article in South Carolina. No libel suit followed it. The other day a state senator of New York was accused of seeking a bribe. The state senate proceeded to apply to him a coat of whitewash. The New York newspapers unqualifiedly denounced the senator as guilty and ridiculed and lampooned the verdict of his fellow senators. Thereupon the senator was indicted, tried and convicted and sentenced to prison by a court and jury. President Mellen, of the New York, New Haven and Hartford Railroad Company, has been the target in recent years of more persistent attacks than any South Carolinian has been since 1876. A few years ago such private citizens as Mr. Rockefeller and lesser financial lights were repeatedly cartooned as vultures. Charles F. Murphy, who holds no public office, was time and again cartooned as a convict in stripes wearing a ball and chain, by a New York daily. Yet the press of South Carolina is believed by many intelligent South Carolinians to be rough in its treatment of politicians. One would not like to contemplate the conditions that would have followed in New York and

Pennsylvania had politicians been accorded treatment so gentle from the press as the press of South Carolina is accustomed to accord them. It is fair to say, however, that the reading people of this state do support their newspapers with praiseworthy loyalty and liberality. I doubt if the daily press in any American state is more generally read by those who can read than is the daily press of South Carolina. Moreover, our newspaper readers give more attention to the editorial page than do those of most communities.

The newspaper as an educational agency is scarcely second to the public school, the pulpit and the hustings. It is appalling to reflect that so large a part of our white population, not to mention the Negroes, are by force of circumstances deprived of it.

XI

That thirty or forty per cent of our people are moved only by the spoken word makes them the natural prey and asset of the demagogue and he has the assistance of the intelligently vicious element who prefer bad government for its own sake. Even the better sort of politicians, fearful of the power of the ignorant vote, is restrained from speaking the whole truth on the stump and so a tribe of trimmers is bred, whose influence to check progress is but little less hurtful than that of the wilful poisoner of public opinion. How absurd is our state's claim to belief in press liberty is illustrated by the fact that within the last quarter century the dispatches of correspondents to newspapers published in other states have been subjected to censoring by armed and uniformed soldiers, the plea of the state government being that they might incite disorders within South Carolina's borders. Nothing stands in the way of repetition of such incidents, but still our wiseacres lift their eyes in superior disgust and horror at the performances of the Russian Czar's police.

Another form of encroachment on press liberty is the bill introduced in the legislature to compel newspapers to print corrections offered by politicians and others of statements which they believe or allege to be erroneous and injurious to themselves.

The politician claiming to be aggrieved is, by the terms of the bill, to be the judge of the length, breadth, thickness and quality of the correction. The bill is manifestly one of expropriation. It is a measure to enable politicians who do not control newspapers to take possession of the papers owned, established and conducted by other men. It is a confession by politicians that the views they represent are so antagonistic to those of informed readers that they dare not attempt to establish newspapers of their own. Any man has a right to set up a printing press, but no man can conduct a newspaper save at enormous financial loss unless he have the support of a considerable part of the reading population. The defamers of the South Carolina press would have a press of their own but for the knowledge that this support is beyond their reach and those of them who have money have no purpose to support it out of their own pockets. To confiscate space in the newspapers they despise and convert it to their uses seems to offer the prospect both of advantage and delight.

XII

Meantime these defamers furnish on the stump luminous examples of what newspaper manners should be. Condemning the press for using harsh language, they go about the state from town to town besmirching one another with accusations and epithets often that would humiliate a fish-woman's pride in her vocabulary. They do not ask the legislature to pass a law compelling opposing candidates to utter orally a correction of a slander; they apparently desire that the freedom of throaty billingsgate be forever unabridged—and they will be content with permission to introduce their billingsgate into newspapers maintained by other people and which, with all their defects, do not descend into the pit of vulgarity not uncommonly occupied by themselves as they shout their claims for public office.

The thrifty measure of expropriation mentioned, if enacted, would have the effect of giving newspapers printed in Georgia and North Carolina towns near the South Carolina border and circulating in South Carolina an immense advantage in the publication of political news relating to this state. An independent

South Carolina journalist would easily find a place on a Charlotte newspaper in which he would express his opinion freely, and the newspaper, protected by Federal laws, would circulate in this state, but it is of no concern to the enemies of the South Carolina press that they break it down while building up the press of other states, if they can obtain by confiscation part possession and control of the former. The amazing incident in the history of this measure is that it has received the votes of many legislators who ought to know better. That it should be advocated by men who look for aggrandisement to the ignorant and vicious vote is to be expected; that it should have the support of one man of intelligence and character is disappointing. The explanation is that even good men are sometimes weak enough to try to propitiate embattled ignorance.

XIII

The one other peril of the press is that it be captured from the rear. The establishment and successful operation of a daily newspaper requires a great deal of capital. A consequence is that newspapers are frequently owned and controlled by persons not directly interested in newspaper making. In the investigation of the sugar lobby in Washington the other day there appeared a letter from one of the managers of the beet sugar industry to General Manager Melville E. Stone, of the Associated Press, entreating Mr. Stone's good offices in behalf of the sugar tariff. In the letter the sugar beet manager remarked that he was himself a member of the Associated Press. That is to say, he owned or controlled an A.P. newspaper and it goes without saying that his newspaper was more intent upon conserving the interest of the sugar beet people than upon serving the general interest. Although the press of South Carolina has been remarkably free from such sinister outside influences, it is not to be disputed that they do exist and operate numerously in many parts of the country, if to a less extent than is supposed. We may have at any time in South Carolina, unless we guard against it, this sort of newspaper corruption. It occurs to me, for example, that had backers of the late state dispensary been sagacious enough to invest half a million dollars of the money they wasted in riotous living in a newspaper of capable equipment, the life of that reprobate institution would have been prolonged for a number of years.

XIV

From motives of self-preservation and for the protection of the people it is the plain duty of the press to guard against the line of subtle attack indicated. The weapon of this protection is publicity. Nothing that is open and above board is likely to be permanently dangerous. A railroad company may without dishonor own and operate a newspaper, provided the fact of ownership be published. While the recent act of Congress requiring statements of ownership to be printed by newspapers was perhaps clumsily drawn and works unnecessary hardships, I, for one, rejoice that it was enacted and that it successfully ran the gauntlet of the courts. I believe in publicity, and I believe in every doctor taking his own medicine. Secret newspaper ownership is the most serious menace, general in character, that the craft must oppose, and a press recreant to the duty of opposing it is unworthy of public confidence. The menace of ignorance is local, not general—it does not exist in Wisconsin or Massachusetts.

The ideal newspaper is that one whose editorial control and ownership are combined in one person, that person being a newspaper man without other important financial concerns.

XV

Recurring once more to the freedom of the press as menaced by ignorance in South Carolina, I venture to suggest a remedy. The newspapers and newspaper men must, of course, do their utmost to prevent prejudicial legislation, but editors and publishers would as well bear in mind that the defeat of a foolish and malicious bill is only the application of a soothing lotion to a malignant symptom. It does not cure the disease. If this paper contains anything calculated to arouse the people of South Carolina to the truth that the freedom of the press concerns even more their interest than that of the newspaper makers, I am fully aware as I write that it will never reach the ears or eyes of that section of our population that I would most like to influence, unless in form so distorted as to be unrecognizable by its author.

The printed word is a pointless weapon against the rank and file of ignorance arrayed and inflamed. If the press is to survive as a free agency and if civilization is to survive in South Carolina, newspaper men, together with all unselfish and patriotic men, must endeavor to reach ignorant people by other means than newspapers. They must mingle with them, join their societies and win their sympathy by personal association. They must not wait until election year to gain the acquaintance of the ignorant voter; they must beware of the notion that it is legitimate to stave off a political disaster by corrupting the weak with money, thereby multiplying the numbers of the corrupt. In short, they must give of themselves, not merely of their pocketbooks, to the elevation of the people of the state, and they must give without a sense of condescension. They must reply to the mouthy dema-gogues by word of mouth in words of truth and soberness, and trust in the final survival and victory of virtue in South Caro-linians however they may be momentarily and occasionally led astray.

XVI

As most of you know, I conducted a weekly newspaper for a number of years in a South Carolina town. Within half a mile of my office was a community containing about one hundred and eighty white voters, men of the same race and social antecedents as mine. The price of my newspaper was a dollar a year. I had not more than ten subscribers in this community, and of them seven were officers of the industrial company employing the one hundred and eighty. Editors here will testify to similar conditions elsewhere. My newspaper had no more influence among these people than it had in a colony in New Zealand. Their wages were sufficient to allow them to buy the newspaper without discomfort to themselves but, in the new environment in which they were placed and with the arduous work in which they were engaged, they were without inclination or time to read a newspaper. I can well perceive how disheartening and blighting to ambition was the toil upon which they had entered. It was my duty and would have been for me the part of discretion to go among them and, since I could not help them through my newspaper directly, to help them in such ways as I could command. That is the duty and that would be the wisdom for all of us who love our state and would strive to prevent its division into two peoples to practice.

Meantime, we may and shall get help from without in the form of intelligent immigration, which we should encourage, but so long as our next door neighbors shall remain slaves to ignorance, the state of South Carolina will not be free and restriction upon the freedom of the press will be a present and continuing danger.

ARE THE NEGROES FREE?

(1914)

The Kosmos Club was established as a club composed of professional men in Columbia, S. C., and professors at the University of South Carolina who met for the purpose of serious discussion. William Watts Ball, a member of the club, gave this address on the status of Negroes.

AT the outset, let me tell you that I do not argue, (no matter what I think) in this paper that the Negroes ought to be free or that they ought to be slaves. I hold that, apart from the question of human slavery, Garrison and his gang of Abolitionists needlessly forced a war and prevented peaceful emancipation. They assailed the contract between the states, the Constitution, whereon American society was founded. Mutual regard for contractual rights, though an element of evil be included in the contractual terms, is essential to the safety of society and who sets himself as a judge to destroy the contractual foundation of a republic can have no vindication unless he succeed in destroying that republic and in superimposing some other and wholly new government upon it. The War Between The States had no such result. The same Republic survived and now it is pertinent to inquire whether or not abolition of slavery is a fact. Manifestly it must be admitted that the institution of Negro slavery has been tremendously modified, that its outer habiliments have been stripped from the blacks, that if a slavery survives it survives beneath a veneer of liberty. Nevertheless, had the Abolitionists not begun, about 1832, their incitement of the South to resistance, there might have been no war and further advances of substantial and genuine character towards Negro liberty than there have been.

"We the people of the United States, in order to form a more perfect Union, establish justice, insure domestic tranquillity, provide for the common defence, promote the general welfare, and secure the blessings of Liberty to ourselves and our posterity do ordain and establish this constitution for the United States of America."

Such is the preamble to the "Covenant with hell," as Garrison called the Constitution, and construed along with the Declaration of Independence we get the definition that freedom in the United States is the right to the pursuit and enjoyment of life, property, and happiness for ourselves and our posterity.

When the great war ended there was evident reluctance on the part of the South to grant to the Negroes full liberty, as was pointed out by Mr. Carl Schurz and others, and as was shown by legislation like that in what was called the "Black Code," enacted by the white South Carolina legislature in 1865. That the Negroes were not prepared to exercise with even fair judgement and ordinary discretion the offices of citizens was plain to the whites and the absurdity of the opposite contention by Senator Wade, Thad Stevens and that school of "Radical" Northern politicians stewing in their own "pizen" was exposed in the course of a dozen years—as was inevitable. Agreement is universal now that the Northern endeavor to clothe the Negroes with citizens' rights immediately after their so-called emancipation was pitifully and ridiculously unjust to them as well as to the whites. Of course the Negro could not be free in 1865 or 1870 except while the whites were enslaved by federal bayonets and in time the whites won back ascendancy and freedom in spite of the bayonets. White slavery or extermination was the only way to full Negro freedom and the North had neither the wish nor the stomach for that sort of warfare. The North, as a whole, has never loved the Negro and even the Abolitionists were for the most part victims of emotional excitement induced by exaggerated emphasis on an abstraction.

But, are the Negroes free, in 1914—here in South Carolina which I shall assume to be a commonwealth typical of the South. Let us see.

The Negroes are practically without the right of suffrage. That will not be disputed.

The Negroes cannot serve on juries.

The Negroes are no longer allowed to form a part of the State's militia forces.

The Negroes receive one dollar for common schools and colleges to seven bestowed upon the whites. Their contributions to public education are practically so great as their receipts from the educational funds. They get back what they give.

Until a few years ago, Negroes could be imprisoned for breach of contract. A federal decision annulling the South Carolina and Alabama labor contract statutes was a small gain for freedom.

The Negroes hold no civil offices in the State.

There is no denying the plain fact that a great proportion of the white people of South Carolina hold in the back of their heads the right to visit summary punishment on Negroes for certain crimes—a right which the more lawless class asserts as to numerous crimes and misdemeanors. Here is a special if unlawful crime code for the Negroes.

Every decent white man and woman maintains and exercises a right of treating all Negroes as inferiors. Thus, no white person wishes or dares to address a Negro as "Mr.," "Mrs." or "Miss." At the same time, failure by Negroes in formal politeness to whites is severely and instantly punished by the individual and the punishment is usually admitted as proper by the courts.

Purposely, I do not enter "jim crow" laws in this catalogue. They are not incompatible with the fullest liberty as the term is known in practice among all peoples. Two peoples of different colors or tribal or national extraction may live in the same territory, enjoying equal rights but apart socially. It may be inconvenient to afford them always separate and equal accommodations, but it is always possible. It is no invasion of the rights of a Christian to forbid him by law to eat at a hotel table maintained for Brahminists—if an equally good table is provided elsewhere for the Christian citizen. It is an infraction of a citizen's rights, whether he be black or white, to subject him forcibly to undesirable association.

Let us consider the economic side.

The unskilled Negro's wage in South Carolina is premised

on his necessities. He is paid for farm work on the same basis that the farm mule is paid—that is, he is given shelter, usually of most indifferent quality, and an abundance of coarse provender. Practically he is denied the right of demanding or fixing his own wage as is proved by the fact that Negro labor organizations in rural districts (to an extent in towns) are always promptly suppressed. The average Negro began with a low living standard, he is content with it and he is discouraged rather than encouraged to improve it; hence, the holding of his wage to the fodder and corn level is comparatively easy.

North and South the Negro is denied entrance into most trades and industries, not by statute but by the infinitely sterner custom. Negro carpenters, masons, joiners and brick-layers, barbers and shoe-shiners are decreasing rapidly in the South. In the North they were never numerous.

North and South the industrial treatment of the Negroes is identical in motive but reversed in operation, a difference due to difference in numbers.

The North segregates the Negroes in the industries. It allows Negroes to serve as domestics, as porters in Pullman cars, shoe-shiners in white barber-shops, in a steadily decreasing number of hotels and restaurants as waiters, occasionally as hostlers and coachmen and as servants in private families. Invasion of any industry by numbers of Negroes is resented, indeed it meets with armed resistance. From Wilmington, Del., to Coatesville, Penna., along the Mason and Dixon Line and the Ohio river west, as far North as Springfield, Ohio, Springfield, Ill., and Springfield, Mo., is a lynching belt. In Coatesville, where whites killed and burned a Negro man-slayer a few years ago there are 6,000 white laborers and 3,000 Negro laborers. Where the Negro coal miners press against the white coal miners, there is bloody conflict. The race question on the border over which the slaves were smuggled is an industrial race question now similar to that between the white laborers of the Pacific Coast and the Oriental immigrants.

In the South the white laborers are segregated. The cotton mills protect white fugitives from the farms who run from the

Negro's low living standard and wage. We reserve all railroad train and street car employment for whites. We can't segregate the Negroes on the farm; they are too many. The plumber's trade in the South is a growth since emancipation. We exclude the Negroes from it. In 1860 every gentleman would have owned a skilled plumber and that is a principal reason that I sorrow about the result of the war. We are steadily driving the Negroes out of all kinds of work except domestic service, farm labor and heavy unskilled work, as in railroad building and excavation.

In the North the Negro enjoys political rights. Industrially, his state is far harder than it is in the South. His exclusion is more rigorous. If the North gave the Negro a chance in industry, millions instead of thousands of our Negroes would immigrate. In time, we may circumscribe the Negro's activities in the same fashion; the chauffeur's trade is the only one that the Negro has won in the South and that is of no consequence numerically. The Negro chauffeurs are few in the North—the white unions attend to that.

But the Negroes are staying on the farms in the South, because they have nowhere else to go, and thereby they are making progress toward industrial freedom. On that will be built in time other freedom. The exceptional Negro, one in ten or twenty, thrifty and diligent, in South Carolina, where only one in three acres is developed and the density of population is only 49 to the square mile, may become a land-owner in half the time that the equally thrifty and diligent white man can, because the Negro is content to live on half as much and produces equally as much. Thus we have 21,000 Negro farm owners in South Carolina and only 45,000 white farm owners, the Negro farms being, however, one third the size, as an average, of the white farms. Today, as I was writing this paper, there came to my attention a Negro farmer in Orangeburg, owner of a store, a five room house and a dozen mules. He owes no money, has turkeys, chickens, sweet "taters," corn, hay and other foodstuffs in plenty, 440 gallons of sorghum syrup, has 69 head of hogs and 40 bales of cotton.

The man with goods always gets his rights in the end—half a

century from now the Negro land owners are very likely to be free politically. That is Booker Washington's gospel and it is a true gospel. This, however, may not in haste be set down to the manner of Yankee or Lincoln emancipation. When the war began free persons of color were paying taxes on property assessed $750,000 in Charleston; it is in no New England abolitionist's mouth to say that had the South been let alone, the slaves would not gradually have been liberated between 1830 and 1900 and that they would not have been in better position now to accumulate property. The active and angry feeling that moves a part of the white population against Negro progress now might have been avoided. In the New York public library hangs a poster issued by one signing himself "Democratic Workingman" during the war, quoting by way of argument against the Southern slaveowners a saying of Robert Toombs that in time slavery would be automatically abolished—that white labor in competition with it would become so cheap that men could not afford to own slaves. In the South the Negroes have the nominal right of contract; they cannot be forced by law to work (though we utilize the vagrancy ordinance device against them to a limited extent in towns) but I submit that the mass of them get out of life little more than the "roughness" necessary to sustain life. The exceptions are the Negro property owners (5,000 owners of cabins in towns perhaps, besides the farmers) and the domestics. The cooks and lackeys are not only free but despotic—though it should be remembered that all domestic service, in the present order of society, partakes of slavery. White or black, the flunky wearing your livery consents to be badged as his master's man, the servant's regalia the outward and visible sign of acknowledged inferiority. Your faithful servant like your faithful dog accepts your kicks as well as your guardianship and tidbits. Those who have the best Negroes and who treat them better than the millionaire treats his white servants make them "know their place" and their service is admission, usually, that they are slaves well fed and kept fat. The average Negro whether cropper or wage tenant, whether kindly or unkindly handled, gets from year to year only his rough and rude keep. A Negro, craving freedom, likes to lease from a non-resident landlord. He obtains a measure of freedom in that way but rarely is capable of managing a farm and his position is not improved; he wears out the farm and does not escape from the lien merchant's mastery whether cotton sell at seven or seventeen cents.

However, many more Negroes are gaining industrial freedom in the South than in the North where they are given political rights. The property owning Negroes will be free some day and in a State of 19,000,000 acres of land—13,000,000 of which are not under plough—Negro farm owners will increase at a constantly accelerating rate.

The North, then, is successfully keeping its Negroes in economic slavery by a policy of stern though unconfessed exclusion. The South is failing in a similar, though franker policy because of the sparseness of population and the abundance of land.

If it be admitted for the argument's sake, that what has been said makes out a case of practical slavery for the Negro, what about the poor white man—the tenant farmers particularly? Politically, to be sure, they are coddled; they are long on political freedom, but economically they are in the chains of the Negro and it is submitted that economic slavery eventually becomes political slavery. Our segregated white wage-earners are, of course, held down by the chains of the white tenant farmers; the 35,000 white tenants are a reservoir of labor overflowing to the mill villages; I bought ten lovely ducks today that came from a farmer selling out to move to the "factory."

The white tenant, like the Negro, is paid only the provender and shelter for himself and family; he can obtain only the "nigger wage" and, meantime, he can't live like a "nigger." In short, I believe that Senator Toombs' prediction, if he uttered it, is being realized; the white labor on the farms has arrived at an irreducible minimum which is the level of the Negro's and that for the 35,000 white tenant farmers, unless conditions change, there is literally no hope on the farms. To be sure, the exceptions will emerge from the tenant class and become land-owners just as the exceptional Negroes do—but there will be many more such Negroes, first because there are 76,000 Negro tenants, and, second, because the Negro holds to the Negro living scale while scuffling to get on his feet while the white man must all the time support his family as "white folks."

Look forward a hundred years: behold the farm lands owned by 50,000 white farmers and 100,000 Negro small farmers—the trade of the latter sought by the merchants, their deposits solicited by the banks, their political position assured because they are well-to-do taxpayers. Can you fail also to see 50,000 Negro tenants and 50,000 white tenants and that with the Negro property-holder admitted to his full political rights, as certainly he will be, there will cease to be discrimination in favor of the white tenant and against the Negro tenant?

The problem before the South is to save the poor white man; the same problem perhaps then but vaguely seen, that existed before 1861.

There are two solutions:

First. School and train both Negro and white so that the Negro's living standard will improve and with it his wage and productiveness and the white man will not be dragged down. The white can then withstand Negro competition. We can, I hope, depend on the white's native superiority to keep ahead of the Negro.

Second. Immigration of whites. Our white tenants as a class are a scattered and beaten people. They are without class consciousness. They are not organized in unions—they can't unionize separately from the Negro laborers. Recruit them with 50,000 Belgians or other white men, with their families, and the Negroes, if they be, as is said, a weaker people, will be crowded out or driven to Negro districts so that there shall be white labor segregation on the farms as in the mill villages and other towns.

Politically, we have segregated the whites by the state primary in which the non-property owner and the illiterate can vote, taking from the white the motive to get a little learning and gather a little gear while we hold out that lure to the poor and ignorant Negro and persuade him to get the ballot by the schooling and property route.

Under our present economical and political system the Negro continues very nearly a slave but chains are being steadily forged for the poor white, too, while a real emancipation is the certain prospect, through industrial progress, for thousands of Negroes.

I don't think the Negroes are free. I think they ought to be free, too—but I am chiefly concerned that our white civilization appears to be resting in part on a white slavery and one with constantly strengthening shackles.

BACK TO CALHOUN
(1917)

This penetrating analysis of suffrage, representation, and the idea of the concurrent majority was read before the Kosmos Club, Columbia, S.C., March 27, 1917. It was printed in 1925, together with the paper "Back to Aristocracy," under the title of *Essays In Reaction*.

SOUTH CAROLINA's need of a new state constitution is generally recognized. The constitution of 1895 was made by a convention called with the avowed purpose of confirming and tightening statutory devices for the disfranchisement of the Negro majority, and a constitution taking its place must be delimited by similar considerations. Suffrage and taxation will be two subjects of importance in the work of the next constitutional convention, but detailed discussion of them is not here undertaken.

Of suffrage, it suffices to say that it should be rigidly limited, and the chief test for enfranchisement should be literacy, or education, through the present qualifications fortified by perfected registration statutes and a form of the "Australian ballot." The present alternative property qualification has ceased to assist more illiterate whites than blacks, and to serve its original purpose it would require radical change. The qualifications, whatever they be, should contemplate only honest and just administration in conformity with the federal constitution. For white supremacy or ascendancy the reliance must be upon the natural and inherited advantages of the whites unaided by resort to laws savoring of fraud in design or administration. If a Negro, Francis L. Cardozo, speaking to the constitutional convention composed in the main of Negroes, in 1868, in advocacy of compulsory school attendance, could use these words, referring to the white people, "We know when the old aristocracy and ruling power of this State get into power, as they undoubtedly will, because intelligence and wealth will win in the long run," surely the whites, all of them members in the South of a racial aristocracy, after 42 years of realization of Cardozo's prophecy, may not fear to rest their case on just laws. Besides, the Negro majority of voting males of 30,292 in the State in 1890, five years before adoption of the constitution, had been reduced to a majority of 8,500, July 1, 1916, according to the census bureau's estimate. So the menace of Negro supremacy has vanished. The continuing and greater menace is white illiteracy and its attendant evils, even if we leave the low state of the Negroes out of the account.

Dealing with the second great subject, taxation, a constitutional convention should for the most part confine itself to clearing away the obstacles to reform and revision imbedded in the existing constitution. The General Assembly should be allowed freer play. The constitutional school tax should be retained only if the condition that its proceeds be expended in districts of its collection be eliminated. If the requirement of identical assessments by the state and subordinate municipalities (an innovation in 1895) be adhered to, it should be accompanied by another that the assessing agency be free of local bias. The delocalization of assessments is of prime concern; so long as wards, townships and counties shall compete with one another to reduce assessments, equity cannot be hoped for. The assessing body, more than all others, should be isolated from partisan and local influence. The "uniform property tax" should be abolished and the classification of objects of taxation permitted. Maximum levies for the state and its divisions might be fixed as a check on prodigality.

Running through and controlling the taxing and assessing laws should be the notion of the state as the unit to be sustained and developed, in contrast with the afflicting and deadening one now prevailing, that every township, town and county should spend the last penny of its public contribution on itself, regardless of the continuing servitude to ignorance and degradation of other districts with which they are inseparably connected and inextricably involved and whose delinquency must necessarily react upon and infect themselves.

The end chiefly sought in this paper is to impress the expediency of a third characteristic of a new constitution—a restoration, in part, of the powers formerly lodged in the General Assembly with consequent, not proportionate, diminution of those with which the executive is now clothed.

Briefly, the plan is that the General Assembly, directly or indirectly, elect most of the heads of the state departments—including especially those which presuppose in the officer expert or technical training. Whether the General Assembly chose, for example, the state superintendent of education of, say, nine members, which would select the superintendent, would not affect the principle involved. That principle is that in this commonwealth, owing to circumstances that differentiate it from most of the others of the Republic, government residing in the General Assembly is safer than government residing in one man.

The election of boards, which in turn would choose the officers, would be preferable to election by the legislature and the value of the plan would be small unless this were the method ordinarily employed. Members of these boards should hold office at least six, eight or ten years, they should serve without other remuneration than payment of actual expenses, and they should be so constituted by law that during no single administration of two or four years could the composition of one of them be completely changed. If, for instance, the board consisted of eight members, the terms of two should expire at the end of each two years.

Obviously, the plan contemplates the removal of departments of the state from factors of partisan politics so far as is possible. That election by popular vote of an educational expert or an expert in military affairs is an absurd thing is almost self-evident. It were as well to elect a professor to the chair of bacteriology or Greek in a popular primary as to choose an insurance commissioner in that manner. By chance rather than design the legislative method of choosing the insurance commissioner is in practice but, contrarily, the commissioner of agriculture is elected by the people.

The notion that the people are fit to choose directly all officers is palpable nonsense. They who profess it do not believe it. The average man would regard as worthless shares of a banking or cotton mill company if he and hundreds of other shareholders were permitted to vote directly for the cashier and the treasurer of them, respectively. Conservation of commercial properties requires that the elections of officers be delegated to directorates. While the General Assembly might be considered a directorate of the state, delegation by it of power to select office-holders would be the better scheme. It would tend to sterilize the elections of partisan politics; compensation of members of the boards to actual expenses would be proposed, save that it would assuredly be rejected.

A board should be constituted for each important department of the state requiring the service of experts or specialists, as charities and corrections, education, military affairs, agriculture, labor, health, taxation and revenues. Boards with more specific and limited functions and powers might also be created.

The time has come when there should be a department of civil service, similar in its office and duties to the federal board, and with ampler authority to put the merit system into operation in respect of minor posts.

So much for statement of the plan. Upon what principle may it be supported at a time when the tendency is toward concentration of power in the executives of the American states by means of the "short ballot"? Without admitting that the tendency is good anywhere, the contention that in the Southern states, particularly in South Carolina, the residence of power in the General Assembly is salutary is proved by experience.

In our periods of worst government, exclusive of the eight years of Reconstruction, the General Assembly has usually been conservative and honest. Sometimes it has been mistaken, sometimes lacking in a sagacious leadership, but as a rule it has been a bar to dishonesty. No Democratic or white legislature has looted the state treasury or permitted it to be looted by others. That the state "dispensary system," when its directors were elected by the General Assembly, proved corrupt and that its corrupting influences acted in some degree upon the legislature itself, must be confessed, but it is not here held that government by legislature is perfect. A dispensary system remaining in the hands of the executive department would probably have become more corrupt—and more powerful—than did the system of malodorous memories. Furthermore, it is to be said that at the present stage of our democracy, it is hardly likely that any kind of mercantile or other business or anything apart from the circumscribed offices of government would be conducted competently and with scrupulous honesty by the state. South Carolina has not yet fully proved an ability to govern well on narrow and conventional lines and exploration of strange fields, until respect for law shall markedly improve, is pretty sure to end in disaster. So long as that it is nearly impossible in South Caroline to convict a man who burns his house in order that he may collect upon a fire insurance policy, honest conduct of a state fire insuring company may not be hoped for. In the last 40 years perhaps 4,000 or 5,000 white men in the state have fallen at the hands of other white men, but the number of white men that have suffered the extreme penalties of the law which the people have made could be counted on the fingers of the two hands and perhaps not more than one in 15 or 20 have suffered any penalty at all. We are in the primer of law enforcement in South Carolina.

Observers of periods of bad government in South Carolina since 1876 could scarcely have failed to reflect that conditions would have been intolerable had the General Assembly been in sympathy with the executive. That reflection has in fact prompted the preparation of this paper. Sometimes, to be sure, we have had executives personally superior in character and usually in intelligence to the average legislator, but the truth survives that the legislature as a whole is nearly always conservative and representative of good citizenship. The day may come, perhaps it will come, when the General Assembly will be corrupt; corrupt state legislatures are not uncommon phenomena in the United States, but no signs of change for the worse in this respect are visible now in South Carolina.

The social constitution of the state changes slowly. The outlook is that for a number of years it will continue rural and agricultural by a two-thirds majority, and there is nothing upon which to forecast for the next quarter century so considerable a change as has been wrought by factory construction in the last. We may with relative safety and certainty use the data now before us and build upon them a new constitution to endure so long as documents of that kind ordinarily endure in America.

If the General Assembly has been the fortress of praiseworthy government, what is the explanation? There must be a reason for it. Why is not the General Assembly so unscrupulous, so selfish, so evil and reckless as the executive is when his ruling motive is personal, to reward followers, to punish opponents, to place a premium on misdemeanors and crimes by loose extension of clemency?

The explanation is to be found in the representative form of our government, modeled on the government of the Republic. In a word, the General Assembly gives to South Carolina something akin to Mr. Calhoun's government by "concurrent majority" while the executive is elected by the "numerical majority." Government by "concurrent majority," as Mr. Calhoun describes it in his *Disquisition on Government*, is based upon representation by groups, as differentiated by geographical features, population, industries or interest. In the Republic the equal representation of the states in the Senate and the possession of votes in the electoral college for each senator, according to Mr. Calhoun, tends to protect the smaller states against the absolutism of the numerical majority of densely populated states or sections and gives to it the definition of a "constitutional democracy."

While counties are not patterned upon states, the same plan is imitated as to them in the disposition of legislative representation in South Carolina. As the State of Nevada, with a population less than that of the most populous of the South Carolina counties, has two senators and votes in the electoral college corresponding to them, as New York has, so the small agricultural county of Calhoun in South Carolina has a senator as has the great county of Spartanburg with its city, manufacturing towns, and agriculture, too.

Meantime, while the white man's primary system lasts, this

excessive representation of counties of heavy Negro population in the legislature is present in the lower house as well as in the senate. Beaufort county has 1,071 white voters and Oconee three times as many, but Beaufort has representation in the legislature for its Negro population; hence it has the same number of members of the House that Oconee has. In the same way, Beaufort has equal representation with Oconee in the Democratic state convention that creates and controls the party election machinery and sends delegates to national presidential conventions.

The result of this arrangement is good, not bad, much as it clashes with theories of extreme democracy. By reason of the concentration of about one-third of the white votes in ten northwestern counties, the menace of sectional government might raise its head in the state. The sudden coming into being of a segregated and class conscious industrial vote has already presented a stubbornly vexing problem. That the distribution of political power is not founded exclusively in population or in white population has been repeatedly proved in recent years; it is a fortunate circumstance that Bamberg, Hampton, Edgefield, Georgetown, Clarendon, Darlington, Beaufort, Lee, Barnwell and Calhoun have a strength in legislatures and conventions disproportionate to their white or total population as compared with that of Charleston, Spartanburg, Anderson, Richland, Greenville, Pickens, Oconee and York.

The historic number of members of the House of Representatives is 124; it has not been changed since 1790. The number of senators is now 45; so late as 1876 it was 32, but since then 13 new counties have been carved out of the older counties. (At this time, 1925, the counties number 46; therefore the Senate has 46 members and the General Assembly 170.)

It follows from the senatorial representation and representation in the House based on total population (though only the white vote has weight in primaries) that in elections by the legislature the numerical white majority in the state is robbed of its mastery and the power is fairly well placed throughout the nearly 31,000 square miles of territory. This balance will not be seriously disturbed. In the early days of the state primary, the strength of the small counties was conserved by the election, in a primary, of delegates to a state convention. The arrangement was unfortunately superceded by the direct state primary, but it may be taken for granted that the small counties would not submit to a further stripping of their weight in the state convention and certainly not in the legislature. Attempt to effect such a change in the party constitution would probably end in party disruption.

The history of English constitutional liberty has been the history of contest by the people against the executive, the king. In that way arose the power of the parliament. Privilege was wrung from the hands of the king first by the nobles, and prerogative was steadily trimmed and whittled to all but contemptible proportions. Long ago the preponderance of power found its secure home in the House of Commons and since 1832 the people have carried on a progressively successful battle for aggrandizement at the expense of the classes. The last obstinate stand for executive absolutism was made by George III against the Whig statesmen, and the American Revolution was, in notable degree, a phase of it. Intense jealousy of the executive was a fruit of it, and in South Carolina government by the legislature lasted from 1776 until 1865.

In the former year the colonial legislature framed a constitution predicated upon the assumption that the quarrel with the mother country would be composed. This not coming to pass, a second constitution was framed two years later which was operative until 1790. Both of these had no higher sanction than legislative enactment, but they contained the skeleton of a government that ever since has survived, despite wide alternation in method of choosing its officers in the later years.

The "president" under the first constitution and the governor under the second were elected by the General Assembly and so were the other officers of the state and the magistrates and sheriffs of the counties. The colonial General Assembly consisted of one house and the first state constitution provided for a "legislative council" which the General Assembly would elect, as well as a privy council. So came into being in South Carolina the bicameral system.

A distinction was made in the manner of choosing the law and chancery judges, the General Assembly electing the former and leaving the latter to be commissioned by the governor, subject to removal by the General Assembly. The governor's term was four years, but he was ineligible for reelection until four years after its expiration. The government having been born in the stress of war, naturally its head was looked upon as in some sort a military chieftain, a circumstance that the repeated references to him as "governor and commander and chief" in the early constitutions accentuates, but even his military authority was cabined and confined. Military officers above the rank of captain were chosen by the General Assembly and the governor was only allowed to appoint subordinate officers as necessary with the advice and consent of the privy council. South Carolina had had her lesson in the despotic exercise of authority by the colonial governors and would take no chances for the future.

The constitution of 1790 was the product of a convention and, while it included far-reaching advances on its predecessors, among them the abolition of primogeniture and of all religious tests, it held with few changes to the method of electing the governor and other officers. The election of chancery judges was restored to the General Assembly. "All the other officers shall be appointed as they have hitherto been until otherwise directed by the law" is the language of this constitution. The governor's term was made two years with inelegibility for reelection until the lapse of four. He was required to reside at the capital only when the General Assembly was in session.

The right of suffrage was based on the holding of real estate or the payment of a three shillings tax by non-holders of real estate in the districts of their residence. This property qualification, however, was repealed in 1810. Governors and lieutenant-governors were required to be holders of real estate and plural voting by owners of land in more than one election district was permitted until 1833.

The attorney general was one state officer appointed by the governor—a provision manifestly sound in its wisdom as he is the official adviser of the governor. It should by all means be revived in a new constitution unless the people are prepared to say that lawyers should have a peculiar claim to the governorship itself.

Moulding the future of the state more than anything else was the plan of representation known as "the parish system." Some seventeen parishes were made election districts, each with a senator, the parishes of St. Michael's and St. Philip's, coincident with the city of Charleston, having two. The up-state districts, about nineteen or twenty, each had a senator, though Marlboro, Chesterfield, and Darlington together had but two. The parishes generally had three representatives to two for the districts, and members of both houses had to be freeholders. The preponderance of strength in the parishes inevitably kindled envy, which grew in intensity as white population in the up-state districts increased, until, by amendment in 1808, representation was based on white population and the amount of taxes raised in the election districts. Thus the parishes were given representation for their slave property, and much the same end is attained as by the present system, under which, in practice, the lower counties have representation for their heavy majorities of non-voting Negroes. No change was made by this amendment in senatorial representation, the parishes remaining senatorial districts as before.

While the white population of interior districts steadily increased and, doubtless, resentment was felt and spoken against the power exerted in the senate by parishes of minute electorates, the system seems to have aroused no serious and general opposition. Slavery rapidly extended in the interior and broad landed estates multiplied, bringing the up-countrymen and low-countrymen into close economic and political communion. When the state seceded there was little to separate the districts from the parishes in the disposition toward slavery, if two or three semi-mountainous districts be excepted. The saying that "Secession was born in the parishes" had little more than a rhetorical foundation.

Mr. Calhoun, himself an up-countryman, concludes his *Discourse on the Constitution and Government of the United States* with a description of the government of South Carolina to illustrate the wisdom of a constitutional democracy founded on "the concurrent majority." Discounting that it idealizes the parish system and remembering that it was penned in 1849, it may be accepted as, on the whole, a fair and balanced portrayal of fact. However unfashionable it may be to set up Calhoun as a political guide in these times, I make bold to say that his doctrine has not lost vitality so far as his own state is regarded and I commend it to you.

That the time was ripe for the wiping out of the parish system in 1865 is not evidence that it had outlived its usefulness in 1849, and the truth that stands out is that the senatorial representation of counties today, together with the representation in the house and the state conventions, accidental and perhaps temporary though it be, for the non-voting and disfranchised Negroes, still gives the doctrine life, though in greatly modified form.

The convention of 1861, the same that passed the ordinance of Secession, made no substantial changes in the internal arrangements of the government and may be omitted from this discussion.

The convention of 1865 was held under the proclamation of President Andrew Johnson and its mission was to conform the state to the new conditions resulting from war in a manner harmonizing with the opinion of its status entertained by him. It was composed of native white South Carolinians of prominence, elderly men being prepotent in influence. Benjamin F. Perry, throughout his long life a staunch Union man, was the governor and was looked upon as the spokesman of the President. The convention, as was expected, promptly declared the institution of slavery abolished. The federal constitutional amendments, clothing the Negroes with the right of suffrage, had not been adopted and the convention, following the advice of the governor, proceeded in the theory that the Negroes would never be citizens and neglected to take action with a view of enfranchising even the exceptionally worthy of them, as had been cautiously proposed by Mr. Lincoln. "The Radical party of the North," said Governor Perry in his message to the convention, "forget that this is a white man's government and intended for white men only, and that the Supreme Court of the United States has decided that the Negro is not an American citizen under the federal constitution." At that time free persons of color in most of the Northern states always had been and still were without the ballot. The downright refusal of the convention to consider any of the Negroes as potential citizens of the future had the effect of further infuriating that element of the Northern people most intolerant of the South.

Governor Perry did not mince words in condemning the aristocratic form of the South Carolina government, particularly in the election of the executive and the presidential electors by the legislature. Recommending changes as to these, he said that "the minor offices might be filled by appointment, and the people relieved of trouble, loss of time and demoralization in making these petty elections." "The Governor," he advised, "should live at the seat of Government." "The General Assembly of South Carolina," he said, "is the electoral college for the state as well as the legislative body. They have the election of the governor, electors of president and vice president, lieutenant governor, United States senators, judges and chancellors, all state officers, magistrates, commissioners of roads and bridges, poor and free schools, commissioners and masters in equity and various other offices. This embarrasses legislation, occupies a great deal of the time of the members, and is productive of evil consequences. The most of these elections and appointments should be taken from the legislature."

The convention followed the line indicated as to the election of governor and lieutenant governor and presidential electors, and for the first time gave to the executive a qualified power of veto, which since then he has possessed.

Governor Perry also denounced the parish senatorial system, declaring that repeated efforts during the past 75 years had failed to reform it. By way of contrast he pointed out that one parish having only 20 or 30 voters, whose combined population and taxation entitled it to one member of the lower house, had equal representation in the senate with the district of Edgefield with its 3,000 voters and six representatives.

The parish system died hard, but after the warmest contest

of the convention, it passed out of existence, and the low-country was divided into districts after the manner of the up-country. The principle of legislative apportionment on population and taxation was retained. The oath required of officers of the state was reformed, that part of it declaring by implication the allegiance to the state paramount to allegiance to the United States, incorporated about 1834, as a sequel to the Nullification controversy, being excised. Property qualifications for membership in the legislature were abolished and a proposal for an educational qualification for suffrage was defeated on the plea that it would disfranchise large numbers of white men.

Surveyed as a whole, the new document was a forward step in democracy, quite so great as the people were prepared for at the time. It left the election of all the important state officers having administrative duties except the governor and lieutenant governor as well as the judges of the higher courts to the General Assembly; and, but for the unhappy though entirely natural lack of provision that would have arranged for a gradual enfranchisement of those Negroes who might prove competent to vote, the constitution would have been wisely proportioned to the times and circumstances of the commonwealth.

While even greater enlargements of popular government than those contained in the constitution of 1865 would in time have followed the War Between the States, it remained for the convention of 1868 to be the vehicle to bring them—with a too great swiftness and in indigestible quantities. That convention was called by Brevet Major General E. R. S. Canby, in charge of the 2nd military district with headquarters in Charleston, pursuant to the "Reconstruction acts" of Congress, of 1867, and it was composed of 115 or 120 delegates, three-fourths or more of whom were Negroes and the others carpetbaggers and scalawags. In their election, the whites, being for the most part disfranchised, did not participate.

The convention assembled in January, in Charleston presumably that it might be under the protection of Canby, and its proceedings were carried on nearly altogether by a score of delegates of whom all save six or eight were black men. Signs of incipient graft, in the election of the convention's attendants and in the printing, were not wanting, and in the government that they set on foot nearly all of the leaders and the majority of the delegates were developed in the course of eight years as freebooters, thieves, rascals, brazen and gluttonish looters of the public treasury. Among them were differences in degree of viciousness and a very few, doubtless, were honest men and so remained but, had the law been enforced without lenity against them by the Democrats after they came to power in 1876, with rare exceptions they would have worn stripes. Nevertheless, when one hears the average South Carolina office-seeker ranting about the rights of the "people," one familiar with the work of this convention must acknowledge that the ranter does not know (perhaps would loudly deny if he did know), that it gave to the people a large part of their rights so far as the form in which they are now exercised and enjoyed is considered.

The constitution of '68 made manhood suffrage universal and practically without restriction. It provided that all the state and county officers, with the exception of the county treasurer, auditor and magistrates and the circuit and supreme court judges, be elected directly by the people. In introduced the homestead exemption, authorized a free school system with a two mill tax for its maintenance, abolished imprisonment for debt, included an antidueling clause in the oath of office, prohibited judges from charging juries in relation to facts, opened public educational institutions of every grade to all persons without regard to race or color, forbade lotteries and made the estates of married women separate and independent.

The provisional governor, Judge James L. Orr, formerly speaker of the national House of Representatives and later minister to Russia, the same who had received next to the highest number of votes cast for president of the Secession convention seven years before, addressed the convention upon an invitation extended not without bitter opposition.

Judge Orr, believing it the better policy for the white people to participate in the government through the Republican party than not to participate at all, had allied himself with it. His address was noteworthy for plain-speaking and that grasp and vigor that he usually displayed. He told the convention that they and those whom they represented were on trial and strove to warn them against reckless departures.

Among other things, he urged that the suffrage be based on education with an alternative property qualification—exactly what the Democrats incorporated in the next constitution 27 years later, in 1895. He also advocated a homestead law and it is inferable from his language that he expected that it would be of more beneficial import to the whites than to the Negroes.

The convention adopted in general a reproduction of the constitution of Ohio—but did not merely gulp it down. For more than two months the delegates drew their per diem and indulged their propensity for harangue and disputation, and the speeches of some of them gave ample evidence of native ability and of study, too. It is incontestible that ideals of democracy were sincerely entertained by many of them and they found occasional expression in suggestions that were rejected.

For example, W. J. Whipper, a Negro of Beaufort, proposed to strike the word "male" from the suffrage clause so that suffrage might, indeed, be universal in South Carolina, and Daniel H. Chamberlain, then attorney general and afterwards governor, the ablest delegate and one of the better white men of the convention, contended for the election of judges by the people on the ground that the general electorate would be less easily corrupted than the General Assembly.

Nor were all of the delegates destitute of the conception that a democracy to be efficient must be erected on an intelligent electorate—that use of the printed or written ballot presupposes ability to read and write. The principle of compulsory school attendance, after an interesting debate notable especially for the speech of F. L. Cardozo, a mulatto delegate of Charleston who had been educated in the University of Edinborough and who was later state treasurer, disclosing remarkable understanding and prescience, was incorporated in the constitution, but the condition appended that it be operative when the school system of the state should be sufficiently organized and improved made it a dead letter.

The committee on suffrage favorably reported a literacy test for the ballot, to take effect after seven years, in 1875, but this was too severe a trial for the virtue of the convention. The leaders, foreseeing that its adoption would be the doom of Negro supremacy, with savage unanimity pounced upon it, with the result that it was eliminated by a vote of 104 to two, most of the members of the committee joining in apology for or condemnation of their own report.

A clause permitting the truth to be given in evidence as a defence to prosecutions for libel founded on publications relating to public officials and investigations of their conduct was a slight advance made in the direction of freedom of the press—enlarged by the constitution of 1895 to admit evidence of the truth in all actions and prosecutions for libel.

The election of directors of the penitentiary was left to the determination of the General Assembly and the appointment of those of other institutions and that of the superintendent of the state asylum for the insane was given to the governor, by and with the consent of the Senate.

These provisions were rewritten in the constitution of 1895, with embarrassing consequences to the asylum that brought about a transfer of the election of the superintendent to the board of regents in the last two years—an illustration of the danger of delegating the power of appointment to the executive when the office to be filled demands a man of special training and equipment.

The white people came into power in 1877. The mongrel state government had, of course, utterly failed to establish a free school system worthy of the name and it was left for Hugh S. Thompson, elected superintendent of education in 1876 and governor in 1882, to organize it. No attempt to educate the races together, as contemplated by the convention of 1868, was made except in the state School for the Deaf and Blind and in the University. It caused the instant resignation of the faculty and the suspension of the one and drove the white students from the other. The white General Assembly promptly enacted laws having the nature and effect, in part, of literacy tests and the Negroes ceased to vote.

The convention of 1895 was, as has been said, called to devise more effectual and permanent disfranchisement of the Negro masses, and this was done by the adoption of the alternative literacy and property qualifications. For two years oral interpretation of the constitution was allowed so that white illiterate adults then in being might not be deprived of the ballot. In the terms of the law Negroes were extended the same privilege, but as to them there were "mental reservations."

Except as to the suffrage, the features of the constitution of '68 were, in the main, reaffirmed and preserved. Barriers to prevent mingling of the races were raised, but the homestead law, the free school system and various other fundamentals or contrivances of popular government that had been introduced under the glint of Canby's bayonets were perpetuated. There was no going back toward election of officers by the General Assembly that had until the day of the scalawag and carpetbagger distinguished government in South Carolina. The white people had become not less intoxicated with democracy than the mongrel mob were, and they clove to it without thought of the channel through which it had come to them—making it, though, an exclusive white possession.

Other important if not basic laws were introduced in the new constitution to meet new social, commercial and industrial conditions. One innovation, the dispensary regulations, precluded for the future enlightened legislative treatment of the traffic in intoxicants. The people in 1895 were infatuated with the dispensary system and their leaders were stupid enough to force into the organic law a clause having the sharply defined lines of a statute, thereby cutting off progressive reform of the liquor traffic save by a narrow path. This provision, grounded on assumption of final knowledge of a subject that has baffled social reformers for uncounted centuries, affords an accurate gauge of the mental and temperamental limitations of its authors.

The makers of the constitution of 1895 fully expected that its suffrage limitations would be effective after 1898. Two rebellions against the state primary system had already taken place. That the primary would last more than 20 years, having the effect of nullifying the suffrage restrictions so far as the whites were concerned, they perhaps did not dream. Nevertheless, this has come to pass. The white primary is the real election and in it the illiterate and propertyless participate. The suffrage as an incentive to gain literacy and property has been taken from the whites and left to the Negroes. Perhaps in no other modern state has been such unrestricted manhood suffrage, so far as the white race is concerned, as in South Carolina.

In the belief that universal literacy of the whites would be needed to protect the state from the Negroes, education was the dominant note of the proceedings of the convention of 1895. The constitutional school tax was raised to three mills, with the lamentably astringent condition attached that its proceeds should be expended in the locality of collection, so insuring for South Carolina educational progress by counties rather than as a commonwealth. South Carolina is strong for local option in everything except the whiskey traffic. Senator Tillman had formerly proposed a $3 poll tax, but this highly aristocratic suggestion was too much even for his usually unquestioning followers. He did not adhere to it in 1895.

The growth of the primary has upset the calculations of 1895, the white people have more and more wallowed in democracy, and the state being now racially aristocratic, the educative influences of democracy have been, as hinted, cancelled—the illiterate whites being deprived of motive to emerge from ignorance.

Having sketched generally the constitutions, a few particulars merit attention. Despite the jealousy of the executive in the Revolutionary period, the pardon power was conferred on the governor. As he was elected by the General Assembly, it was perhaps reasoned that he would not dare abuse it—but, more probably, it was given to him because it had to be lodged somewhere and could not be conveniently exercised by the General Assembly. The expedient of a pardon board had not been thought of in those times. In a land of democratic institutions, as an executive power, it is an anomaly. In Great Britain it belongs to the king on the theory that public wrongs are breaches of "the king's peace." So read the indictments. In this country, it is "the peace and dignity of the state" or of "the people," that is broken—so read the indictments—not "the governor's peace and dignity."

More than once in this state and in other states this awkward departure from the principles of American governments has blossomed in shameful and dangerous abuses. Governors have taken the disposition of criminals to be their peculiar and personal province and there is almost irresistible tendency even on the part of good governors to review the evidence, hear new evidence and retry criminal cases already passed upon by juries. That executive clemency is permitted solely as a corrective of the rigidity of the law they forget.

While machinery for the application of modern penology to convicts is desirable, to make the governor the sole or chief instrument of it is a stupid recourse. In the United Kingdom of Great Britain and Ireland the pardon power belongs to the king in no more than a technical sense, it has long been delegated and is now exercised only upon recommendation of the secretary of state for the home department or the lord lieutenant of Ireland. In some of the American states it belongs to the governor and in others to pardon boards. The convention of 1895 made provision for a board of pardons but gave to it no more than an advisory power. Manifestly, in the hands of an unscrupulous executive the power to pardon is the power to punish, see the case of King Henry II and the Archbishop of Canterbury, and it is not less than astonishing that the people of a democratic commonwealth allow this contradiction in government to continue, susceptible as it is of being turned to the destruction of the courts and juries and pregnant as it is with peril to their very freedom. A new constitution in South Carolina should certainly place the larger part of the pardon power in the hands of a board elected by the General Assembly.

A defect in the present constitution (and in all its predecessors) is that it has no provision by which the General Assembly can convene, except in regular session, without the initiative of the governor. A governor, therefore, may run amuck ten months in the year without danger of impeachment.

General Assemblies should be prohibited from electing their own members to other office and members should be ineligible to such elections for a period after the expiration of their terms.

Recapitulating, it is emphasized that the transfer of the power to appoint officers from the executive to the General Assembly would take from the people no power that they now hold, except in so far as the governor is more likely to be the product of the numerical majority of the whole state than is the General Assembly. This objection is academic—the people's interests are safer in the hands of 170 men, or boards of their choice, than in one man's hands.

It is proposed to take out of the people's hands only the offices calling for considerable special equipment. Popular election of the governor, lieutenant governor, secretary of state and other officers for whom general training suffices would not be interfered with. Muster ground fisticuffs and gander pullings having lost their vogue, the people must have "races" preceded by ranting in the good old summer time.

The small counties being preponderantly agricultural, the plan would entrench the farmers more than ever in government—it is a "farmers' movement" here advocated far more than was that of 1890.

If the principle of electing the commissioner of insurance by the General Assembly is sound, the practice of electing railroad commissioners by direct popular vote is ipso facto unsound. The General Assembly elects the superintendent and the directors of the penitentiary while the governor appoints the regents of the state hospital and they elect its superintendent—wherein appears a conspicuous hodge podge of antagonistic principle and practice. The legislature delegating the choice of executives to boards, each board's composition changing by the entrance of one or two members at intervals of two years and no board's composition being subject to complete change during the life of any legislature, danger of a board being packed corruptly by a legislature would be small. Membership of the governor in certain boards, or all of them, is a detail for consideration. To elect the members of the boards would consume less of the time of the legislature than is now used in legislative elections.

The plan as sketched is not set forth as the wisest for all the states or as an everlasting insurance of good government. It is offered as probably adapted to conditions now prevailing and likely to persist for two or three decades, and it is proposed as the correction of the blind and blundering excursion into democracy in 1868 for which the people were not prepared and which the white people in 1895 ratified and in many directions carried further. It is open to objections and no more is claimed for it than superior merit to the plan of government now operative. Proportional party representation might be suggested as preferable, that being almost unheard of in South Carolina, its explanation, much the more its application, would present insuperable difficulty.

If the foregoing proposals are altogether bad, the condemnation of the state government from 1790 to 1868 as vilely and unspeakably bad is included. If they cannot be defended, the conclusion is unescapable that it was South Carolina's supreme misfortune that the scalawags, carpetbaggers and Negroes did not enjoy the opportunity to make the government democratic half a century or so before it was given to them by the "Black Republicans" at the instigation of Thad Stevens and his crew.

BACK TO ARISTOCRACY

(1919)

Read before the Kosmos Club, Columbia, S.C., in 1919, "Back To Aristocracy" is especially valuable as a key to William Watts Ball's views on two great issues of government: the relation of property to liberty and fitness for the suffrage.

PREFATORILY, you are asked to receive this paper as indicating a bent of mind rather than an irrevocable and fixed opinion. Factors in any political equation change so swiftly in these hours that the program of an evening may appear inadequate and old-fashioned at the dawn of the next morning. So the writer has employed himself to present an argument based upon premises which he reserves the right at any time to reconsider and repudiate. Nevertheless the bent of mind will expose if not impress itself.

Two years ago, before this club I read a paper entitled "Back to Calhoun," written with a constitutional convention in view and bringing into brief retrospect the constitutions of South Carolina beginning with that of 1776. In that paper it was pointed out that the government of South Carolina had been notably aristocratic in form until 1868. In the early days the state of South Carolina not only had property qualifications for holding office and for suffrage, but until about 1833 plural voting was permitted and legislative representation was based upon taxable property as well as population until 1868. Thus a parish in the low-country having less than one hundred voters was represented in the General Assembly by one senator and by as many members of the House as an up-country district of two thousand voters might have. As the General Assembly elected the governor, the presidential electors, the judges, nearly all the state officers, and some of the county officers, nearly the whole power of government was lodged in the legislature and it represented property, largely slave property, as well as citizenry. It was held that the administrative fruit of this system was good, not bad, destructive though it was of modern notions of democracy. Mr. Calhoun, in his *Disquisition on Government* praised it as a successful example of government by "the concurrent majority," which, with transcendent power he contended, is preferable to government by the "numerical majority."

In 1868, when the white people were disfranchised, a convention called by General E. R. S. Canby, commanding the state as a military district, composed of one hundred and twenty delegates, about two-thirds of them Negroes, the few whites being either carpetbaggers or scalawags, met in Charleston and adopted a constitution substituting a form of government, which, for that day, was the last word in democracy. Universal and unrestricted manhood suffrage was provided and the ignorant and property-less man, black or white, was endowed with equal ballot power with the intellectuals and capitalists. Curiously enough, W. J. Whipper, a Negro delegate of Beaufort, with a vision of democracy half a century in advance of his day, and attuned to 1919, proposed that the word "male" be stricken from the suffrage clause of the constitution so that half the population, the women, might not be disfranchised, but his proposal was defeated.

Twenty-seven years this constitution was operative in South Carolina and as soon as the white people regained control of the state, after eight years of misrule, they not only accepted the democratic regime, but took boundless joy in it, became drunken upon it and turned their backs upon all their old customs and traditions. To be sure, they seized this democracy of Negro fabrication and introduction as a boon fit for exclusive white employment. By one device or another, they promptly eliminated the Negro vote, induced upon the Negroes the habit of not voting, mesmerized them into a political slumber, creating a government racially aristocratic, but entirely democratic as far as their own race was concerned. The white man was allowed to vote in primaries and so to gain and hold office, wholly regardless of literacy or property.

The constitution of '68 made nearly all officers elective by the people, but wisely excepted the fiscal offices of county auditor and treasurer and the justices of the peace, but even these exceptions were repugnant to the new notions of democracy that took possession of the minds of the white men. They put them into the primary and soon it became as much as the political life of a politician was worth to suggest that any office, however it might require expert and specialized equipment, should not be filled in a primary election in which every man apparently twenty-one years old and having a white skin was allowed to vote. Nor was it customary to ply a youth of ruddy countenance with embarrassing questions about his age when he appeared at the primary poll. Between 1877 and 1895 it was fully understood that at all hazards racial aristocracy must be preserved and it was fully understood that its fortifications were legally fragile, so the convention of 1895 to strengthen the disfranchisement of the Negroes was called.

In those days was little fear of indulgence in aristocratic expedients and even that "tribune of the people," Captain B. R. Tillman openly advocated, for a time, a three dollar poll tax, a proposal that was unpopular, not so much that it was undemocratic as that it gave the anti-Tillmanites a specious war-cry. The convention of 1895 deliberately restricted the suffrage by writing into the constitution an educational qualification coupled with an alternative property qualification. Harking back to the ancient superstition that military service should guarantee the right to govern, a provision was inserted whereby until January 1, 1898, the suffrage could be conferred upon illiterate persons who could construe a part of the constitution when read to them, the plain and avowed aim being to avoid the disfranchisement of veterans of the Confederate armies.

Twenty-four years ago the makers of a new constitution had no illusions about the flimsiness of the foundations upon which pure democracy rested in South Carolina and, calculatingly, they contrived voting restrictions that they thought would destroy it, not that they did not love it, but that they believed that it was not a plant to be safely nourished in a mixed population. The preponderant wish was that the white people should be made universally literate in a generation, so the three mill school tax

was written in the constitution. Lest the Negroes in equal numbers should learn to read and write, compulsory school attendance
was not considered. The white voters having "split" in 1890 and
1894, it was apprehended that the firmer disfranchisement of the
Negroes would be followed by subsequent divisions of the white
people, as they would be relieved of the menace of Negro domination, but what happened reversed this prognosis. After 1895
the state primary system grew stronger instead of weaker and
the racial white democracy, built upon what was no more than
"a gentleman's agreement" and rooted in vague alarm at the
consequence of appeal by two white parties to Negro voters, was
crystallized. Thus about a quarter of a century the white party
has held together and sometimes evil government has been
endured lest resort to the general election call down greater evils.

The fear of Negro supremacy long ago vanished, but the
larger fear that the admission of the Negroes to the polls, the
mass of them being easily corruptible, would react in the political
corruption of the whites, has steadily increased. Probably about
50,000 or 60,000 Negroes might legally qualify to vote now and
the number of literate and property holding whites is about
two and one-half times as great, but the belief is that perhaps
five-sixths of the Negroes could be misled by demagogues and
controlled by money or whiskey. Thus the balance of power in
politics would be transferred to unscrupulous white leaders
skilled in manipulating the prejudice and passion of the ignorant,
the weak and the vicious. So the white racial party has lived,
the white people depriving themselves of a habit and privilege
of independent thinking as well as action, and political anemia
and stagnation, inseparable from a one party system, have been
accepted in preference to a hazard of more serious ills.

This maintenance of a separate white party has been worth
the cost, and its perpetration should be encouraged. Some day
it may collapse under strain, but the longer that day is post-
poned, the better.

Meantime, democracy has flourished among the whites voting
in the primary and knowing it to be the real election, and the
ballot, as an incentive to gaining literacy, has been removed from

them. On the contrary it has been and is held in the hearts of the Negroes as a distant but certain avenue to political enfranchisement. Although, naturally, white illiteracy has been reduced, it is only within the last half-a-dozen years that the people have awakened to the necessity of aggressive efforts to wipe it out and compulsory school attendance is not yet fairly started.

It is not the aim of this paper to emphasize the Negro question, but it is impossible to discuss the political future of the state without recognizing it as part of the background. It is assumed that the "war amendments" to the federal constitution will never again be seriously assailed. If any feeble thought of their repeal lingered in the South, it vanished with the participation of the Negroes in the European War and it would be surrender to stupidity to indulge the notion that race discrimination in political affairs will at any time be lawful. Nor will sex discrimination anywhere long be tolerated.

The suffrage laws and their administration in South Carolina not only must, but ought to be, in future fair and impartial to both races and sexes and there should be no contemplation of recourse to intimidation, force or fraud for the disfranchisement of any man or woman in coming time. If this be admitted as a major premise, and it is a major premise of this paper, what are we going to do about it? How are we going to insure good government, with which most of us hold white government to be synonymous?

The answer is "Back to Aristocracy" or, at the least, to hold fast to the aristocracy that we have in political affairs. As already said, politically every white man in South Carolina is now an aristocrat, because the humblest white man occupies a position superior to that of the most intelligent or wealthiest Negro. Thus, exacting that "Mister" be applied to the humblest white man and denied to the Negro of wealth and education, we have made it a title whereby all white men are raised to a *noble* class! The Negroes remain a vassal race, the War Between the States having failed to change their essential relationship to the white race.

If the white ascendancy shall be preserved, it must seek a new formula for the future and the aristocratic government must be less racial and more political. The way out of the wilderness will be to define the ballot as the privilege of trained intelligence, or of property, or of both, and in that case the maintenance of white ascendancy will turn upon whether or not white superiority is a truthful assertion or an empty boast.

By way of illustration, if the successful passing of such a written examination as is usually given to a grammar school boy or the payment of taxes on property assessed at one thousand dollars instead of three hundred dollars were made the qualification for suffrage and more Negroes than whites met the test, it would be difficult to escape the conclusion that the Negroes were better fitted to govern than the whites are. In that event the claim of white superiority would become ridiculous and the right, if asserted, for the whites to fall back on brute force would be laughed at. Indeed, if such a result were to be recorded, it would prove that the whites had lost the power of control even by muscle and courage, as in this age successful fighting demands a skill founded on education. There is no hope for the cave man with his club in a contest with machine guns.

It is not necessary for me to assert implicit and complete faith in the ability of the white man to take care of himself against all comers, especially in a conflict of knowledge getting and property getting, even if his many centuries of start ahead of the Negroes be disregarded.

Pre-supposing that the present social order will not be disturbed in the United States, that we shall not have the destruction of private property, and proceeding on the assumption that the federal constitution will last, the next thing to consider as a fact is the world-wide and sudden infatuation for democracy and how we are to be affected by it. The world is to be made "safe for democracy" and in the utterance of the resounding phrase, our chief apostles of Democracy (with a big D) in the United States do not distinguish between men as they are subject to classification by education, color and achievement. So far as our definitions go, democracy is to be no less safe for the ignorant hordes in Russia, Jugoslavia, Bulgaria, and Rumania than for the universally literate Germans and Englishmen.

In the stertorous cry that democracy shall prevail everyone joins and no one halts to give limitation to the word, to say whether government shall be representative or by direct voice and vote of the people, and the residue of inference is that universal manhood and womanhood suffrage is to be established. To this there is and could be but one response, and it reverberates around the world. The clamorous demand is, in the first place, for self-determination and in the second, for government by all the people, in the African and Asiatic jungles and mountains as well as in the so-called civilized nations of the West. Inevitably the demand in the United States is especially loud, and that it should be taken up gleefully and enthusiastically by the newly arrived immigrants from Europe, of a dozen nationalities, and by the American Negroes, is at least the natural development.

Amid the noisy acclaim of democracy, many, if not most, of the American Socialists are turned "Reds" and are already abandoning their former moderate position that reforms may be had by lawful means, through appeal to the ballot, and saying that the American brand of representative democracy is none too good to be overthrown by force.

The Negroes, speaking, for the present, through publications in the North, and encouraged by the "parlor Bolsheviks" on the one hand and those doctrinaires who think they inherit a commission to guard and pet the former slaves, on the other, are saying that they are not only the most abused and outraged of all peoples, but that they should be instantly lifted into the seats of authority. They are taking for granted that the rest of the population should and will, by way of showing forth fruits meet for repentance, feed them henceforth on fatted calves.

The universal insistence everywhere is that one man is as good as another, which may be true, but, more than that, it is proclaimed that one man is as well fitted as another to exercise the office of government, notwithstanding that the medium of exercising it is the printed ballot, and the right of property to be heard in government, which though not in its own strident accents, has always been recognized in the United States, is now quietly ignored. The truth that men and women may be and are represented in government though they do not cast a ballot is forgotten if it has not come to be denied. By implication, the indictment is brought that a great majority of the people, including women and children and a variety of smaller classes who have not voted, have been immemorially the victims of an oppression as cruel as it was vast.

In substance the indictment is that representative government is a monstrous failure, for which mankind should spend the next century or two in apologizing and doing penance. That is the atmosphere in which we are living and which many people, who ought to know better, seem to regard as healthy and salubrious. If the American people tacitly and too long assent to these foolish notions, their Republic will fetch up in wreck, and it is high time that we consult our chart lest we lose our course in the roaring winds of the day.

Excepting our own Republic, an off-shoot of England, the English government and civilization is the most successful, if not the most virtuous of modern times. At any rate, it has endured longer than any other. It has better weathered the storms, its people have suffered less from war, from slavery, and from poverty than have those of other nations and the average of their generations the thousand years that it has been a going concern have gotten more out of life, despite all its handicaps and sorrows, than have the generations in any other land. England has had her Wars of the Roses, her Cromwellian Revolution and many another calamity, but they have been as nothing by comparison with the agonies of continental Europe in the same cycle, and today England is at least as free as any other country. Yet England has never had popular government, has always had, and still has, a governing class.

If it be said that all the people of England have not all the time been happy and prosperous, that one need go back but half a century or less to discover the working people in poverty or three-fourths of a century to find them in a state of abject misery, so far as creature comforts are considered, worse than that of the black slaves in the United States in the same period, the indictment is true, and yet when all is said the evolution, the progress, toward freedom and happiness, though even now the way to go be long and weary, has been safer, surer and attended with less pain than in any other land save those whose civilizations are mere projections of the English system.

In 1832 when the first Great Reform Bill was passed the total electorate of England and Wales was 435,391 out of a population of six million adult males. In 1867 a second bill was passed and it increased in two years the number of voters from 1,353,000 to 2,243,000 and for the first time a large part of the British working class was given a share in government. Prior to its passage but one man in five was allowed to vote. The bill gave the ballot to all householders irrespective of the value of their holdings and to all lodgers that paid not less than $50 a year for unfurnished rooms.

Even this measure, however, left the agricultural laborers without the voting franchise. In 1884 a third Reform Bill gave the vote in the counties to all householders and to those who paid at least $50 a year for lodgings, and it swelled the electorate from three millions, in round numbers, to five millions.

The Electoral Law of 1918 gave the ballot to women over 30, under certain restrictions; reduced the residence qualification and restricted plural voting to the casting of ballots in not more than two constituencies. "Although Parliament is elected (now) by what is practically universal manhood suffrage and voting in Great Britain is considered a property, not a natural right, there are still property qualifications for voting as *the expansion of the suffrage was brought about by the contraction, and not by the abolition, of the property qualification.* In order to be permitted to vote, a man must be a land-owner, a householder, that is, the head of a family occupying a house, or a lodger paying $50 a year rent. Plural voting is permitted, for a man has the right to vote in constituencies in which he possesses landed property." (Schapiro.) The whole power of government has come to reside in the House of Commons and the ministry, the latter being its creature, the House of Lords having been stripped of its power of absolute veto.

In the Nineteenth century the overwhelming majority of the lower classes could neither read nor write, and it was not until 1870, following the passage of the Second Reform Bill, that the Foster Education Act establishing a national system of popular education was enacted. In 1850 about 30 per cent of the men and about 50 per cent of the women were illiterate, but, when the Foster Act became operative, illiteracy rapidly diminished, and now, with schools free and attendance compulsory, it is practically non-existent. The number of voters in England and Wales in 1917 was 6,771,364, in Scotland 884,909 and in Ireland 701,475.

Had the suffrage been conferred on all males of voting age in Great Britain in 1832, at a time when the great majority were illiterate and while appalling poverty and wretchedness prevailed among the working people, it is likely that the British system of government would have been disrupted and destroyed. Government in South Carolina was destroyed, except in so far that it survived under the protection of military force, between 1868 and 1877, and the Negroes of South Carolina were little more illiterate than were the British masses in 1832. It is not intended here to suggest that the British were not then superior in capacity to govern than our Negroes were and are, but the British Parliament had the wisdom to perceive that universal enfranchisement of an ignorant people was incompatible with the perpetuation of an orderly and civilized government.

The democratization of the British masses has come to pass in the last 87 years, but it has been gradual, it has been extended from the top downwards and, generally, the laws enacted by a parliament elected by the aristocratic and middle classes have graduated the extension to the social and educational improvement of the masses, sometimes responding to pressure from them not exerted through the ballot. The ballot in Great Britain has not been given to the people except as clearly they were in a fair degree prepared to use it intelligently, and we have seen that even in this year of 1919 it remains closely interlaced with property-holding. The right of the land-holder to vote at least twice, if he have land in more than one parliamentary district, is still retained. This is the principle upon which government in Great Britain is erected, notwithstanding that there is no racial embarrassment to British democracy.

The enlargement of democracy in Great Britain has been so rapid in the last thirty-five years that it is too soon to say that the British system will endure in the coming years without tremendous modifications; not yet have the working classes had time to express themselves fully at the polls. The war in 1914 checked in considerable measure the rapid changes that were going on, and we may look presently for their resumption.

Disestablishment of the English church may be forecast as assured, and assent to the control of the House of Commons by members chosen from the landed aristocracy and the business and professional classes may come to an end. The labor class is already numerous enough in the House to hold something resembling a balance of power and it is possible, though not probable, that Great Britain will awake to a realization that the advance of democracy has been in late years beyond the speed limit commensurate with safety, as safety has been historically defined in John Bull's Island.

The impressive truth that shines out in this story of 87 years of popular aggrandizement is that the British upper classes could be trusted to deal justly with the people, that they held the government as trustees for the people, that they did not misuse their power, that they distributed it liberally, if prudently, not gripping it and hugging it to themselves as a divine endowment. When the hour struck, when British common sense dictated that the hereditary House of Lords had outlived its usefulness, the governing body, the Commons, proceeded virtually to demolish it, with scant ceremony, and the inference is fair that they will suffer the bulk of it together with the trappings of royalty that remain only so long as they shall serve a practical, if secondary, purpose.

The representation of the states in the United States Senate and in the electoral college, fixed without regard to population, is obviously opposed to pure democracy and, whatever its design, in its results it clothes property as well as men with power in legislation, and in choosing the executive. In the states the same scheme is adopted and in "Back to Calhoun" it was pointed out that the counties, not the people, control in South Carolina. Also it was pointed out that in this state the counties having non-voting Negro populations are enabled to exert a weight in government through the legislature and the state conventions wholly disproportionate to their voting strength in Democratic party primaries. Thus the rule of the numerical majority is counter-vailed and that of the "concurrent majority" maintained.

In the United States one is not driven to the South, where the Negro population is in part disfranchised, to find the earliest examples or the most persistent of non-democratic government in the states. Thrown on the defensive the last 60 years in relation to suffrage laws, the tendency in our part of the country is to assume that we are the only sinners against democracy, when the plain truth is that disfranchisement had early precedents in the North, especially in New England.

If that things equal to the same thing are equal to each other be axiomatic, the taking from one-half of the people one-half of the effectiveness of their votes is equal to stripping one-fourth of them of all their voting effectiveness, or to complete disfran-chisement when measured by results. This, approximately, is what has taken place in Rhode Island. In 1910 Providence and three other cities with a combined population of 341,000 had four state senators, whereas the remainder of the state with a population of 201,000 had 34 senators. Providence, with a little more than half of the state's population, had one of the 38 senators and 25 members in the Lower House of 100 members. Thus, "the Republican machine finds it easy with the support of the million-aire summer colony at Newport and the street railway corpora-tions to corrupt the French Canadian and a portion of the native element in the rural towns and maintain absolute control of the state government. The majority has occasionally protested by electing a Democratic governor, but he has not been able to accomplish a great deal, because until 1909 he did not have veto power or effectual means to induce the senate to ratify his appointments." The quotation is from the *Encyclopaedia Britannica*, Eleventh edition.

Since colonial times this system has placed the control of Rhode Island in the rural districts and racial and religious prejudices have prevented its abolition. The foreign factory operatives and the Roman Catholics have generally acted with the Democratic party and the native Protestants in the rural districts with the Whigs or Republicans. The armed insurrection led by Thomas W. Door in 1842 was a protest against it. The struggle has been going on for more than a century and, while great progress in modifying the system has been recorded, the government of Rhode Island remains much less democratic than is that of South Carolina. Even now the Rhode Islander must have property of the value of $134 over and above all incumbrances in order to vote, and the legislature is controlled by the rural voters. While the citizens of Providence may go to the polls and cast ballots, the scheme of representation reduces the weight of the ballot 50 or 75 per cent.

In Connecticut much the same plan, based on the federal system of legislative representation, is retained and the rural citizen has two or three times the ballot power of the man in Hartford or Bridgeport.

Massachusetts has always had an educational qualification, and although occasionally Democrats have been elected governor, the General Court, or legislature, that meets on Beacon Hill, is invariably Republican.

In 1916, young Mr. Gerry, of the historic Democratic New England family of that name, was elected to the United States Senate in Rhode Island, and last November Governor Walsh was elected from Massachusetts. The latter is the first Democratic senator from the state since the 1850s. These two elections were made possible by the amendment of the federal constitution transferring senatorial elections from the legislature to the people.

These undemocratic systems in the New England States are not wholly unobjectionable. They have led, for instance, to corruption of the rural vote, particularly in Connecticut, but they are conspicuous illustrations of the retention of state rights, and they have protected what New Englanders regard as their property rights. It is not for the Southerner to condemn them as unrighteous and wicked, but they ought to silence outbursts of New England pharisaism against the South.

Naturally American democracy is purest in the far West, in states of new settlement, in which the people had an even start only a few years ago, and the class differences are comparatively small. Two Colorado miners, both pioneer settlers, one of them now a rich man and the other still poor, are much the same type. Two or three generations must pass before class crystallization shall harden and be distinct. In the Western states the population was in the main literate from the start. The late James J. Hill amassed seventy million dollars, but he was a railroad brakeman. The bright vision of unadulterated democracy will begin to fade in the West, especially if foreign elements continue to pour in too fast for assimilation by the native stock.

Again, let it be stressed that the contentions of this paper do not bear against men who would consent to the demolition of the existing social order, that is, to the destruction of private property rights. Necessarily the Socialist advocates universal and unrestricted manhood and womanhood suffrage, the abolition of state lines, and popular, not state or county, representation in government.

This proposition is here submitted for your consideration: if representative government be destroyed and the vote be placed in the hand of every man and woman, irrespective of their property stakes in the community, the destruction of private property rights, as we know them, will be the implied consequence. If non-property holders come to be the large majority and one man's vote counts as much as another's, the majority coming to be class-conscious, the obliteration of laws protecting property-holding must follow. In other words, universal suffrage plus destruction of state and county unit power in government would open the way to the realization of Bolshevism, (except in so far as that it is minority rule by force) and here let me say that Bolshevism is not an ideal to be denounced outright as unholy;

that one have no faith in its expediency is not conclusive of its iniquity.

Of course, if the majority of the people should be and should continue property holders, universal suffrage would not imply the destruction of private property, the minority would be overcome at the polls, but it is suspected that the advocates of pure democracy proceed on the theory that the non-property-holders will be the majority and that they look to universal suffrage as the weapon with which to minimize property-holding and to set up a "social" or Bolshevist state.

The Rhode Island electoral and representative system is close akin to the Prussian system. Under the Empire, Prussia controlled Germany—with the fundamental difference that the Prussians employed their system to maintain the Hohenzollern autocracy. In England the governing class, rapidly coming to be co-extensive with the people, vests the Parliament and its ministry with all power; in Prussia, the governing class gave to the Reichstag only advisory power and left the real power in the hands of the hereditary Prussian King and the Bundsrat, or House of Lords, a body whose majority membership he dictated. So in South Carolina and other Southern States, we have had and still have class political government by which our "junkers" retain control. Except during the radical and military period, 1868-77, the power of government in this agricultural state of ours has never departed from the land-owners.

Can we without misgiving contemplate its departure? I answer, "No." Therefore, universal and unrestricted suffrage is not to be thought of. Safety demands that we steer away from the infatuation even of universal white democracy. There is perhaps no immediate emergency calling for the jacking up of the qualifications for suffrage and it is thinkable that for the present we may look to literacy as a sufficient qualification for protection, but, at least, there must be no let-down or weakening of the qualifications we have and those must be more rigorously enforced. If need be, the restrictions must be increased and tightened and our people should accustom themselves to the thought that the ballot relating itself to property-holding contains no element of injustice.

Until 1833 plural voting was permitted in South Carolina and if dire necessity arises we may have recourse to it again. The Fifteenth amendment to the Federal Constitution reads:

Sec. I. The right of citizens of the United States to vote shall not be denied or abridged by the United States or by any state on account of race, color, or previous condition of servitude.

Sec. II. The Congress shall have the power to enforce this article by appropriate legislation.

For a Constitutional convention to grant the right of the owner of lands in two townships, or two counties, or two Congressional districts to vote on the same day would be an expansion, not an abridgement, of the suffrage and, as we have seen, it would be the adoption of the present English plan. Such a step would be no more radical, in essence, in the direction of class government, than the adoption of the alternative property qualification was in 1895, and that the latter has never shocked us as radical is explicable only by the circumstance that it has never been of common resort. Had the racial primary not grown to be practically the sole means of government, and had the Negroes been generally literate, the alternative property qualification might have proved of considerable importance. That is to say, had there remained an illiterate and non-property owning group of whites, its resentment would have been sharp.

If the existing order of society, founded on the right of property holding, shall survive, it is doubtful if a literacy test alone will suffice for its protection. Literacy is certainly no bar to Socialism or at least it has not so far proved a barrier to it. The literate Socialist is more dangerous to the property holder than the illiterate, and the probability is much greater of the permanent establishment at an early date of a social state in Germany than in Russia or in Hungary.

This paper is not designed, let it again be emphasized, to point a solution to the race question in the South. It purports to submit to your consideration a broader and stronger program. It denies that government should take account of color and declares that question settled forever in the United States. No laws should be passed or ought to be passed that would exclude from a voice in government any man (or woman) who establishes possession of character and trained intelligence, and *it sets up that the acquisition of property is one of the proofs of those qualifications that cannot, without disaster, be ignored.*

To save what we call our white civilization, we must rely upon the natural racial qualities of the white man, and if, with them, his ascendancy cannot be sustained, and without appeal to force or fraud, it will have to disappear, and ought to disappear. Consequently, we must look forward to the sustaining of government by the superior class and trust to its demonstration of superiority in manner harmonious with what we conceive to be the eternal laws of God. We must have faith that this ruling class will rule justly, as it has ruled in England, and that it will extend to other classes the implements, or weapons, of government as they demonstrate capacity and skill to employ them.

W. E. B. Dubois, the Negro educator, has proposed the erection of a Negro state in the former German colonies of Africa, which the National Association for the Advancement of Colored People has endorsed, (in passing, we endorse it, too,) and it is interesting to observe that he advises that "this reorganized Africa be under the guidance of organized civilization. The governing international commission should represent, not simply governments, but modern culture—science, commerce, social reform, and religious philanthropy." He conceives that "the principle of self-determination which has been recognized as fundamental by the Allies cannot be wholly applied to semi-civilized peoples," but asserts that "it can be partially applied." That is admission that not all people are capable of self-government. In carrying out this African program, he further says that "the public opinion, which should have a decisive voice, should be composed of various classes of intelligent Negroes throughout the world," "the chiefs of the tribes of German Africa," "the educated persons of Negro descent in South America and the West Indies," "the independent Negro governments of Abyssinia, etc.," among others, and one of these classes he defines as "the twelve million civilized Negroes of the United States."

There is an absence of warrant for this definition of the "twelve million." Civilization is a relative term. If the twelve million could be removed bodily, in the twinkling of an eye, to Central Africa, could they, with no white civilization to lean upon and none to imitate, maintain a civilized state? One would like to see the experiment tried. Dr. Dubois' scheme is a pointed illustration in support of the contention that pure democracy is a fantastic dream.

If we are to have in the United States, and especially in the South, government resting on intelligence and property, *accepting property acquisition as an essential evidence of intelligence*, precaution must be taken lest property gain ascendancy over men. Vigilance and the practice of justice may avert that danger; so, it is held, the history of England proves. Again using South Carolina as an example, it should be comparatively easy here to prevent the too great growth of landed or other estates. Surtaxes may be placed upon non-resident holdings, and other ways whereby land ownership would be limited are of facile contrivance. With but one-third of our nineteen millions acres under plow, it would be practicable to effect a multiplication of small holdings, of fifty, one hundred, or five hundred acres as the maximum, if the people were so resolved.

The Socialists say that the chief barrier to their progress is the small farmer and in this great country the number of land holding farmers might in time be made five or ten times what it is. So the Republic, in the states, might be impregnably fortified against the advance of the socialistic spirit.

In the United States we have never had a peasant class, in the European sense. The small farmer is as independent as the owner of what would be an English manor; hence we have the groundwork upon which to enlarge a land-holding system whose every member, regardless of the number of his acres, would belong to the same class and have the same economic and political interest, provided always that check be placed upon the over-enlargement of individual estates. In 1790, when the whole country was agricultural, a check was provided by the abolition of primogeniture, and similar devices of law, no more radical than that one was in its time, could be the resort now.

Anticipating the objection that this paper raises a false alarm, that no danger confronts a restricted ballot and representative government in this country, the only answer is that in regard to that is difference of opinion. Some of us see the world about to plunge into an abyss of democracy. Russia, for example, apparently would destroy the institution of private property and have democracy at the same time, temporarily ostracizing and punishing former property holders, including peasant proprietors. More moderate socialists would first cauterize from the human mind the notion of a natural and rightful relation between property and government, and, having insidiously induced this conviction, their next step would be to blot out private property holding by means of the ballot.

Opposed to this is the idea that the acquisition of property is one of the highest evidences of intelligent selfishness, that it is the indispensable evidence of it and that in intelligent selfishness human freedom has its birth, growth and stability.

The title "Back to Aristocracy" is not accurate and comprehensive. It has been chosen as a challenge. Older countries in which "Aristocracy" refers to a class of landed gentry, usually holding by inheritance, laugh at the use of the word in America, looking upon all property owners in America as bourgeois, and recognizing that as yet an American proletariat is but dimly defined.

It is scarcely needful to say that I have employed the term without reference to the few American snobs who call themselves "arisctocrats," and to the American demagogues who roll the term under their tongues with the object of inflaming prejudice among men who are themselves aristocrats or capitalists or bourgeoisie in the economic and political sense. For the purpose of this argument, the ruffian landowner operating a five mile or 20 mule farm, in South Carolina, exploiting his labor perhaps more ruthlessly than does the multi-millionaire owner of an iron foundry or street car system, as ignorant, coarse, and brutal as

Henry Fielding describes "Squire Western," is no less aristocratic than was that representative British tough of his day.

The challenge is that we look forward to government in the United States, and especially in the South, by the best men, men able to understand and to exercise the best governing processes and who may be trusted to extend and enlarge their own group steadily by taking in those men outside of it, as they reveal fitness for the suffrage by evidences of education and property acquisition.

The maximum requirements for admission to this political aristocracy should be as low as is consistent with safety, that is, they should be just as high as is necessary to prevent the capture and over-running of the government by the ignorant and irresponsible. If the protection of the government of South Carolina shall demand that we make property holding as well as education a definition of citizenship responsibility, we should not hesitate so to make it, having recourse, if need be, to plural voting, such as we once had, and to the restoration of more of the agencies of government to the General Assembly, so that the state government will approach the form that it had prior to 1868.

It is expedient that we combat and withstand the hysterical tendency toward undigested and amorphous democracy, to which our own white people have been succumbing the last half century, by candidly telling and preaching the truth that we cannot and will not have it. I am, for myself, far from convinced that a government, though it be based upon an entirely literate democracy, but one taking no account of the existence of the rights of private property in the delimitation of its electorate, would be secure in any state of the American Union, unless we concede that the establishment of the Social state is a thing to be invited.

In consideration of the special conditions in the Southern States, we are compelled to be in greater or less measure opportunists and to adhere to a vision of government that, in these times, would be denounced as reactionary, Bourbon, fossilized and barbaric—in short, that would be subject to all the hard names with which the vocabulary of the latterday saints of democracy and "up-lift" howls and reverberates. Our state government is already aristocratic, we are already constitutionally "dug in," we have but to hold our trenches, digging them deeper and extending them if need be, as occasion appears, and, with this in mind, speak plainly, without apology, boldly defending our electoral and political system whether it be derided as aristocratic or branded in terms more scurrile by the demagogues who tickle the ears of the groundlings.

COMMENCEMENT ADDRESS: COLLEGE OF CHARLESTON

(1925)

William Watts Ball, Dean of the School of Journalism at the University of South Carolina, 1923-1927, gave the commencement address at the College of Charleston, May 12, 1925. The commencement was held at the old Academy of Music.

THE military victory in the World War, one has said, was France's, England won the political victory, the United States the economic victory, and the religious victory went to the Roman Catholic Church. Whatever the truth, if truth it have, of this summation of the results of the conflict, it could not apply in fullness on this side the Atlantic. If America has gained an enormous economic victory, economic world conquest for the time, it has lost none of the political and military prestige and power that it had; their enhancement is inseparable from economic expansion, and it is clear that its internal religious adjustments and cleavages have not been upset.

Here are visible no signs of seeking refuge in churchly authority. No new interest has been kindled in "a library of dogmatic theology" which, according to Ruskin, "Titian put into the backs of a row of archbishops." On the other side, in countries where the interlocking of church and political power survives, where guideless peoples are still foundering in the muck and slime that the war left, it is not surprising that men and women uneasy and adrift look in companies toward to the spiritual organization that appears most stable. On the continent of Europe breaking away from Protestantism seems not to be hard, and it is reported to be common in practice.

The economic victory of the United States is complete and overwhelming, a fact incontestable, little as we of South Carolina may share in it, much as we squirm in the grip of high costs, with its usual accompaniment of good profits already quite vanished from us. We happen to be a frayed edge of the cloth of gold, but the country is rich. One is tempted to say that it is noxiously, disgustingly rich. Even in South Carolina few of us, poor as we think ourselves, and are, can afford to live as we lived ten years ago. That we couldn't do. It isn't done. So, in *forma pauperis* we luxuriate.

We, or most of us, think in terms of property-holders, small or great, of houses and fields, mortgages and stocks, forgetting, as always, the existence of the cooks, the servingmen, the swingers of picks and pitchforks. With us lingers the attitude, if nothing else, of those forbears of ours who thought in the language of a British squire and imitated his habits. It is worth mentioning, though it be shocking, that poor and embarrassed as are the South Carolina landlords, South Carolina labor has profited immensely from the war and its sequelae. The wage hand on the farm and in the mill is getting more than formerly. In short, if the whole people, black and white, all sorts and conditions, in South Carolina, be considered, the emergent truth is that South Carolina, too, is, relatively, rich.

More important than any other legislation enacted in the United States in the last quarter if not half century are the restrictions on immigration. Those measures are getting next to us. We are feeling their operation every day. When we and our neighbors refuse to maintain the cook's wages, she and her sister cooks go North. There, cooks are wanted. The supply, hitherto unfailing, from Europe, is now scant. So the labor supply is scant in all the spheres of industry and when a Northern employer puts his lips to the telephone, the receiver is already at the ear of the Southern worker. The labor market of South Carolina is linked with the coal mines of West Virginia and Pittsburgh. No man is so poor that he can't go for a job wherever a job is looking out for a man, and there is every sign that this condition has come to stay. No bold prophet is needed to say that in 20 years or less laborers will be transported through the air from places where labor is slack to other places where the demand for it is urgent,—which is no more than an aspect of the economic victory peculiarly affecting, perhaps disturbing, us of a commonwealth where much more than a century population has been nearly stationary.

The other nations have surrendered, unconditionally, except Great Britain, to the Dollar. The question is, and it is one of exceeding gravity, can the United States endure it? In so mighty a victory of the Dollar, how far down shall we be dragged spiritually? The legend on the coin, "In God We Trust," has never been thought of seriously as the coin passed from hand to hand. It may be that to place it on the dollar smacked of flippancy, but the new question, raised in these times, is whether or not the Dollar will not actually resent the legend's presence as mockery of Dollar dignity? In what degree are things hitherto held sacred in danger? That is the inquiry.

Before 1917 our want of "preparedness" was incessantly dinned—yet, with comparative ease, military victory came to the United States. Of the economic victory no one was thinking, certainly not in 1914 when King Cotton went into the streets and begged—one could see a bale sitting in the lobby of a New York hotel pleading, for sweet charity's sake, to be purchased lest the Southern planter starve. Nor did this victory concern even the financiers in 1915. Thereafter they began to take notice.

The economic victory being wholly unforeseen, unless by a few prescient and forehanded capitalists, what was our "preparedness" for it? Our preparedness against its evils and perils? At best war is a gross thing. The effort to idealize it may have a mitigating influence on its horrors—the last war may have been, after all, less cruel than those waged by Kubla Khan's ancestors, but "it hardens all within us" and one suspects that the resulting indurations are tougher and thicker, if surface smoother, about the souls of the men—and the women—on the home front than on the men in the trenches paying the glory price. How did we prepare for the after-horrors of victory?

It must be confessed that we went rather far in some of our home front sacrifices. The crushing, the lynching, of common, everyday, liberties, is an incident of all considerable wars, and there need be no regrets wasted about that—even the semi-intelligent perceive that war cannot be waged without the stifling of thought, that the mobilizing of national resources must include those of the human mind, that the sudden concentration of physical force cannot go on efficiently while intellectual forces are allowed their peace-time latitude of discussion and disagreement. When war breaks out, freedom must go into temporary eclipse, lest it go into permanent eclipse, presupposing that the country's point of view is right.

Some things, nevertheless, should be too holy to touch even for "winning the war." Religion and its instrumentalities are among them, unless the war is itself religious. If the preaching and waging of crusades for avowed religious objects has been proved unwise and unmoral, if it has ceased to be righteous to go forth to rescue the Holy Sepulchre, the employment of even a part of the methods and paraphernalia of crusades in a war, which, much as it was defensive, was a secular war, is not easily justified. But the Stars and Stripes were paraded in most of the churches. Sometimes the altar almost was *swathed* in political emblems. The flag, shall I say impudently, nudged and jostled the Cross. Not only were the things that belonged to Caesar rendered unto him, but the things of God were rendered unto Caesar with them. How far the American people were adopting some of the derided manners of their enemies may not be measured, but a posture of humble suppliance to the Almighty that we might be right was very nearly displaced by one of assumption that our national will was become known to us as the will of God. Almost we tried to apply the selective draft law to Deity. No, we did not say it in words, but we decorated the temples of the Lord with the trappings of politics—and only now are men bold enough to speak of it above a whisper.

The church allowed itself to be drafted for propagandic purposes—in ways far apart from its natural offices of extending succor and comfort to the suffering. Surely the church should be in the highest and the broadest sense social—but it should beware lest it sink to the level of a social club.

That, after the great war, the church should adopt or imitate its methods and, for that matter, its vernacular, was inevitable. The church had seen a vision of the Republic's resources marshalled. For the church militant to seize upon the device of the "drive" and employ it on the scale to which Americans had learned to think—in millions—was a natural step. Indeed, the effort was made, devoutly, to prevent the submergence of the idea of spiritual in carnal growth—but the church, I repeat, was thinking in millions.

It is hard to think, spiritually, in millions. Colossal numerals are corrosive. Since 1918 there has been a great deal of taking thought about the wherewithal the church shall be clothed. The church has not escaped the incrustations of the economic victory, and the church is mentioned because, if such be *its* fate, one may not hope that other institutions, mere universities, colleges, and schools, shall have immunity from them. The ugly fact is that many of them have been smirched, some of them engulfed.

The great "drives" in behalf of the benevolent agencies have fruited in many splendid demonstrations. Buildings are imposing. Figures are mustered in appalling array. Men have perhaps been photographically, radiographically and statistically saved. And in the saving process, their virtues have been X-rayed, graphed, and canned. The completeness of the operation is not gainsaid.

Yet something is lacking, and very much at that. One hears, on the sidelines, jeering as well as cheering. There are vulgar onlookers with thumbs in their cheeks. What is worse, there are ruffians with blackjacks in their hands.

In South Carolina has been no marked increase in violent crime; perhaps there has been some slight diminution, in recent years, but it has to be confessed that, for a civilized country, South Carolina already had crime to the saturation point before these new conditions arose. In the metropolitan cities and the richer states, crime wave has followed and overlapped crime wave. Everything that could be done has been done. Pistols are prohibited. Whiskey is prohibited. The motorcar remains unprohibited, just as though the bandits that infest New York and Chicago and operate with a daring and success never dreamed of by Dick Turpin and Jack Sheppard, could get along without gasoline. Womanly sweetness and gentleness, too, have been brought into government, accompanied by generous and sanguine predictions that politics in future would be antiseptic. Nothing has been left unlegislated, nothing unregimented.

Still things are not just right.

If they were, there would be no room for intolerance, organized and aggressive intolerance, for intolerance always is rooted in fear. What more curious development in the midst of the triumph of democracy, if the shattering of thrones welded in blood and iron can be so described, than a sudden return, in free countries, to the religious proscriptions of a century and a half ago? The General Assembly of South Carolina in 1778, adopting a new constitution, disestablished the English church, but it was far from adopting "disestablishment." "The Christian Protestant religion," it reads, "shall be deemed and is hereby constituted and declared to be the established religion of this state." Strange words do they seem? Twelve years later, in 1790, a convention of the people adopted the constitution under which the people lived 75 years and by that instrument all religious tests were abolished; then and not until then Jews and Roman Catholics came to be citizens on equal footing with Protestants in South Carolina. Singular that these tests remained so long in South Carolina? How singular? What is the measure of the singularity? It is certain that, were the way open, the religious tests would not now be reenacted—but what if the reverse be postulated? If, in 1925, religious tests were in our constitution, would they be, by popular vote, abolished? I hazard the opinion that they would be, for the majority is not yet irrational, but I couple with it the opinion that the process would be accompanied with stubborn and heated opposition.

How far have tolerance, and freedom of opinion, advanced in South Carolina since the year of our Lord, 1790? And St. Paul tells us that "Where the Spirit of the Lord is, there is Liberty."

Intolerance raises its head and it is a reaction of fear. So is the agitation that is called Fundamentalism; the resort to popular legislatures to define, confine, and delimit the steps of learning.

"It is fear, Little Brother, it is fear," that has made these quaint notions vocal, ululant, in 1925, and it is fear that, however foolish, may be explained.

To the people, all does not seem right with the world. There is not the old sureness that God's in his Heaven. To old-fashioned people who, for the most part, are right-living people, even if they do not carry searchlights in their foreheads, the signs are evil, menacing. The riches, the education, the art, the luxury, the rising walls of the churches, are on every hand—but so are the crimes, the social, the family disorders. The family itself, except perhaps in this little commonwealth pendant to the edge of the mighty Republic, seems not secure on its foundation. There is much groping by these old-fashioned folk, panicky, it may be, and phrenetic, so that sometimes they bump rudely against other people as good as or better than themselves. Anyway they remember, vividly, a world of a few years ago that was not altogether bad, that contained much that was to them solacing, pleasant, precious, and the sudden destruction of all those things they would prevent.

Were one of these people asked the cause of his agitation (and his silly behavior, if you please), it would not occur to him to talk about the "economic victory"—he has not heard of it. Prating of the nation's preparedness for it would set him agape. Perhaps he would not "find a formula," but he might put his finger on the disappearance of reverence. That spirit has gone out of men—and women—or at least in most men and women it is weak. Whether the prevailing irreverence is a symptom, or a cause, one doesn't know, but it is a fact. One feels, sees, hears it, everywhere.

It does not become me to sermonize, I do not wish to usurp the preacher's place. I have alluded to the church because sacredness begins with religion, and I am trying to point out that it is the want of reverence for anything, or for all things, that should make us "view with alarm," that, whether the cause or the symptom, should arouse concern. What if the scornful answer be that men past middle life are always reminiscent, reactionary, conservative, harking to the "good old times"? Whether the great war brought on the suffocating tides of materialism or materialism brought on the war, the problem that we grapple with is a despiritualized world. We know with what precipitation the Americans came down from the mount and its vision of the League of Nations. The descent was not even graceful.

Cutting the strings and throwing off the garments of superstition may be desirable, but even that may be done with too much haste.

There may be an exposure of nakedness and an abandonment to shame, and it is left to fools to deny that in manners there is more than the usual unseemliness, that in the common standards of honesty, of obedience to law and observance of virtue, there has been a decline. One is tempted to say that something may be gained by searching for precedent because it is precedent, because it is old, because it has been tested.

Yet one is sometimes driven to believe that South Carolinians have been teaching their youth to forget. Let me disclaim sectionalism, I think I may call myself an American—without apology—but with it I claim the right to love the South and hold it to be *superiorly* American.

The other day, in my hearing, a thinking and observant man, come some years ago to the state, said that he had read the Constitution of South Carolina, of 1790, that it was a noble document, that sound state government was about as fully insured by it as was possible by human prevision. He was reminded that an earlier admirer of it was Mr. Calhoun, and it may be profitable for us to recall something of it and its fate. Under it, governors, judges, nearly all state officers, some of the county officers, U. S. senators, and even presidential electors were elected by the General Assembly, and representation in the General Assembly was based, not on manhood suffrage, but on suffrage in combination with property. In the way, low-country parishes, with small white population, checked the political power of the districts of large white population. The system was resented, often bitterly, but as slave property increased in the interior, the resentment softened. Undoubtedly the general results were good; nowhere on the globe was government purer than in South

Carolina between 1790 and 1865, or 1867, and to say that it was unprogressive is to indulge in the gibberish of the uninformed. By 1849, when Mr. Calhoun wrote his *Disquisition on Government*, he was able to hold it up, with great pride, as fruit that proved the wholesomeness of his theory that "government by the concurrent majority" is more desirable and more safe than government by the numerical majority. He said that government by numbers was charged with the perils of tyranny, that it was not defensible that rural populations, for example, be exposed to the will of populations crowded in cities or in manufacturing districts.

One need not look to the parish system of ante-bellum South Carolina to perceive the wisdom of the principle. More than half the population of Rhode Island lives in a single city, but that city has scarcely a fourth of the whole number of members of the Rhode Island legislature. So, until the federal constitution was amended no Democrat for 75 years or more was elected to the United States Senate, in Rhode Island, though the election of a Democrat to be governor was at least occasional. So, in Connecticut, Massachusetts, New York, and other Northern states, the rural districts are clothed with legislative power disproportionate to the number of their voters. That, they say, is subversion of democracy (democracy in the broad, non-party sense), and, more than once, in Rhode Island, the divided people have all but come to blows about it—once in the last twelve months. So it is denial of democracy—our Southern denials of democracy are by no means original sin—and it is cleancut, pointed vindication of "Calhounism." Possibly the statesman imported some of his philosophy from the Litchfield, Connecticut law school—anyway, it is in full flower in New England—and we Southerners ought to uphold our New England brethren in it, though it operates disastrously to the Democratic party.

In 1868 a constitutional convention, called by General E. R. S. Canby, in command of South Carolina, then a military district, met here, in Charleston. Most of the white people were at the time disfranchised and did not participate in the election of delegates, so the convention was composed of about 80 Negroes and 40 Carpetbaggers and Scalawags—deliberating under Canby's guns. Despite its corruption and comicalities, its unceasing wrangle, its proceedings were not uninteresting, but the sole conclusion come to by it was the adoption of the constitution of Ohio, almost verbatim. That was a democratic constitution. Of course it abolished property representation, adopted universal manhood suffrage (if one Negro could have had his way, it would have adopted universal woman suffrage, too, half a century ahead of the Nineteenth Amendment), and South Carolina set out in a path strange to her. After eight wretched years, the prophecy of another Negro delegate, was fulfilled and "the aristocracy of intelligence and wealth re-captured the state" — redeemed it.

Then what happened? Did the white government restore the constitution of their fathers? Such a course was not so much as mentioned. The white people hugged the importation from Ohio. They caressed it, they gloated in it, they wallowed in it, and in 1895 they re-enacted it, adding clauses designed to exclude the Negroes from its beneficent provisions. So drunken has South Carolina come to be on this bootleg democracy from Ohio, that it is now almost felonious to hint that honesty and efficiency in government would perhaps be promoted were elections of county auditors and treasurers taken out of the primaries and again appointed by the governor, by and with the advice of the senate, as the constitution in terms prescribes. Reverence—affection—for South Carolina's past? We are subjugate to the spell of Ohio's democratic notions, woven about us when Canby's bayonets were at our throats.

Infatuated as were leaders and people in 1895 by the foreign notions introduced in 1868, the state has, accidentally perhaps, escaped some of them. Under our present constitution, representation in the legislature is based on black as well as white population. Consequently, a county like Beaufort with 1,000 or 1,200 white voters has equal representation in the General Assembly with Oconee, having four times as many. Every county, little or big, has one senator, and our Democratic party conventions, controlling and contriving the party machinery, have a representation proportioned on that of the counties in the legislature. The result, and it is a happy one, is that although about fifteen counties out of forty-six have a majority of the white voters and may elect a governor or United States senator in a primary, the remaining thirty-one have an entrenched majority in both houses of the General Assembly—and the General Assembly elects the judiciary and, of course, levies the taxes and spends the revenues.

It is popular to sneer at legislatures. They are, indeed, far from perfect, but the people have good reason to be grateful that government in South Carolina rests, for the most part, in the legislative body and cannot be taken from it, so long as the people of the smaller counties are vigilant to protect the constitutional rights that they now enjoy. The system is a denial of democracy, but from an orgiastic democracy most of our political woes have sprung, and the modified Calhounism, the government by concurrent majority, whereby this state is not controlled by population crowded in urban or industrial centers, has been and is the commonwealth's salvation. Recognition of this truth, with attention flowing from it to the selection of members of the legislature, would insure to South Carolina clean and efficient government, at least so long as the present racial and social constitution of the state shall be unimpaired.

The most incompetent and the most vicious of executive officers that may be elected will be comparatively harmless in South Carolina if the people see to it that legislatures and constitutional conventions are composed of good men. In these bodies our government is lodged, and in the majority of the counties, not of the people, lies the power of controlling them. These bodies, if they wish, may make of the governors what they were, in the main, before 1868, holders of honorary posts which did not require even so much as their residence in the capital city.

Why should we be ignorant of these things? Why should we forget them? Surely we are not ashamed of "Calhounism"? The barrier to return to the government under which the state so long flourished is not insurmountable, not even difficult. We shall have a new state constitution before many years pass and the delegation of the principal agencies of government to commissions elected by the legislature and at the same time utterly removed from partisan legislative influences could easily be accomplished, provided there were the will to do so.

To say that the state and the country suffer from too much democracy is unpopular. The use of the word has been unfortunately misleading. The concept of pure democracy was scarcely thought of anywhere in the American colonies or the early states, certainly not in South Carolina, but so incessantly has it been harped on of late that the notion of delegated, representative, government has all but vanished.

In a word, forgetfulness, upstart daughter of sneering ignorance, is the political sin of the time. Students and leaders in this day, in South Carolina, assume that the institutions of proved worth were abandoned because they were unworthy, and much as orators indulge in flamboyant declamation of the state's past, there is no searching of its merits, only a tame acceptance of the condemnation of it, from outsiders, as dead, unpractical. "Reaction" this will be called, but it is a curious thing that, with all our just denunciation of the period of "Reconstruction" after 1865, so much of it was allowed to survive, and still survives, to our constant vexation, to our possible undoing. Were one to propose a return to plural voting, legal in South Carolina as late as 1833, one would be laughed at, yet in emergency resort has been had, temporarily, to ballot laws that were evasive, while that at least was honest and frank.

No one would have wealth too much exalted, no one would erect a golden calf for worship, but property may be a sign of virtue, the possession of a vine and fig tree may point to the possession of frugality and hardy honesty, and there is in truth nothing, so far, in mankind's experience to show that civilization is separable from private property. There may, there should be, new and frequent measures to curb it, it should be given no chance to get the upper hand, but if it have a right to exist, its right is to be defended. Nicolai Lenin and his followers were unwise and wicked to cut the throats of the intelligentsia, but they were not unlogical. If trained intelligence is to be tolerated, certain masteries will come with it, including a certain mastery of property. Our problems, in this state, have changed since 1860 not nearly so much as may be lightly fancied, and it is folly to throw away lightly the keys to their solution.

Perhaps, though, one should not speak in terms of "the state." There are those who would abolish the American states—some of them, one suspects, dwell in South Carolina.

It is trite to say that the times are out of joint, that crises are to be faced. Yet I shall, I do, say it. We can't live without politics; politics is a *modus vivendi;* only the loose-minded deny it. When the scoffers at politics are the majority is the hay-making time for demagogues and grafters. The sad truth is that public opinion in South Carolina is rather sadly demoralized just now. If one may venture to speak in terms of the state, to think in the ancient manner of a South Carolinian, it is well to recognize that leadership is at low ebb—and states without leaders languish. A long time, one does not like to say how long, has passed since a brave and informed, mark I say informed, leader has told the people the whole truth. To do that would require a man of parts, a man of distinction—a man of more than the hour and immediate office.

Common school education is an excellent, and indispensable, lubricant for popular government, but lubricating oil is not fuel, not motive power.

The need is for unpopular leaders—especially in politics. They will have to be heroes—men willing and able to take punishment, to endure defeats, and bide their time. In time of peace, the hero is the man in the minority.

No imminent danger confronts us that this country will be seized by some foreign prince or potentate. Nor is there peril of violent revolution and overturn from radicals, Bolshevists, or other horrid spectres bodying forth from the agitated hearts of one hundred per centers. Yet there are greater if more insidious perils. We run away from them. We do not tell ourselves the truth. Where is the courage in a legislature of this century that 100 years ago brought about the impeachment of a brave old judge, a hero of the war for Independence, whose intemperance had made him incompetent? Where is the stern virtue that would require of every public servant that in matters relating to money he avoid even the appearance of evil? Who holds with old Walter Scott, after he had, through no fault of his own, incurred a debt of more than half a million dollars, that a public man is disgraced if he do not meet his financial obligations? Where is the leader so armed in honesty that he would lay down the rock-hewn rule that honesty begins before charity, that there is no merit in making free, even for the widow and orphan, with what is *not* thine *own*.

The mob is abroad and busy. It is a light-minded, hysterical mob of nitwits. It has a hundred banners and every one of them advertises a nostrum. Its addled members fool themselves with silly phrases, with gauds of rhetoric, with vain repetitions of tawdry slogans. One does not object to things that are new; there must be progress and adaptations; occasionally a new principle is discovered and deserves acceptance, but most of the principles and the standards were discovered long ago. The American mob is not making worthwhile discoveries. It is not saving the world or saving itself, despite its self-righteous outgivings. For most of the old institutions and customs at which it jeers, it is offering no improving substitute.

The need of the day is for men—and women—to speak and write the hard, biting truth. Much of it is to be found in the history lately behind us. The spirit of irreverence has bred ignorance of it; we have turned from precious inheritance and we are become an imitative, poll-parroting people. Now and then there is a faint gleam. It may be that a poetry society, the very name of it a jest to the one·hundred per centers, contains more of a hope than a catalogue of commercial triumphs, and a community having a college that dares to remember its yesterdays may have tomorrows.

The nub of what I have tried to say is that a good start was made in this country. When the colonies became states they formed a republic and it set out on the right track, in the right direction. Despite jolts, jars, near derailments, it has kept going and ought to go on a long time. There is enough in its constitution and history to keep it going. The danger is in ignoring its vital essence, and ignorance is impiety. Never was patriotism so vociferous as it is nowadays. The chattering of the catch-words is deafening and, nearly seven years after the last war, unsuspecting, well intentioned gentlemen are actually subject to threat if they neglect signs and salutations, if not genuflections, to the flag. Now, the fact is that everyone loves the flag, but another fact is that it is difficult for the affections to attain a healthy growth in the midst of distracting noises.

"Americanism" is doubtless an excellent thing. One reads a great deal about it in the magazines; it shrills through "the rant and twaddle of the daily press." One asked to define it would perhaps be confused, as was the law student asked to define the rule in Shelley's case. "I don't know what it is," he said, "but I think it has something to do with poetry." So, if I had to define "Americanism," if my diploma depended upon it, I should say that it had something to do with Lincoln—and that would be as good as the magazine writers and the orators can do.

One doesn't hear of Englandism, Scotlandism, or Britainism. The older peoples do not find it necessary to convince themselves of their patriotism by chanting it. Need one drone "Every day and in every way I grow a better and better American" in order to sterilize him of the germs of treason?

One said of Mr. Gladstone: "You have so lived and wrought that you have kept the soul alive in England." Not the soul of England, not the English or the British or other stereotyped, trade-marked soul, but—"You have so lived and wrought that you have kept the soul alive in England." It was a great saying.

The soul in the United States and in South Carolina was not born yesterday. If with reverence and zeal it shall be kept alive, we need have no fear for the flag.

TELLING NEWSPAPERS ABOUT THEMSELVES

(1926)

William Watts Ball spoke on criticism and problems of the press at a small gathering of Vanderbilt University faculty on the evening of May 11, 1926.

WHEN two and one-half years ago I began to teach journalism, after spending a third of a century practicing it, I found mapped out in the catalog of the University a course in the history of journalism. Two or three histories of American journalism, all written by newspaper men, were in my library, and three or four of the British press. None of these was fitted for a textbook. What of the history of the press, in general, the world press? No such creature was extant. A letter to a young friend in one of the best equipped schools of the country brought the response from her professor of the history of journalism that he knew of no such book—he "only wished that he did." So, not exactly imitating the method of the book reviewer of Editor Pott, of the Eatonsville *Gazette*, I turned to the *Brittannica* and found some twenty pages that were a present help in time of trouble, but surely it is singular that the press of the world has aroused no historian to write a book about it—at any rate no historian writing in our language. A professor in one of the schools of journalism is now said to be engaged in such a work, but one has misgivings about it—newspaper men (all, or nearly all, professors of journalism are practical journalists) have not, usually, the historian's temperament, or method.

Newspaper men the last two or three decades, especially the last, have been much and increasingly given to writing books about themselves—textbooks, biographies, reminiscences, memoirs, and the like, and some of them are delightful reading. Histories of great newspapers have been written. They are of absorbing interest, filled with good stories of humor and of adventure, and they fling many a penetrating pencil of light on political history. Such books as Mr. E. P. Mitchell's, Col. Henry Watterson's reminiscences, Don C. Seitz's *Life of Pulitzer* will be relished keenly by laymen and the books of Wickham Steed and of J. A. Spender, of the London press, will enrich any cultivated man's knowledge of affairs, but inevitably they tell of the pressman's press from the pressman's point of view. Not many newspaper men tell tales out of school.

Besides a very few doctoral dissertations of minor import, not half a dozen books about newspapers, by others than member of the craft, in the last 20 or 30 years have appeared. *The Brass Check* of Upton Sinclair, is a clever assault on the American press. It contains some accusations not to be dismissed with a sneer, but it has on the whole the convincingness and sincerity of the squeal of a pig in pain, which somehow one does not take seriously.

Almost the search is vain for light on the press cast by students outside of the ranks of the profession, or the art, or the trade, whatever this newspaper making is (the journalists don't quite know, and it doesn't quite matter)—"almost" because the two books of Dr. Lucy Salmon, of Vassar College, *The Newspaper and the Historian* and *The Newspaper and Authority*, are scholarly and immensely valuable breakings of profound silence of scholars on the subject. The works of that woman, advanced in years, published lately, have the unmistakable signs of competent research. She has delved deeper than any English writer about newspapers (I do not know what has been done in other languages) even if she has come up a little dry.

Why this negligence of scholars, they who have dug into and upturned the earth and stones of Egypt and of Babylon, of the mound builders of the Americas? Library shelves are weighted down with histories of the law, of medicine; the critics do not give a rest to the pulpit; but, so far, the scientific hammerers and chiselers have let the newspapers severely alone. It is to the mighty loss of the newspapers, and therefore, to the public. What is the explanation?

Well, the newspaper is young. St. Paul was sitting at the feet of Gamaliel nearly sixteen centuries before the embryo newspaper saw the light, and more years passed before it began to emit light. It would be against the proprieties for a newspaper man to set up that in the last three centuries newspaper progress has outrun that of the law. Anyway, there is time remaining for the press to catch the attention of investigations.

Or another explanation may be that the erudite look on the press is superficial. So it is, especially the American press. In some sense a newspaper is a complex concern, a combination of metallic machines, the post office, telephone and telegraph wires, human machines, and some other humans less machine-like in varying degrees, manufacturing and selling, by wholesale and retail, a product technically called circulation and a by-product called advertising, the product consisting of printed information, opinion and entertainment. Newspaper making is an intensely practical and enormously speedy operation; unavoidably the product is superficial. But it might be less so. The point is that in the last 60 years the press has grown to be a monster. It ought to be watched. You ought to watch it. If the university cannot, or will not, make it behave properly, to what shall we look?

Or still another explanation of the silent treatment of the newspaper by scholars is that they are a wee bit afraid of it, and this is not said frivolously. Why shouldn't they be? Virtually, the bullying ability of the press is unlimited. That tale I do not tell out of school, because, perhaps you know it already. The power of the newspaper, on the editorial side, is its incessancy. It always has the reply, every day in the year, and through the years. One takes issue with the editor. The editor "sits pretty" and, within his chamber, may laugh. He need not reply today, or tomorrow. At his leisure he may pick off his antagonist. "You may fire, Gridley, when you are ready," the Admiral said at Manilla. The editor is always ready, and he need not cease firing. If in ruder times, a "fighting editor" was sometimes of service about the shop, the sense of helplessness in the newspaper's enemies may account, in part, for the ruffianism in which they occasionally indulged. That the newspaper's manners were beyond reproach, that it spoke in the modulated accents of polite society, may have had the greater effect in exasperating. The ruffian was angered that the editor "showed him up"; the knowledge that the more he roared the more he would be showed up, maddened him.

Newspaper territory is parcelled out. The citizen of Tennessee does not easily gain a hearing in an Ohio newspaper, and if he does it is of small value to him. His neighbors read the newspapers of Tennessee. That in Memphis or Nashville may be two newspapers of opposite opinions, or even hostile to each other, is not perfect protection to the outsider. A newspaper will take care of itself in a quarrel and fight on till both its legs are hewn in two, after the manner of Witherington's at Chevy Chase, but it tires of taking care of its friends.

To be sure the gross abuser of editorial power at length destroys himself, but he may destroy many a brave but half armed assailant meantime. It may be glorious to bandy words with a newspaper, but seldom is it war. Indeed it may occur to one that every gentleman of controversial temperament should have his own newspaper; without it he may find himself in awkward predicaments.

Again, the newspaper man is looked on, by the laity, as a mysterious person. Otusiders have the "stereotype" of a magician when they consider him; they garb him with occult powers, usually exaggerating them rather absurdly.

None of these suggested explanations, possibly, have to do with the silence about the press, but the silence is indisputable. Everyone talks of the newspaper, everyone coddles it, or curses it, but it is seldom that anyone gets close to it, "under its hide." The layman buys his copy of the paper, peruses it, resents or approves its contents, but the press as an institution is a distant acquaintance, it passes him afar off. It was Mr. Pulitzer's theory that an editor should have few friends, few personal contacts, to employ the over-employed word of the day. The editor should be a monk. How could the editor have friends and not make concessions to them? Eat salt at a senator's table and "show him up" next day? Who can think of independence without isolation? Not on your life, thought Joseph Pulitzer, and it is hard to disagree with him. The smaller the community the more the personal contacts and the more difficult to avoid entangling alliances of a friendly and loving nature. In the two centuries in England, and the somewhat shorter period in this country, that editors spent much of their time in jails, they must have been relieved of many annoyances and embarrassments. The scholar's aloofness causes not the least discomfort to the editors; they like it; that they are left to themselves, except by themselves, yields an atmosphere delicious for chop-licking.

Yet the press is under suspicion; from long distance it is under fire from hostile guns unequipped with rangefinders. Seldom do these shots make a hit, and they are without disciplinary or remedial effect. To reply to the vague accusations, some of them grotesquely false but most of them with more than a grain of truth, would be wasteful here, but a few may be referred to, for illustrative purposes, at any rate.

"They say" (and we all know who she is when I say "They say") that the press is "commercialized." That's a fact. The establishment and conduct of a daily paper, even in a town of 25,000 people, do, in these days, require a considerable investment of capital. Things have changed since that marvelously prescient and practical Scot, James Gordon Bennett, set the *Herald* going with $500, to make it in time the most powerful newspaper in the Western hemisphere. Mr. Bennett would need millions now where hundreds sufficed in 1835. One can't palter with millions, or with hundreds of thousands, for that matter. If from this flows an absence of personal responsibility, of individual responsibility, of "heart," there are offsetting benefits. Besides, there may be other than the mighty, the monstrous, if you like the adjective, organs of publicity, co-existing with them and restraining their bad habits, of which I hope to speak in another lecture. For the moment it is enough that the daily newspaper is "big business," a family of Titans in an age of commercial Titans. If they are wicked Titans, surely the reason is the more that they be not left to indulge unmolested their wicked passions. Who shall show them up?

What is the University here for?

"They say" that the newspaper is subservient to the advertisers. That never was true in any important sense; in recent years it has ceased to be true at all, for the simple reason that the newspaper has come into complete and accurate understanding of its powers. Every publisher now knows that his strength lies in his readers, which is to say, his buyers, those thousands or hundreds of thousands who, as has been said, every morning or afternoon hold a primary election and reelect him or impeach him. So long as he is reelected, the advertising will come, no doubt about that, and subservience to space-buyers (who pass on the cost of the space to the consumers) cannot be hidden. No merely knavish publisher "sells out" to the advertiser; to do that he must be a fool too.

That he may have "innumerable trepidations" when, in the solitude of his office, he is attiring to meet his readers, his buyers, in the gray dawn of the coming morning, when transmuted into a printed sheet, he is flung upon the doorstep to be taken up and scanned at the breakfast table, is another thing. He may sell out to *them*, day after day, and in the process sell them out, and the traffic may be in its long effect worse than an occasional lending of indulgent ear to an advertiser. When the newspaper is guilty of corruption, the newspaper readers, who, for example, insist on being served with trivial or libidinous reading, may be the chief corruptors; the newspaper conforming to their demand, the corruption comes to be mutual and reciprocal. It is in "giving the people what they want," if it be more light, or more rich, more gamy food than is good for them, that the publisher is likely to sin. His case is notably similar to that of the theatre, which may be given over too much to gross vaudeville.

Again "they say" the newspapers, are shallow, they are ignorant; they are not truly informing. In this indictment may be, indeed, is, substance—how much substance one does not undertake to measure. "Could it be maintained that a person of any education could learn anything from a penny newspaper?," Lord Robert Cecil, later the Marquis of Salisbury, scornfully asked when in 1855 Bulwer Lytton, Milner Gibson and Gladstone were pressing in the House of Commons for the repeal of the newspaper stamp tax, "the tax on knowledge," and his question is derided as exposing the temper of the incurable British tory. Yet it may be asked seriously now, in this American democracy. The answer would, of course, be yes; the educated and the uneducated man, too, must learn from the penny newspaper, or they will not learn at all, of current affairs. Certainly they cannot let the day pass without knowing whether the coal strike is settled or not settled, whether the revenue bill is passed or not passed, and not yet has the radio or other vehicle been perfected to bring them the essentials of information.

No one will dispute the indispensableness of the newspaper. The answer that one may learn something from the newspaper, however it show up mid-Victorian toryism, does not satisfy. Does this newspaper inform sufficiently? Is its looseness, its flimsiness, its tin-canning and tom-tomming, wholly excusable? Is it really doing the best possible in the circumstances? A distinguished Southerner was packing his bag. His charming and second wife came into the room. "What are you doing, John?"

"Going down to the Powhatan club tonight for two or three days with George and Henry, for a little fishing."

"No you are not, John; you can't go on that kind of a trip now."

So the old warrior sent a telegram to his old warrior friend. It read:

"Circumstances over whom I have no control will prevent me joining the party."

Is the newspaper's obedience to its readers, to the extent that it is given, inevitable? Is it service or dis-service? Are the readers "circumstances" over whom it has no control? The question is addressed to the court of last resort, the university.

The foregoing are a few of the plentiful and searching criticisms of the press. The press is being raked fore and aft, but almost entirely by itself. In raking is hope. The magazines the last half a dozen years have overrun with discussions of the press, its virtues and faults—and the faults have had the far greater attention. A dozen or more books have been written on the subject. Lights, burning, blistering lights from every direction have been turned on every part of the newspapers. They have been dissected in mass and, often, in particular, and it has been and is a magnificent agitation. To be sure it is full of promise. It guarantees progress, it makes improvement certain. No other trade, or profession, or calling, is so fortunate. No tribe of clever or merciless writers turn the law, or medicine, or the pulpit, inside out. They are, for the most, allowed to stew in their juice—and they stew. The press is extraordinarily fortunate, if not happy, in being the daily and weekly recipient of more dosing than all the other professions together.

It is all, or nearly all, self-dosing. The press needs to see itself as others see it, and those others not casual, gaping, emptily gazing onlookers, but clear-eyed seers and searchers, armed with all the weapons and curative instruments, too, of the trained and serene, detached investigator. The press would be looked, not at, but through.

A few months ago it was announced that the University of North Carolina was about to begin a survey of the textile industry in North Carolina, and on the heels of the announcement came another that the textile industry was averse to it. Indeed, it was said that the textile industry had filled the moat and lifted the portcullis, so to say. Wherefore, one's suspicion is aroused that within the castle walls is something interesting that, one day, will be told of by some man or thing that will creep in, to the industry's dismay, and sense of injury. But we are not concerned with the textile industry.

A survey of the newspaper press of Tennessee, by Vanderbilt, or another university, would, one makes bold to say, be welcomed. Materially, it has no secrets. Every day, morning and evening, it tells the story of itself; the facts and the figures are between the lines and, laid on the table, need only to be assembled. Twice a year the larger newspapers are required by federal statute to publish the names of the owners of their outstanding shares and bonds, together with a sworn statement of their circulation. The old time "circulation liar" has disappeared from the cities and is rapidly becoming extinct everywhere. Newspapers advertise their circulation; they are members of a bureau of audits and it is decidedly more efficient in getting at the truth, about sales and subscriptions, than are the federal and state agencies supervising banks. Besides circulation, they have advertising space to sell, and nothing else. Space prices are determined by the quantity and quality of circulation and, if not completely standardized now, they soon will be. Anyone with a little patience and a measuring stick can tell, in a year or less time, any newspaper's approximate income.

With hardly more difficulty, the outsider can tell, with sufficient attainment to accuracy for practical purposes, the cost of newspaper production. The price of white paper, the principal item in the bill, is as public, to those who inquire, as is the price of cotton. The union labor scale prevails in the mechanical departments and is, of course, no secret. A day's work by a printer, in thousands of ems, can be learned about as easily as one can learn about the number of pounds of cotton a farm-hand picks. Salaries, telegraph tolls, cost of press services, postage and the factors in overhead present no vexing puzzle to the investigator, the variants are not great except among communities of widely differing number of inhabitants.

In short, a newspaper, much as the saying may surprise, literally has no private business; it cannot long conceal its financial embarrassments if it have any. They show on its face. To the eye that is at all practiced, the anemic, the languishing, or the hectic look is as plain on a newspaper as it is on the countenance of a sick man or woman. Physical survey of a newspaper is child's play, and perhaps there is no other great industry that is so transparent, albeit, for the reason that the observers of it are always casual or habituated to accepting it as a magical institution, little is known about it.

As a physical, business entity, the newspaper could not fool the people if it would, and the greater the newspaper perhaps the smaller is its privacy in this aspect. Yet surveys of the material side of the press would have value; the results of simple research, from detached and competent agencies, would have value both to the public and the press itself, as they would have, in the end, to the textile industry were the scales dropped from its eyes.

The far more important field for newspaper study is that of its work, its relations to the people whom it serves. This, in my guess, would bring forth not much that is sensational. There would be little or no revelation of corruption; there might be of weaknesses almost as bad in effect as evil is. Ponder these few questions.

Do the people read the newspapers? Or read the headlines? Or skim them? A few feeble studies in one or two cities, limited to inquiry in a street or ward, have elicited an estimate that the average business or professional man devotes 20 minutes, perhaps 30, in a day to newspaper reading—but the studies have not gone far enough to ground safe inferences.

What parts of the paper do the people read? Are they interested in crime stories? The layman usually magnifies grossly in common talk of publicity of crime. In fact, crime occupies a relatively small amount of newspaper space—measure and you will see. It is risky to talk about a newspaper without a measuring rod in the hand. Still, the newspaper may give to this kind of news too much space—possibly too much even for its cash register's health. It is highly probable that the publisher, looking ever from within the counting rooms through the window, makes numerous blunders from which its purse suffers.

Any survey of a university would include the scholastic degrees of the instructors as indicative of their preparation, which, though far from a sure sign of competency, is worth while. Journalists are supposed to be engaged in educative work. Undeniably, their opportunities to educate are inexhaustible. What is their preparation? What percentage of them have the bachelor's, the master's, or the doctor's degree?

Nor am I here concerned about the technical training of schools of journalism. Some 40 years ago a young bank clerk in London felt the call of the press and, against the advice of family and friends, he turned his back on the money changers and proceeded—not to a school of journalism (the oldest of them was opened in 1914)—but to Jena. Thence to Berlin. Thence to the Sorbonne. Thence to Rome as a correspondent of a great newspaper, where he was equipped to meet on equal terms ministers of finance, and of foreign affairs. Later, resident for years as a correspondent in Vienna, he wrote the authoritative book on the Hapsburgs and the Dual Monarchy. Then Wickham Steed returned to London to be foreign editor and, finally, editor of his newspaper, the *Times*.

In the United States are the most accomplished newspaper technicians, master mechanics, of journalism on the globe. They have kept 50 years ahead of the rest of the world. Only since Steed's and Northcliffe's time has England begun to catch the flavor of American enterprise in catering to popular taste for reading, but—how many Wickham Steeds has American journalism developed? With the exception of the man whom I quoted at the start of this lecture, where is the American journalist who has written a book as sound and informing as J. A. Spender's *The Public Life?* A John Morley in American journalism in the last generation? Or a Reeve, or a Lowe, or anyone of hundreds who have written for the ponderous sheets of Britain? Yes, we have had and have the keenest, the cleverest, the most audacious and successful news getters and distributors that the world has seen— but bright and entertaining, scrappy, shimmery reminiscences are the most that they have left to prove the possession of attainments. If our newspapers are not manned by educated writers, it is high time that they were exposed. And the light should be turned on them from without.

Newspapers commonly say that they are independent. They do not habitually, or at least not so loudly, boast of themselves now as they did a few years ago, but they are not shy; they preach advertising, and they practice their preaching. For that they are not censurable, but why are their claims and their boasts not tested? Since the marked improvements in their manners set in some years ago, and that improvement is indisputable—no Greeley nowadays denounces a Bryant as a liar and villain— they seldom apply tests to one another.

Are the newspapers of Tennessee, of South Carolina, outspoken about public affairs always? Do they expose, fearlessly, vices in government, state and municipal, at their own doors? Editors, of course, are "fearless"; that is the adjective universally applied to them—have they without exception denounced religious intolerance when that sort of denunciation seemed desirable? Indeed, their sole mission is to crusade, but it may be that sometimes they joust with the windmills when dragons are threatening the lives of and liberties of those whose guardianship they have assumed.

What, exactly, are the newspapers, our newspapers, doing and saying?

Assessing, appraising, and assaying surely are offices of the universities. They have the test tubes and the measuring rods. They are professedly fond of pyschological tests. It should be practicable to survey the utterances and the silences of the press; to count and tabulate the times the newspapers have spoken bravely or have not spoken at all. A table showing how many newspapers in Tennessee condemned the last lynching, or condoned it, how near the plain-speaking press was to the scene of the mob's outbreak and how far away from it was the silent press and the extension of the table to the lynchings of a year or five years, would be interesting. In exceptional cases, it might be embarrassing, but the survey could be made impersonally; the group press of a district or a region could be dealt with. The Behaviorists should have the time of their lives with the publishers, editors, and reporters.

How much of their space do the newspapers give to crime? How much and how far do they pander to a lust for salacious reading? I think their sins in these respects are not grievous, certainly not in our Southern and rural commonwealths, but I don't want to think; I want to know.

What are the universities here for?

They are breaking into the secrets of rocks with hammers. Their crowbars are prying open graves so ancient that time has eaten away the incrustating hallowedness. They are splitting atoms, writing prehistoric history; footing up the accounts of all the ages in their schools of economics. Research! research! research! is the watchword that drones from sea to sea and across the seas.

Nothing is so near to the people as the newspapers are. Nothing is so active, nothing buzzes so closely about us as the press. It can't be screened out or off. It can't be kept out of our houses, our bedrooms, our bathrooms. There is no escaping its eyes, its ears, its touch. It is the licensed, the obligated watcher, the elephant child of "satiable curiosity." It ought to be watched in turn, for its own sake, for the people's sake. The "freedom of the press" is an exaggerated and abused phrase; there is a freedom of the press from the scrutiny of competent, judicial observers.

The university that pioneers in telling the newspapers about themselves will be their benefactor and the benefactor of the people. The glory of pioneering is not to be despised.

DRUNK!—AND—A DEMOCRAT!!!

(1930)

Though he made his home in Charleston after 1927, William Watts Ball had many ties of friendship in Columbia. Hence in 1930 he was invited to address one of the meetings of the Kosmos Club. He spoke on the problem of prohibition, against which he had fought for many years in his editorial columns and which he regarded as an invasion of states rights.

A LITTLE while ago I responded to an invitation to appear before the judiciary committee of the national House of Representatives and "testify" (no oath was taken) about the prohibition regime. Parenthetically, let me explain that I refused to accept payment of my expenses from an organization opposed to prohibition— they were paid by the newspaper employing me. Although I said nothing that I had not written time and again, indeed too often from the point of view of interesting journalism, I returned from Washington to discover that I was, if not the only "wet" in this state, certainly the most notorious—in the opinion of many excellent folk, the most infamous; I have tingled with a singular sensation, for the most part merry, in particulars, depressing.

Of especial offence was my saying that I believed that "conditions under *national* prohibition were worse than those under the saloon system at its worst." Naturally, the qualification that I would not advocate restoration of the saloon has been ignored— I say "naturally" because one must look for jubilant assumptions from eager critics. Not unexpectedly to me, the saying is interpreted that I said that drunkenness and drinking are more common now and the consumption of intoxicants greater than in 1892. It would have astonished me had prohibitionists kept the thesis in mind and confined discussion to its terms—it would have revealed a growth in temperance which I am not prepared to observe.

Whether more liquors are consumed or less is, to my mind, of minor import—I set out in my "testimony" by saying that I would oppose prohibition laws if I thought they could be enforced, that "success of enforcement would be a symptom of pernicious anemia in American character." I of course hold that they are not and will not and should not be enforced.

Granting, for discussion's sake only, that prohibition is right, is national prohibition right, is the "national" idea either right or expedient? Dismissing that I believe in state rights as essential to South Carolina's liberties and prosperity, dismissing that the law is of the nature of a statute and therefore cancerous in a virtually rigid constitution, I denounce the Eighteenth Amendment as contradictory to facts of which men must take judicial cognizance—as of the rising and setting of the sun and the change of seasons.

The peoples of the world do not live in the same age. The South Carolina of 1930 is not the South Carolina of 1830 or 1730. This is not the world of the Grand Monarch or of Alfred the Great. The Roman Catholic church is not the church of the Thirty Years war nor is the Methodist church or the Episcopalian the church of John Wesley. It is equally true that the Chinese are not now living in our age, nor are the Russians. Either may be ahead of us, or behind us, I do not know, but I do know that a difference of 5,000 miles—with different origins, history and environment and behavior influenced by them—may mean to the peoples a difference of centuries. My friend Courtenay Carson miserably failed to make Einstein's theory plain to me, but I can understand that relativity has a significance and that a mixed population of 6,000,000 souls, sprung of a hundred nationalities, dwelling in an area of 100 or 200 square miles, must behave differently from my kinspeople in Cross Hill township. It would not surprise me if my Cross Hill cousins nullified a New York ordinance against parking their cars practically wherever they choose in Cross Hill township were it made for their governance. Cross Hill may be a community in advance of New York and of Detroit, I rather think it is, but among and between these communities geography, environment, numerous factors, make as great gulfs as do many years—except as to certain so-called fundamentals on which Americans are said to agree, as that murder, larceny, arson, forgery, rape, burglary, piracy (not one of them mentioned in the Constitution) are crimes. We are on treacherous ground when we speak of "fundamentals"—acts entirely innocent in New York or Georgia are adulterous or bigamous—and felonious—in South Carolina, if committed by South Carolinians within the state's borders in disregard of our constitutional prohibition of divorce.

Is the use or sale of intoxicants moral? Or immoral? No pope or church council can answer the question for me. I believe not only in the private interpretation of the Scriptures but in the private right to reject them. It is my liberty to submit to the discipline of my own church—not its liberty to scourge me with thongs into submission. At most it can excommunicate me, without trespassing on my civil rights. Hence I twiddle my thumbs at teachers and preachers who would talk to me about the morals of prohibition. Hence I must disdain a majority of voters or of a legislature defining morals. The sooner the prohibitionists strip their cause of its morality garb the more progress will they make for it, in the long run—yet it is this mask of morality under which it is hidden that was indispensable to its enactment in law. Subtract now the notion from some of the churches that alcoholic beverages are sinful and the prohibition fabric will topple. It rests on a foundation half religious and half economic—there is a wedding of fervent piety, or pietism, and economic selfishness that is sometimes beneficent and sometimes bestially avaricious. One of my acquaintances is a builder, an imbiber, and a resolute prohibitionist—he says that prohibition enables him to get more and better work out of his hired Negroes. At this point, let me warn you against assuming that I believe in universal suffrage or unrestricted liberty. Prohibition was undoubtedly good for the mass of American Negroes until 1865, and so were many other restrictions on their freedom of action, but I am unwilling to accept partial slavery for their sakes.

My own interpretation of Scripture is that the religion of Jesus is irreconcilable with coercion, with force—that it depends on persuasion. I prefer not to place overemphasis on the change of water into wine at the marriage feast except insofar as it is illustrative of the kindliness and humanity of the Christ, who, seeing the joy of the feasters wane and the host embarrassed, pitied the poor creatures and helped them, but it seems to me that those who allege that Christianity teaches prohibition accuse the Master of deliberately baffling and bemusing his disciples for all time by that miracle. And I say here that the division among Christians about this matter (for it surely exists) is a menace to the whole Christian church, aggravating the unhappy antagonisms within it that are its weakness. The Paulistic argument about abstaining from meat for "my brother's sake" is a perfectly good argument as long as the abstention is voluntary. One does not suspect that St. Paul would have claimed credit for abstention from meat as long as he should have been deprived of it by a Roman guard. Just as I ought to abstain from drinking with some people, as I do, it would be rank heresy coupled with pagan cruelty for me to abstain with an old friend in my house if I had liquor wherewith to cheer him. In respect of him I am under the sense of obligation that the burgesses of Aix were when they voted the last measure of wine to the good horse that brought the good news from Ghent.

"Demon Rum" is a phrase aptly chosen. Excellent people do in reality impute supernatural powers to an inanimate thing. Some of them raise it to the dignity of prince of fallen angels.

Whether the thing have three per cent or 60 per cent of alcohol apparently does not, to their minds, affect this devil's powers—they are omnipotent for evil. A sacrifice of liberty to it resembles demonolatry.

Are prohibition laws expedient? In the great cities they have placed a sector of "big business" in the hands of thugs. It is well known that gunmen and gangsters handle millions on millions of dollars; hence power without intelligent responsibility produces chaos in Chicago. The same thing would come to pass were gasoline outlawed in Columbia, and that it does not come to pass from the outlawing of liquor is explained by the circumstance that the demand for liquor and the money to buy it with are not enough. It has produced and is multiplying criminals in South Carolina. Many an honest countryman turned moonshiner has inevitably turned desperado—though I believe that there are moonshiners, numbers, who are not vicious persons.

The economic argument, that prohibition has largely increased the savings bank accounts and raised the standard of living is, I think, nonsense. So many factors, most of them new, have entered into the life of the American people in the last fifteen years that it would be folly to lay great stress upon any one of them. Restriction of immigration and the rise of the automotive industry are two that have probably affected wages and savings more than prohibition has. However, if the argument were not nonsense, I should be compelled to point out that economic conditions in South Carolina are deplorable, worse than they have been in fifty years, decidedly worse than when cotton sold, in 1896, at five or six cents a pound—banks did not break in those days and people tried to pay their debts—and are caused by prohibition. It would be nonsense to attribute the suicides in South Carolina in the last ten years to prohibition—but suicides there have been.

One hears incessantly the argument that the railroads forbid their employees to drink—especially their enginemen. It is unworthy of rational people. I employ a locomotive engineer. He is an abstemious black man and bears a fine South Carolina name, Walter Gaillard. He is the careful driver of my motor; I do not allow him to drink; I shall fire him if he drink whiskey and I detect it. Also he waits at my table. I do not allow him to eat raw onions. I shall fire him if he do that. There is no man that does not surrender part of his liberty for his job's sake—I surrender a great deal of mine—and some of you surrender more than I do. I dare say you sometimes fret because of it. But all of us at least have the poor privilege of quitting at pleasure and selling books or hoboing. Walter Gaillard has it.

One might preach to a herd of hogs to stay out of a corn field till the corn ripens, not to root it up as soon as planted lest they starve in winter. The hogs would not heed, not though the preaching were continued to a thousand generations. It is necessary to fence the hogs out of the field, or kill them—that is prohibition. Human creatures, once nearly as savage, greedy, and as improvident as hogs, allow the corn to ripen and then lay it up for winter. Enginemen were abstainers long before the adoption of the Eighteenth Amendment, and thousands of automotive enginemen are sober men, practically all of those employed as drivers—do you hear of drunken drivers on the bus lines? Do you explain it by saying that they have no access to bootleggers? A prohibitionist woman gleefully said in Washington the other day that Pierre Dupont does not allow his workers in powder factories to drink whiskey—it did not occur to her that the prohibition is even sterner against smoking cigarettes.

It is not necessary to fence men from liquor. American legislation should distinguish between hogs and humans. Men should be educated in temperance, and they were. In South Carolina they were more temperate in 1890 than in 1880 and still more temperate in 1910. The motor vehicle, a new and splendid mechanical invention, could have been used to incalculable effect as an incentive to sobriety. Driving on the highway is a privilege, not a right. From the befuddled mind and unsteady hand the privilege should be withdrawn. The craving for gasoline is greater than for alcohol, it is the rarely exceptional man who would not give up his cup rather than his car. We wets hold that the disorderly person, whether from alcohol or mental incompetence, should be kept off the road, and more so the disorderly car. Americans have rejected this new facility of education, which might have been received with thanks as a gift from Providence, and have fenced themselves, the whole herd, from alcohol instead. They treat themselves as unteachable hogs, and if one break through the fence they lock him in a sty and, if he resists, kill him. They do not say, "You may drive if you will behave decently," but "We shall convert you into a decent man by decree of the majority, by a count of noses, by the ayes and nays." They have abolished the principle of "Hope of reward and fear of punishment" as the motivation of human conduct by reducing it to fear of punishment alone. Incidentally, our highway commission reports prohibition liquor as a factor in from ten to twenty per cent of highway accidents. "Driving while drunk" is a common offence, and moonshiners and bootleggers, the progeny of the law, break the speed laws as a business necessity.

"But we should obey the law because it is law, otherwise we shall have disrespect for all law with ensuing anarchy." I reply that most of the liberties we have were gained by disobeying law. In 1735 the jury in New York disobeyed the law in the Zanger case and these colonies had freedom of the press forty years before Charles James Fox, Erskine, John Wilkes and Horne Tooke won a measure of it for England. The seven bishops defied the law of James II—

"And shall Trelawney die? And shall Trelawney die?

Twenty thousand under ground will know the reason why."

A little boy in Laurens, I used to beg empty cigar boxes from stores, the revenue laws were young then and the storekeeper always carefully cancelled the stamps on the boxes before giving them to me. Now thousands of stamped cigarette containers are flung away hourly—no one cancels the stamps, but the law remains intact. A lawyer of Philadelphia writes in the current *Harper's* and proves that that the average man in his town breaks laws enough daily to subject him to fines of $2,895.67 and imprisonment for five years were the laws enforced, and so perhaps do you. He cites the statutes, and does not mention prohibition or automobiles.

Who of you, called upon to go on a long and lonely drive at night, with your daughter or your wife, is conscious of guilt if you place a revolver in your hip pocket? Fifty years ago, when lawlessness was rife in South Carolina—or rather when there was more shooting and not one fifth as much stealing—much was expected of the prohibition of carrying concealed weapons. It failed. Then the carrying of pistols not of prodigious length was prohibited. It failed. My young friend Clem Ripley went to a hardware store and asked for a pistol. The merchant was a devout man, a Presbyterian elder and a dry, and did not know Ripley, who asked, "I have no permit to buy—can you sell me a pistol?" "Oh, yes, I'll sell one to *you*," and the merchant wrapped it. In South Carolina no one is arrested for carrying concealed weapons unless already in custody for another offence—yet I think that the essential criminality in a hip pocket pistol is far greater, unless the circumstances are unusual, than in carrying a hip pocket flask. To carry a flask to a dance is nasty, obscene, but one does not carry it to kill with. The concealed weapon law, good in itself, is practically incapable of enforcement, and, besides, white men in South Carolina have never consented to submit to searches necessary for its enforcement—therefore the Negro buck is not held up and searched. It would be a waste of time to talk about the speed laws—suffice it that an automobile not advertised as capable of breaking the speed laws would not be salable in South Carolina. Many good laws are disregarded; bad laws ought to be defied. Who shall say that a law is "bad"? Well, keep your eyes open and you will find out. The good laws in the criminal code have survived.

What of the laws against smuggling? Who of us free traders would not ignore them if we could do so without forswearing ourselves and getting caught? Have not some of us bought smuggled cigars when they were offered, and are not the best of our women sometimes swindled by peddlers whose selling song is that the laces and Irish linen napery were smuggled? Yes, if it could be done without perjury and without punishment, I would like to stump South Carolina for smuggling, and if I could pilot a ship loaded with necessaries and luxuries for our people impoverished by the "robber tariff" safely through Dewees' Inlet to our shores I would do it delightedly. Were not Boston patriots smugglers—was not that the "spirit of '76"? Mussolini's word is law in Italy—were he to proclaim prohibition should the Italian merchants obey and the Italian peasants plow up the vineyards? If Mussolini did, it would be the end of him.

Thoreau, as a protest against enforcement of the Fugitive Slave Law, refused to pay his taxes in Boston and went to prison, and Emerson visited him.

"Henry, why are you here?" asked Emerson.

"Ralph, why are you not here?" asked Thoreau.

I think Thoreau's protest was against the wrong law; the blood of slaveholders is in me and I have no recantation, but I honor Thoreau's disobedience. And you gentlemen teaching in a civilized institution of unmixed race are so doing because you are law-breakers, as your fathers were.

Who shall say what law is "bad"? Keep your eyes open and you will find out. The bad law dies the death, and the law books are white with their bleached bones.

Drunkenness, or the excessive use of intoxicants, is a disgusting vice; I have scant toleration for it; like many others I have seen it among my kinspeople, of an older generation. It is not the only vice, or the most damnable. When the typical prohibitionist talks about the "consumption of whiskey", it is with the assumption that all consumed does evil. Not one of them will concede that the "social glass" can possibly contribute to the sum of human happiness. I think it can and does. If the evil and the good of these beverages could be set off on two sides of a ledger, the record being of the last 5,000 years, I cannot say on which side the balance would be found. In fact, I am much too old to KNOW much. KNOWING is itself often intemperate. Of the alcoholic beverages consumed in England or Canada, I doubt if one tenth of one per cent results in drunkenness—but here the proportion is greater, for the ban causes people to get whiskey to get drunk. To be sure one has sympathy for the dipsomaniac, for the hypochondriac, the neurasthenic, the paranoiac—and for the nymphomaniac (these sad creatures are not so rare)—yet we really cannot contrive legal inhibitions that will protect them. If the human race is to be saved by force, the logical procedure is to weed out the weak with surgery and slaughter—one can imagine a form of prohibition that would speedily insure approximately universal continence, that would extirpate lechery. It is not advocated. The problem of procreation could be solved as it is solved on the horse and cattle farms of Blue Grass Kentucky—the strong men prohibiting the weak. It might be a noble experiment for the human race as it is for four-footed thoroughbreds—but I am no prohibitionist.

The use of intoxicating beverages is beyond a doubt rapidly decreasing in England and since prosperity has come to Ireland it is said that great numbers of public houses have had to close. Besides our country, only Finland has prohibition, and a month ago a mid-European diplomat told me that he had lived five years in that country, that its liquor conditions were wretched, that in the interior the population was insistently dry, that a great and profitable liquor smuggling industry had sprung up in the coastal region and towns, that coalition of the drys and the smugglers now fastens prohibition on the country. This confirmed the description of an American writer published recently in a magazine.

"Were the liquor question vigorously presented in South Carolina by both sides before a referendum with personal and extraneous issues excluded, how would South Carolina vote?" The experienced politician (not a Charleston man) to whom I addressed the question paused, then said: "It would be close—but you would have to reckon the bootleggers and moonshiners on the dry side." Finland over again. I shall not name the man, for he may soon be a candidate. I do not wish to embarrass him; he may run as a dry—but he gave me a drink of raw white whiskey out of a bottle that he had ordered at a hotel. I could hardly stomach the stuff—but I was polite.

Many of the moonshiners are good average countrymen—usually very poor. One of my country friends tells me that some of the moonshiners in his county are excellent citizens, school trustees, supporters of the church. These men manufacture but do not deliver. The bootlegger comes with a truck, pays for the stuff and hauls it to town. Moonshining has lifted them out of insolvency and poverty. A considerable sprinkling of farmers are making profits, and paying their debts, even educating their girls and boys in college from the business. Nevertheless, they are outlaws and tend to become desperadoes. It is shocking to me that thousands of the yeomanry of South Carolina are converted into criminals—in barroom days not more than 1,000 or 1,200 persons were engaged in the lawful liquor business, if so many, and moonshining was confined to three mountain counties. Moonshining was scarcely a noteworthy South Carolina industry—most of it was done across the North Carolina line.

Of the corruption of officers one knows little. Rather often in

Charleston when carloads or boatloads of fine liquors have been seized, it has been commonly reported that much of the seizure was distributed. One of my reporters obtained a supply, so he as good as told me, and sent four bottles, including one of champagne, to his father, a Baptist churchman and dry. "The old man was mighty curious to know where I got it, but he said, 'It sure was good.' " So the boy told me. The story was that friends of the officers in charge drove up and loaded a case or two in their cars, the officers looking in the other direction. My reporter was on that beat.

Not long ago bootleggers were soliciting buyers of "extra quality" liquor which they said had come from a seized box car. They may have been lying. News of the seizure had been published a day or two earlier. One can only say that when a two or one hundred and fifty dollar a month officer is in charge of a $10,000 stock of goods destined to be destroyed he is likely to be tempted. Doubtless there are honest constables, but one does not hear of prominent drys holding these offices.

Twenty-five hundred trials a year in state and federal courts come to a pretty sum. Maintenance of the enforcement units is expensive. Feeding prisoners costs. In proportion that energies of sheriffs are directed to liquor traffickers they are diverted from other duties. The withdrawal of 15,000 persons, or 30,000, from lawful trade and industry is costly. The annual destruction of unlawful property (stills included) of a selling value of $500,000 is an item reducing the state's wealth—though it please prohibitionists. South Carolina's contribution to the federal enforcement fund of $42,000,000 must be $600,000.

Of the demoralization of youth I shall not speak except to say that I know that the fashion of cocktail parties is by no means confined to Charleston. One young friend of mine was invited to five in two other towns in the last 30 days. A football game is always a drinking time. For the Clemson-Furman game on the Clemson grounds, did not President Sikes ask for a detail of liquor constables? Let me repeat that I am not discussing whether or not the volume of alcoholic consumption has increased—that to me is of small bearing on the subject. The fact is that young people now drink *hard* liquors, thousands of young people. This is not saying that they are drunkards—fortunately the vast majority of persons, young and old, would have good sense and self-restraint enough not to drink to excess though a barrel of free brandy stood at every street corner. Our people, with exceptions, are not born drunkards and cannot be made drunkards.

One cannot discuss this subject candidly. It is "an undercover" subject. The evidence of the prohibition "crime" by its nature must, in large part, be procured by those who make themselves *particeps criminis*. Detection without the practice of deception, duplicity, spying, lying, bribing, is not easy. Hence high-minded prohibitionists cannot and do not participate, except by proxy, in enforcement—and their proxies are not high-minded. One lives in an atmosphere reeking with hypocrisy, cant, and deceit. One fears to tell the whole truth even in this paper—one might betray one's self or one's friends.

The people most ignorant of conditions are the consistent and practicing drys. No one offers them whiskey. They are known, they are marked men. One is cautious in the company of some clergymen and bold in that of others. I have friends who are firmly convinced that little whiskey is consumed in Columbia, or in Greenville.

Were I a dry I would be compelled still to violate the spirit, and letter too, under the conspiracy and other decisions, of the law, unless I were resolved to be a recluse, an anchorite. If I go to a dinner where liquor is served in an ante-room, shall I make a scene though I abstain? If cocktails be passed in a private house and I perceive that the hostess has "stored" and is "possessing," shall I run to the nearest United States commissioner's office, swear an information and ask that a warrant be issued for her arrest? No, I won't do it. I plead for the "higher lawlessness," with Dr. Nicholas Murray Butler—in this case the higher lawlessness of hospitality and common decency.

If it be answered that Ball is a private citizen and under no special obligation to enforce the law, (he's not storing or possessing a "felony" under the Jones Law and shall he be quiescent when a felony is committed before his eyes?), I reply that I have seen a practicing, consistent, resolutely dry federal judge and good man placed in precisely the position I have described, and he obeys the "higher lawlessness" too. He should. Yet he is especially sworn to uphold the constitution and laws. Yes, even the consistent drys are often actual lawbreakers or consenters to law-breaking and connivers at it.

Prefacing that I am neither a hard drinker nor a regular drinker, I affirm to the Kosmos Club these things, stressing that I do *not* write exclusively of Charleston and what I have seen and done in Charleston. In the last four or five years I have been in company with, cumulatively, from 2,000 to 2,500 men and women, in fifty or more gatherings numbering from four to five hundred, most of them socially prominent or representative of professional and business classes, when drinking of hard liquors was part of the entertainment. I have occasionally, rarely, seen beer or wine served. I do not say that all drank—I have not fallen so low as to watch the individual drinker. The abstainers were the exceptions. I have drunk with judges, state and federal, (not with a federal judge of South Carolina), numbers of public officials, United States senators, I think with public prosecutors, mayors, legislators, college presidents and professors, bishops (not Methodist), clergymen and rabbis, numerous prominent bankers, lawyers, and physicians, well known Baptist, Methodist, and Presbyterian laymen, artists and musicians (men and women), authors of celebrity including historians, novelists, critics, biographers, and poets, and with heroes.

Of course I have drunk with editors, some of the most distinguished on the continent. I know but two practicing dry editors. One of them is Josephus Daniels, I think the most dependable dry of national reputation in the South. A member of his staff in an article of a tenor not unlike this paper printed over his name in a magazine a few months ago said that Mr. Daniels did not dictate to his employees about their habits. Josephus Daniels is a man of sense and a fine fellow, and he owns his paper. I have drunk with dozens of millionaires and multi-millionaires. We depend for the protection of our government ultimately on the army and the navy—I would look on an officer in either who was an abstainer as a freak. I have been in company with scores of them, rear admirals, generals, colonels, majors, captains, lieutenants, when they were drinking. Recurring to an earlier statement, do not accuse me of having taken a drink with a United States Senator of South Carolina—I am guiltless of that. In Washington at the wet hearing or on the train going or coming I did not see a drink—no one hinted one, to my disappointment, for I was very tired.

Do not understand that I have tried to paint a picture of ribaldry and revelry. Among all these people I have seen only five or six who had more than they could comfortably carry, though in one company three or four dozen of several hundred were pleasantly exhilarated.

The truth is that among the kind of people that I have described, it is unconventional not to drink, if not a little immodest. Total abstention draws attention to one and makes him feel slightly uncomfortable I fancy.

Nor am I to be understood as saying that everybody drinks. On the contrary, I am sure that the majority of people, now as always, drink rarely and that a great many do not drink at all. Outside of most of the Protestant clergy and others of conspicuous dryness, I think that now, as always, a great many people, given exactly the right setting, as on a fishing party on a boat forty miles from Charleston and from everywhere else, would be persuaded not to be churlish in the presence of a fruit jar.

Jack Falstaff said, I believe, this: "If I had a thousand sons the first *humane* principle I would teach them would be to abjure thin potations and addict themselves to sack" (whatever "sack" was), and that suggests to me one of the two sorriest phases of the condition. There are no "thin potations" and therefore there is no escape from hard liquors. These hard liquors, by the way, make the cocktail party economical. Two gallons of corn whiskey, aged a month or two in a charred keg, cost about $10 or $12 at most and will make a huge quantity of powerful punch—or cocktails—I do not know how many but perhaps enough for forty or fifty persons. Light sandwiches and olives are inexpensive. The same number would consume five or six gallons of wine—but whoever heard of a wine party? With wine, one entertained at dinner and a dinner cost money—it was inconvenient and burdensome to the lady of the house. Before prohibition, cocktail or whiskey parties were not given—at any rate I was never a guest at one.

The second phase is that drinking is now an adventure—a brilliant newspaper friend said to me, "Why, one must take a drink now to preserve his self-respect." Undoubtedly, the young people of fashion are drinking hard liquors, and I am wondering, with apprehension, if we shall have a noticeable number of women inebriates when the present generation under thirty-five shall be forty-five or fifty.

Not forgetting that Mr. Edison and Mr. Ford are prohibitionists, I have presented personal observations of the "experiment noble in motive" (I think no mortal has made a shrewder use of a word than is your dry president's of "experiment," it has soothed millions and may be his sesame for a second term), as a cross section of the American people, or of a mighty part of it—at least of its "upper classes," so-called. I have arrived at the opinion that about 80 per cent of the intellectuals exclusive of clericals and teachers of schools and colleges depending on rural support, about the same per cent of the daily newspaper (100 per cent of those of great circulation), and nearly all magazines that speak politically are against the Amendment and Volstead Act. It is a pregnant fact that prohibition has developed scarcely one potent voice of first rank—one doubts if Mr. Ford's money could create a lastingly popular prohibition magazine. Anyway, no one tries that experiment.

The saying that all of us ought to obey the law, that men of leadership are culpably responsible for conditions, may or may not be true, but in any case it is beside the point. Forty or "forty thousand parson power" sermons and appeals will and do go unheeded, unheard in fact. Men for whom all of us have the highest respect may sit in the city gates and tear their shirts and bellow, but they do not touch and they do not see realities. Moreover, if hortatory exertions can induce total abstinence, why in common sense were coercive laws passed? To talk of "oughtness" in the matter of laws saying "must" is the hollowness of wind blowing through the unloaded barrels of an unbreached gun.

Force is logical. It is always logical. The most logical people in this immediate world are the Russian communists. They do not bellow; they slit the throats of the intelligentsia and the bourgeoisie and shoot daylight through them. The prohibitionists are thrown into panic when Senator Bruce, a wet, slips in an amendment raising the enforcement appropriation from $42,000,000 to $200,000,000. The $42,000,000 won't pacify Chicago or any first class urban community. All this Congress knows; it well knows that the people won't make war, won't pay the costs of war, on the "Demon." To send old Elihu Root, or Nicholas Murray Butler, or Douglas McKay, or even me, to jail would hardly effect a conquest. Half a million handsome martyrs are required. The bootleggers are coming to be looked on as martyrs. I hear of one now in the penitentiary. "How is he getting on?" his partner and successor in business was asked. "He's mighty tired, we are hoping to get him paroled soon," was the reply. "Do they work him hard?" "Oh, yes, he's got a job in Leavenworth." "What is he doing?" "He's manager of the baseball team." I personally know one or two bootleggers home from prison whose "social" standing has not been damaged in the slightest. However, one of them reformed. A federal officer lately told me that Negroes, in this territory, sometimes serve as substitutes for moonshiners and bootleggers—they hire themselves as "goats." Not a bad job for Negroes otherwise unemployed. The drys are not in earnest, they are not logical, but the nullifiers are. Go to New York or Boston, go anywhere, and see for yourself.

Let me repeat that if the prohibitionists would defend their law for the sake of the poor and the working classes, that is their job—but they must reckon with the American Federation of Labor. If their theory is that Americans are not to be trusted to take care of themselves, let them say so and re-enact a modified slavery system.

If my description and the inferences from it are true, or one half true, should we go on with this national hypocrisy, this national clownishness? How long shall we live under a coalition majority of the population composed of honest drys ignorant of facts and lying drys who drink and are dry enough election days to get the honest dry vote? Shall we suffer the cant, the deceit, the corruption—shall we live and move in hypocrisy hiding from and deceiving one another? It is the poisoning of the Republic in the miasmic strata of the air we breathe that I hate and fear.

You ask for a remedy, for my substitute for national prohibition. I answer: repeal the Eighteenth Amendment. Let the federal government protect the borders and shores of South Carolina from trespass as it is bound to do under the old, the undiluted constitution. Let South Carolina make and enforce its whiskey traffic laws, as it does its laws against murder, arson, burglary—crimes not mentioned in the federal constitution, or state. Federal laws against importations of alcohol into dry states were effective before the Eighteenth Amendment was adopted. If South Carolina is incapable of suppressing or controlling the liquor traffic within its boundaries, it can hardly be of assistance to Chicago, Boston, New York, Detroit and Baltimore. If South Carolina cannot be temperate except under a bludgeon of Texas and Kansas, I am for intemperance, rebellion, nullification. Not until I shall despair of South Carolinians as worthy to be trusted with self-government shall I give assent to the proposition that they cannot solve the liquor traffic question for themselves, but as one of them I cannot presume that Massachusetts should not be trusted in the same manner. South Carolina's prohibitionists would say that in their state the law is enforced far better than in the great urban states—unless they have a surplus of resources to expend in those states enforcement in their state must weaken if they send a man or a dollar out of the state for this cause. If their own task of enforcement is a bellyful, so to say, national prohibition needlessly created for them a new host of foes and a peril hitherto non-existent. It is as though Great Britain in the midst of her trials of 1916 had declared war to suppress bull fighting in Spain or booze fighting in Sweden. With the Eighteenth Amendment and the Volstead Act out of the way, time and opportunity will remain for South Carolina to adopt its own police measures.

Dr. Paton, psychiatrist of Johns Hopkins, said the other day that supine consent to national prohibition law would mean the succumbing of the American people to mental disease, or to use his illustration, leave them as a nation, "subject to shell shock", a feeble or hopeless people, of lost power of resistance. I agree with him. The danger, though, is not imminent.

Judge O'Neall, the first great lay preacher of total abstinence in South Carolina by the way, relates in his *Bench and Bar of South Carolina* that when, in the early nineteenth century, the leaders in Charleston were still "Federalists" and the "Jeffersonian" agitation was not yet respectable, old Judge Bay had a son who not only distressed his father by addiction to his cups but by joining one of the new "Jeffersonian" clubs. One night the young man attended a meeting of the club and imbibed heavily. It was a summer night and the friends of the youth carried him home and deposited him on the piazza. At 6 o'clock next morning, the old gentleman, an early riser, came out, and gazing in disgust on the sleeping boy, exclaimed:

"Drunk!—and—a Democrat!!!"

It has seemed to me since my return from a day excursion to Washington that I am so looked upon in South Carolina. Naked and unashamed, and protesting that as I write I am free from the fumes of alcohol, I offer myself for your dissection.

THE CONSTITUTION IS NULLIFIED

(1930)

Changes in the Constitution of the United States and the wisdom of an experiment in parliamentary government in the American states are discussed with great insight and wisdom in this paper written in December 1930.

THE Constitution of the United States, a remarkable instrument in its day, has outlived its usefulness. The attributions of demi-godlike wisdom to the "foundation fathers" were just, but wisdom did not check the process of the suns, or die with them.

In the 140 years the great document has been vitally changed. The changing began early. The nature and purpose of the electoral college as the designers knew them were soon abandoned, and it was converted into a recording device. Sometimes war was the necessary resort, first to break and then reset the document. In later amendments the Republic's texture was raveled and unwoven by extensions of suffrage, for, at bottom, the Republic politically is its voters. Again, the states, forgetting the strength that lay in simplicity, drove into the organic law a regulation of personal habits, such a rule as a ladies' seminary might lay down for the government of girls—the Eighteenth Amendment—which might as well apply to cigarettes or to the length of skirts as to alcoholic drinks.

Here or there, or everywhere, the Constitution is nullified. This not only is openly defended, it is sometimes boasted. School boys are offered prizes to write praise of a pact which discerning men know is heaped upon a relic.

Most of the changes have been wrought by judicial interpretation. Legal writers employ the polite fiction that the Constitution is a living thing and growing. As new circumstances arise judges inject cocaine into an inconveniently obtruding sentence or clause, deaden it, kill it, remove it, and graft living flesh. For a name for the operation, "rule of reason" is as good as another. Without rules of reason can be no advance. "De sun do move," formulae are static, so judges reverently and deftly alter, rearrange, chemically change them. It is unavoidable.

A written constitution, though it embody the wisdom of the ages, cannot long survive its own age. The age of 1789 glimmered out long before the generation of 1930 saw the light.

So the Constitution remains and is venerable, a venerable obstruction. It is large, heavy, difficult to get around. Provisions for remodeling to suit the times were put into it, and experience teaches that they were not of skilful contrivance. The "fathers" sacrificed everything for a degree of stability and with it got ponderous rigidity.

Recognition of this is constantly and fretfully cropping out. The President is inaugurated at the wrong season. Defeated candidates for Congress linger months—"lame ducks" we call them—and measures are proposed to put them out of their misery, but the measures linger. Others opine that cabinet officers should be given seats without votes in congress, but they are dismissed with a "what's the use?" gesture. As for the regulation of interstate commerce no one has better than a dim idea of what it is all about, and had the acceptance of a theory of the tariff long ago forced by sheer political weight been foreseen in 1787 it would have aborted the Union's birth.

This written instrument is a stubborn thing and unresponsive. The United States of 1790 or 1830 moved internally with the slow and solemn ticking of a grandfather's clock. Now the machinery whirls. A hundred years ago few people read, a numerous minority could not read. What did the "masses" know about performances in Washington? They listened to political haranguers and followed them with sheepish if excited faith. An excellent and compensating result was that honest and strong men were often, it may be usually, chosen to represent them. "There were giants" in the thirties, the forties and the fifties. Elected to Congress a Webster found room and nourishment, he grew, he waxed in stature if not in the fear of the Lord. Relatively he was a free agent if for no other reason than that it was hard for his constituents to keep up with him when mails were slow, telegrams a novelty, all travel an adventure. Andrew Jackson set the crowd going, it came along cheering, but always at a respectful distance and little informed about proceedings at G. H. Q.

By 1890 most of the people had learned to read newspapers, the new era of movement and communication was dawning—since then it has taken on staggering proportions. The doctrine that representatives should obey the will of their constituents, hitherto applied as an emollient by orators and editors, had to arrive with it, was now real, logically had to be. A William Jennings Bryan to preach it was inevitable. The sequel was the amendment compelling the states to elect senators by popular vote—thus the constitution had another bone driven into it. Thus it has come to pass that representatives and senators are, as everyone is saying, messenger boys, bell-hops, echoing the home lingo, with dwarfing duties of commercial agents on the side. L. Q. C. Lamar's protest against the attempted dictation of the Mississippi legislature was a gallant utterance—so was the death song of Wantolla, the Lone Wolf, after the battle with the red dogs of the Deccan. It is not mentioned in Kipling's story, but the red dogs always come back.

In 1829 General Jackson was five weeks on the road from Nashville to Washington; the trip now could be made, by air, in as many hours (with less danger, too), but once in the White House a President finds the government's pace scarcely accelerated. The old rules hold it back, while the country, the electorate, travels fast—public opinion on which government is supposed to rest shifts with speed increased proportionately to the quicker speed of vehicles. The so-called "ship of state" crawls like a prairie schooner, which would be no matter if it did not block the road.

In these things is nothing new, they have been said often enough lately, but what are we going to do about it? Nothing at all, and a shrug of the shoulders accompanies the answer as one points to the sacred constitution clutched tenderly in the arms of Chief Justice Charles Evans Hughes, him gazing raptly at the portrait of John Marshall out of one eye and alertly at Justices Holmes and Brandeis out of the other.

Why not try the parliamentary system? Again the shrug of the shoulders. It has worked a long time and fairly well in Great Britain, but did we not improve upon it? British government is adjustable, gaited to the British people, but the thought of blowing up our prairie schooner is impious. Besides we can't do it, we can't get to it; always are thirteen states in the way, most of them likely to be puny, toddling states which other states have pledged themselves to treat as grown ups.

Seventy-five years, from 1790 to 1865, South Carolina had a good government. The legislature, or general assembly, representation in the popular body of which was nicely blended of manhood suffrage and property-holdings, elected the governor, nearly all the state officers, some of the county officers, and "appointed" the presidential electors. As for the governor, ineligible to succeed himself, he was always a personage and bore a bland resemblance to a king of the Britons. He was without the veto power. He was without most dangerous accoutrements, though he did have the pardoning power unrestricted, which was a mistake. A "secretary for home affairs" should have had it. The governor was commander-in-chief of the militia and probably looked the part. He gave parties (1,500 quarts of champagne were consumed at one about a century ago); he came from his plantation or law office to Columbia, the capital, when the general assembly was in session, sent it messages, conferred diplomas at the commencement of the state college (conveniently held while the general assembly was in session), spoke eloquently when invited, and behaved with the decorum expected of a constitutional monarch with an alias in a democratic republic. This governor, like a king, could do no wrong—or at any rate he could do mighty little harm.

The system, modern, progressive, as it was, is not adapted to the South Carolina of 1930. It also was too rigid. An administration lasted a definite period, two years. South Carolina's currents of public opinion shift too rapidly for that nowadays. The commonwealth, all American commonwealths, should have government by parliament, choosing a prime minister and cabinet. The governor could be omitted, unless it were discreet to bestow the title on the chief minister, as a popular concession to pomp. The state senate, like any other house of lords, might be retained for decorative purposes, as needed.

In short, the British system less the two ornamental estates of the realm might be fitted snugly upon South Carolina, with invigorating results.

"Ah," objects a vigilant guardian, "but Section 4 of Article V of the Constitution declares that 'The United States shall guarantee to every state of this Union a republican form of government.'" What would the British government, minus a king and hereditary House of Lords, be unless republican? Perhaps other legal objections would be raised—this paper does not pretend to be a lawyer's argument, and they are not anticipated: one is content to set down that a government carried on by the creatures of a legislative body elected by and representative of the people, the electors, and at all times answerable to that body, holding office at its pleasure, is more nearly and exactly republican than those now established in the United States and its forty-eight constituent commonwealths of sovereignties cramped and growing more cramped as the years pass.

How would it work? If, for example, the prime minister, or governor if he be so called, in the course of a speech to an excited section of the populace should say that the lynching of a Negro for a particular crime was a deed to be praised, it is certain that a resolution of censure would be proposed in the parliament. Passed, the resignation of the ministry and the installation of a new government would follow. Rejected, it would at worst prove that the parliament was scarcely civilized and it might be none the less representative on that account. The parliament would expire at stated intervals of time of course, and a ministry might "go to the country" in the manner customary where parliamentary government obtains.

What happens now? The governor's term in most of the states

is four years. If he be guilty of an utterance or act outraging decent opinion, the sole redress that the people have is impeachment by the general assembly. That process is of extraordinary difficulty, tedious, elaborate, necessarily attended by sound and ceremony. To establish that "high crimes and misdemeanors" have been committed is a huge undertaking. Seldom is it undertaken. A sentence of impeachment carries with it disgrace, an ineradicable taint of dishonor. A senate is reluctant to pronounce it though a house indict and prove its case. Retirement from office as a consequence of loss of a parliamentary majority on the other hand is no more than defeat at the polls. The defeated would have his chance to "come back." An executive protected by a fixed tenure may run amuck—sometimes he does—with little fear of being brought to book and with reasonable certainty that whatever bad behavior he may be guilty of short of overt crime will be forgotten—a nine days' sensation. In the parliamentary system the erring minister must answer promptly, instantly, and his responsibility extends to subordinates in the ramifications of the state's government.

The system would work in an American state as it works elsewhere in civilized states, and the results would reflect the fitness of the people to rule, for, in the long run, no republican or popular government can assay better than the character and intelligence of its creators, the electors.

Whatever the issue—taxation, labor legislation, what not—the process would be the same, but the foregoing illustration is purposely chosen because the question of crime is exigent in most American states. One hears of "the law's delays," of "dilatory practices," the lawyers and the courts are blamed. Courts are agencies of the people, ultimately the people select the judges and make the laws, but the people are failing to correct the errors and evils of which they complain. And why? Manifestly, they are out of touch with government, too far removed from it.

How long would popular interest in football last were all the games played on one or two days at intervals of two and four years? Is it a marvel that the "masses" are concerned less with politics than with football, that the affairs of the state are left for

the most part to the professionals, the politicians, the officehold-
ers, receivers of the gate receipts?

The masses must have games, have always demanded them, always have had them, are stupidly inert without them. What interest they show in the biennial and quadrennial professional
contests is stirred by a press that unduly magnifies them in relation to their news values, a truth that the "tabloids" have perceived, and made the most of. They belittle politics and gain
turgid circulations. In the United Kingdom the attention of the
electorate is constantly focussed on Ramsay MacDonald and his
team, who ever must fight to hold the line and make gains or
Stanley Baldwin's opposition will march down the field across
their goal.

In this republic and its forty-eight constituent republics the
people's minds are on other subjects between elections. No game
is going on except as between the two sets of hired professionals,
who have the grand stand as well as the field to themselves.

Whatever the railings of press and politicians, the great majority, once government is installed for an assured period of time,
forgets it or thinks of it vaguely as secure in a distant fortress. If
contact with a tax gatherer or prohibition agent stir resentment,
in it is an ingredient of hopelessness, a reflection that life is too
short to bother about it. By the time that the next political campaign opens, a variety of issues has accumulated beyond the
powers of mental digestion. They dilute, weaken or neutralize
one another until at last the average citizen casts his vote in
slavishness to party habits or a campaign slogan. The slogan is
potent because it is the expression of a single idea, or emotion,
which, generally speaking, is enough for one man at one time.

Parliamentary government would work in South Carolina.
The state long had its approximation, and even now, though the
people are scarcely aware of it and executives encroach when
they can, most of the powers of government reside in the legislature. The virtues that should flow from the arrangement are
negated by the want of immediacy in the legislature's responsibility. Unconsciously but surely it becomes arrogant and selfish,
a body of wirepullers and logrollers, dividers of spoils. Evidence

of it is the fact hardly disputed that only a member or person enjoying contactual association with it is likely to be elected to a
judgeship or other office to which the legislators are the electors.
Members and senators are "in" for two or four years and while
they are in they take for themselves the goods the gods provide.
Usually there is time before another election for the people to
forget. The forty-eight states are "sisters under the skin."

Thirty odd years ago agitation was widespread, especially in
western states, for the initiative, referendum and recall. It was
denounced as radical. It was in very truth the awkward groping
of a half-awakened people for the parliamentary government that
is their heritage. Were it established in states swift reforms would
be effected, a flagrant miscarriage of justice would bring down
upon the party responsible for the unfaithful or blundering judge
instant penalties, improvements that the people helplessly seek
would be effected, government at worst would be as good as the
people would have and therefore as good as they deserve.

The Constitution of the United States has outlived its usefulness—that is our major premise—and what shall we do about it?
This Constitution was made by the states, it is not the child of
the Republic, the Union. Only the states can unmake it and substitute another. Only an event or series of events that would
simultaneously shock the country from ocean to ocean and from
lakes to gulf conceivably would bring them together in convention to write the document of 1789 from the books and frame
another better suited to the twentieth century. That document,
all its parts, was brought out of the thirteen states. It was in no
sense a fabrication from raw materials, for the bricks had been
moulded and burned before they were carried to the Philadelphia
convention by Franklin, Pinckney, Madison and their fellows.

"Forty-eight laboratories are better than one," said Dwight
Morrow, speaking of the national prohibition "experiment," last
summer. So they are for all constitutional experiments. Would
not parliamentary government be worth trying in a state? Suc-
ceeding in one, it would be adopted in others. Probably it would
work in all. It works in Great Britain, Ireland, Canada, Australia,
the South African Union.

When the forty-eight states had proved its efficiency, some bellwether state leading, it would remain for them to repeat the performance of the thirteen in 1787-89.

The old Constitution would still be revered. A monument would be erected in Washington.

MORE INTENT TO SAVE THE CITY THAN TO SAVE THE COUNTRY

(1931)

In proposing reforms assumed to be beneficial to the American people, reformers time and time again have, in reality, acted to bulwark the swollen cities whence crime and poverty arise. William Watts Ball exposes this ironical situation in this essay.

THE despairing conclusion of Norman Thomas' interesting article about Tammany in the *Forum* for June rests on the assumption that the American city is an organism not subject to qualitative change, therefore its constitutional evils can be corrected by substituting socialism for capitalism and in that way only.

The assumption is disputed. It may be more expedient to tear down New York and the other cities, in part, and reconstruct them than to uproot the existing order of the country. Major operations, removal of tumors, may save them and the Republic too. Or, what is more likely, nature left to itself may save them.

Why "support the enormous load of landlordism" in New York? Obviously, because the people must have homes and shops, therefore landlords. Out of every line of Mr. Thomas' article sticks that in New York are too many people. Are they under sentence to live in New York, in the "slum, the ugliness, the discomfort," in the "vice and crime and misery, which bad housing, unnecessary congestion, and lack of parks and playgrounds create"?

Mr. Thomas means the phrase in another sense, but is not "unnecessary congestion" the key to what he calls "the racket of private landlordism"?

"Two thirds of all New Yorkers have family incomes of less than $2,500; one third less than $1,500," Mr. Thomas says—and why should an American family insist upon living in New York? Some of us having incomes considerably greater than either of those sums would not undertake to live in a great city unless we could afford one of the sumptuous apartments he mentions, for the excellent reason that for half or one third the money we can and do obtain better values—at least we think so. We are not sufferers from urbanitis and in the degree that we are immune from it, so are our working people, our poor.

In New York in 1927 were 552,507 wage earners engaged in manufactures, and the sum of their earnings was $904,646,427, their average wage being $1,637.

Why are they engaged in manufactures in New York?

Why of all places is New York the greatest industrial center of the United States, producing more than 50 per cent of its manufactured values?

There are many answers. One is that the factory workers are so in love with New York that they are willing to support the "racket of private landlordism," enduring life in the slums, the ugliness, the misery, amid vice and crime.

A few small classes excepted, as bakers, daily newspaper mechanics, these factory workers are under no necessity to labor in the city. The factory does not belong in the great city. To be sure, until they are moved into the "open spaces" the workers may remain, and this removal is and will be opposed by New York's "landlordism"—aye, there is the immediate and heartbreaking problem.

About twenty-five years ago occurred in New York the tragedy of the "Triangle Shirt-waist fire," costing the lives of some scores of young women, and it came to me with a shock of astonishment that on two or three floors six or seven stories in the air were employed twice as many workers as in one of our textile plants in South Carolina that we thought of as big. None of these plants is more than four stories, it would be inconceivable that forty girls could lose their lives leaping from windows to escape fire—most of them would be working not thirty feet from soft earth. Why a clothing factory, in the suffocating city, of all places in what is still the roomiest of civilized lands?

At the time of the Triangle fire, workers in the city went to a mill by street car paying a five cents fare or, if it was in a village, they lived in easy walking distance of it. The mill itself was built about the stationary steam engine or on the river bank at the shoals. That is why Manhattan's population, 60,000 in 1800, swelled to 813,000 in 1860 insofar as factory workers swelled it. Railroads contributed to the growth, but their trains ran on rigid schedules and the worker, if he lived miles from the mill, still had to live close to the railroad station.

It is not so now. Our "Main Street," hard, smooth, the year around, stretches from Miami to Quebec and every acre butting on it is as good a factory site as is the bank of the Tennessee at Muscle Shoals. Electric current flows everywhere. In the South, cotton mills always have had abundant space, the company owning from fifty to 500 acres, sometimes 1,000. Land was as cheap almost as water and air—and is cheaper in 1931 than it was when the first mills were built.

New York's area is 197,727 acres, hardly two thirds of an average South Carolina county, and, apart from its offices, stores, wharves, railroad stations, schools, libraries, theaters, and so on, it is just a mill village for 552,000 factory workers and their families, as Pacolet, in South Carolina, with a thousand acres, is for perhaps a thousand families. Pacolet, too, has the stores, schools, theaters, and so on, though it is conceded that New York's are bigger. Some of them may be better.

But Pacolet's working population is no longer confined to the company's land. The village, for the worker's practical purposes, may be as wide and long as the Bronx is with its 27,365 acres, it may scatter over the county. Why not? Travel by motor costs about the same as by subway, and ten miles down to Pacolet is only twenty or thirty minutes. Even now one may see from a Pullman window twenty or forty cars parked under the eaves of a cotton factory. They belong to men and women who live in farm houses two miles, five, ten, from the mill.

Nor, for many kinds of manufacturing, is one big plant longer necessary. Electric power may drive the machines in a hundred little garment mills in as many square miles as it does in New

York, but, as not in New York, about each may spread farms that feed the factory workers, upon which one member of the family may drive a tractor or a mule while another under roof operates a sewing machine. At the nearby railroad station may be the company's office, warehouses, and shipping rooms. The president can reach by motor any of the fifty little factories on the farms in a few minutes, to them raw material may be carried by motor truck and the finished product gathered in the same way. Every establishment is a blend of factory and farm where is some choice of employment, some opportunity for initiative, where a garment worker may raise gardenias if she wish. In these little factories the ingredient of ground rental in overhead is virtually eliminated; 400 or 4,000 square feet in the country scarcely count in the rental of a farm.

Why is New York a mill village? Factories making paper bags, shirts, purses, confections, jewelry, knit goods, a hundred articles, may they not be built and operated alongside of the dairy farms, the milk and the butter, the chicken and egg factories, two hundred miles from Broadway?

The automobile and distributed power are undoing the work of the steam engine, stationary and locomotive. The automobile is as flexible in movement as a snake is—and the commercial airplane has already arrived at least for the convenience of the management. Does not the manager of a state farm in Soviet Russia, as big as a county, fly to his distant fields? Something like the handicraft age may be coming back. Henry Ford, a capitalist not afraid to break outworn rules, has already encouraged the disintegration of the big plant when the process was "indicated."

Nor does dispersion of congested population imply that it must go into the mills. Here is land, millions on millions of acres unoccupied, not the choicest, not the most fertile as a rule, but land on which the family willing to dig a little cannot starve or perish from cold. The talk is not of opportunity to get rich—the clerks, the saleswomen, the messenger boys, the workers in the needles trades had that in the years and months before October, 1929—it is of the way from the bread line and the soup kitchen, the way of the "ranks of the unemployed," out of the slums, the misery, the "landlord's racket." If it is not the road to wealth it is the path from beggary. Here is how it is done, according to the plan of C. O. Splawn, of Rutherford county, North Carolina, on the South Carolina line, published in a newspaper this day:

> "Five acres have been planted to cotton in order to furnish some cash in the fall, two acres to sugar cane which will be cut green for feed, the remainder to corn, beans, peas and soy beans, potatoes, sweet potatoes, onions, cabbage and turnips. A large garden will provide all the vegetables the family can use while the orchard will provide plenty of summer fruit and all the apples, peaches, plums, pears and cherries that can be canned.
>
> Mr. Splawn also maintains a flock of hens, plants some tobacco, grows his own strawberries and eats home-churned butter."

Mr. Splawn will not amass wealth. He will labor with his own hands sometimes under a broiling July sun, occasionally in wet and sleety weather. His wife and children will not be hungry, they will wear comfortable clothes, and their roof will keep out the rain. "Is that the destiny of a free-born American?" Why the question? The breadline and the unpaid rent for the tenement in the slums are the questions.

If Splawn lived farther south he might have an easier time—so easy that he might drop into lazy habits, though one is under no compulsion to form them. The summers, if longer, are scarcely hotter than in the lower East Side.

"Cap'n Aleck's" case is the evidence. He is a Negro, born more than seventy-two years ago, therefore a former slave, and lives in a two story house with his wife on St. Helena, a barrier island, off the South Carolina coast. The old tale is that in 1815 when the news percolated to the ears of the gentlemen planters, after Waterloo, that the French "ruffian," Napoleon Bonaparte, was to be banished to "St. Helena," they met and drew up a formal protest against the outrage of dumping him on them. It probably isn't true; anyway by another war the gentlemen planters lost their lands.

Last year "Cap'n Aleck," who began life as a boatman, sold

from his farm of seven acres vegetables and fruits to the amount of $500, and, besides, he lived. He owns two other larger farms. Mr. Thomas might call him a "landlord racketeer," but he has no automobile. He prefers his boat, in which he has carried thousands of loads of fresh vegetables to Savannah, where he has peddled them. He and his wife, incidentally, have raised sixteen children, all of whom, with one exception, have been sent to the excellent industrial school long ago founded by Northern people on St. Helena. That one "took" a college education.

"These things being true," the puzzled reader interrupts, "why do the farmers murmur; why are they poor?" Well, they are poor, that is why they murmur, albeit this reader driving into the court house square of a Southern town on a Saturday would with difficulty find a parking place. They are poor indeed, nearly all of them in debt, discouraged, hard put to it to pay taxes, and there are many answers. "The one crop system," the old, old speculation of the man who put all his eggs in a single basket is one of them. They have gambled on cotton so long that they have lost the power of turning to another game. Verily, Markham's "man with the hoe" was a cotton "chopper." Now and then from some fortuitous cause the prices rule high a year or two and they are crazed for another decade.

Early in last November I heard an informed citizen describe the destitution in his country—how farm loan banks were foreclosing mortgages, and tax collectors were selling homesteads, how families by hundreds were sick with pellagra for the want of a balanced ration of milk and "greens"; and then arose the most progressive farmer in South Carolina and said: "I know that district, it is within thirty minutes drive of my house. I have traveled it with this gentleman. I confirm all that he says: the people are suffering, they have no milk cows, they raise cotton, and a week ago I saw two things and since then I have been impatient and out of humor. One of my neighbors asked me to see his sweet potato patch, on the same kind of land that these sufferers occupy—he was harvesting 600 bushels from an acre. That day I looked at one of my own turnip fields, saying to my foreman, 'It will make 500 bushels to the acre.' 'No,' he replied, 'nearer

350.' I was not convinced and had the crop measured. The yield was 780 bushels on an acre—about ten tons of turnips for cattle and tons of turnip greens besides."

Another planter followed: "I have nine Negro tenants on my plantation and the other day I looked into their affairs. Each of them had a little cash, four have cows, all of them have food for their families and feed for their beasts to carry them through the winter. By the first day of the new year they will be dependent and begging, for all of the nine have second hand cars, on a Sunday afternoon you will see them with their families strung along about a quarter of a mile distances on the 'big road' mending wornout tires—they will sell everything and borrow more to buy gasoline."

This is but half the story. These farmers must clothe and feed the workers in New York, in all the cities. When they buy cloaks and skirts that the "needle workers" make, they must pay a price in which the urban landlord's rental is included, and if they ship cotton or peaches, the wages of the railroad brakeman enabling him to maintain the "American standard of living" is charged into the freight. If the American annual income be eighty-seven billion dollars and the farmers are receiving eleven billions of it, what would be the catastrophe were eleven billions added to it—and taken from the city dwellers? Yet twenty-two billions would be about the farmers' fair share reckoned by the number of them. Shall justice be done and the cities destroyed? Shall landlords be reduced to penury? Can wages be hoisted?

Shall not every artificial prop that legislative ingenuity can contrive be the resort to perpetuate urban congestion, its wretchedness, ugliness, vice and crime? Release 552,000 factory workers pent in New York and hundreds of thousands of men, women, and children would flee to the open country with them. So they must be coddled, petted, promised insurance against unemployment, perhaps. Their "psychology" must be kept right, or the city itself may be a busted concern.

Their "psychology" is right. A long time ago I, a reporter, rode on the seat with an Irish boy who drove a carriage in a civic procession in Philadelphia. He pointed out to me the pygmy skyscrapers of that day, and the pride of vicarious possession was scarcely less than the real thing. He despised "rubes"—the word "hick" had not been invented. In 1922, in the midst of the "depression" I gave a hitchhiker a lift, a square-shouldered, clear-eyed, frank-faced lad of Brooklyn, a sailor with his honorable discharge from war service in the navy. He was making his way to Norfolk to seek a job, and as we rolled over earth roads south of Lynchburg in Virginia, I said, "Why don't you stop here, go to work on a farm? You can soon own it, be your own master—why do you work for a boss?"

"Humph!" he said, "No farm for me—the farmers have the lowest 'standard of living' of any people in this country." He spoke the phrase trippingly on his tongue, and he was a independent fellow too, for he politely declined a dollar that I offered him as we parted at the next railroad station.

They have, these farmers, a low standard of living, for in the United States are two standards, and the higher is in town, which the farmers make possible—or the town would wilt and shrivel. The protective tariff is but one, if one of the chief, devices whereby the urban wage scale and status are maintained. The countryman buys the protected goods at the town price, including the town rental, and sells—for what he is offered. It is the conflict between urban and rural standards that is cracking the American fabric; the protective tariff is a part of the urban defense. To most countrymen Mr. Thomas' $1,500 income of New York's poor family would seem princely.

Yet the hard "psychology" of the Philadelphia driver and the Brooklyn sailor may thaw. I think it is thawing. The "full dinner pail" having failed some of the "seven million unemployed" may look for full bellies on little tracts of land—despite the piteous outcries last year from the congressmen of Arkansas. Some of these people must be resourceful, must have grit, the stuff that the pioneers were made of, in this land so spacious that every man may be a landlord. Perhaps "Cap'n Aleck," Negro landlord of St. Helena, is not superior to all of them. It may be that thousands are still capable of expelling the notion that the world owes them a job if not a living and of making jobs for themselves.

There are no unemployed on the farms operated to provide an independent livelihood for the man and his family, and that kind are not famishing or begging, in South Carolina, few though they be. The wise ones would not come to the lands with the expectation of getting rich quick and driving a twelve cylinder car, but they would indulge the reasonable hope of bidding a last farewell to the bread line. France teems with farmers of that kind, and the village blacksmith, if "he owes no man anything," is a gentleman blacksmith after all. Likewise, the tiller of his own soil is a gentleman farmer, car or no car.

Pioneers? Hugh Macrae of Wilmington, N. C., has brought them into his state, settled them on lands, sold them lands and helped them, men of divers nationalities. Most of them have prospered, and some have gained wealth. It is his story that one of them, a Dane, after a year of residence, approached him to buy a farm.

"Well, how much land do you want?" Mr. Macrae inquired.

"Ten acres," said the immigrant.

"Do you think you can make a living on ten acres?" Macrae asked, wonderingly.

The man hesitated and answered, "No, sir, I'm not sure that I can, but if I can't I know that I can on five."

Such men are doing just that on five acres in Denmark, Belgium, France, Holland, Bavaria, and in the United States the millions of acres await them.

The Socialism to which Mr. Thomas looks forward implies bosses, and the blood and iron of Bismarck was nothing to Joseph Stalin's. The major premise is that in the United States the average man no longer can take care of himself. Even if it be true in Russia there is no reason to accept it in this roomy country, in which, so far, individualism is not yet bankrupt. If democracy can be saved by the partial disintegration of the cities, leaving them trading, shipping, educational, and artistic centers, the experiment would not be so radical or so cruel as is that of the United Soviet Republics. With sincere and great respect for Mr. Thomas, it occurs to me that unconsciously he may be more intent to save the city than to save the country. His fears and his plans may not be wholly divergent from those of the urban potentates.

These potentates, had not they better look to the reserves back of the front line? Every cotter, every "yokel" as glib fools like to call them, who lives on his own little place mans a machine gun nest against the advance of socialism and its kindred "isms." They are the people sure to respond in the republic's emergency. The city may persuade them to remain a little longer in its pigeon roost tenements, may fascinate them yet awhile with its glamor, but what shall it profit the landlords if they save their rentals a few more years till the city shall lose its soul?

It may be, too, that the experiment is going on. In the last decade California's population gained 65 per cent and Florida's 51. Men are enjoying pleasant flight in automobiles from ice and snow—the saving in the winter's fuel covers the cost of it. Each year the southward stream of low priced cars swells and begins to flow earlier, to turn north later. It breaks into streamlets that stop in the cities—so grow Los Angeles and Miami—but thousands of families are finding lodgement and foothold in the villages and along the countryside.

Anyway, the roads are good, travel is cheap, electric power is everywhere, and the distribution of population is going on. It can't be stopped or checked, and, above all, the land is abundant for every man who loves freedom and is not afraid to work for it, to dig in and defy the landlord's and every city's racket.

THE VERTICAL FRONTIER

(1933)

In 1933 William Watts Ball commenced work on a book on the unrecognized frontier of the United States the sparsely settled lands constitute. Because of the pressure of editorial work the volume was not completed. "The Vertical Frontier" is a chapter taken from the projected book.

SINCE 1890, historians say, has been no American frontier, for by that time the free lands were exhausted. No longer in a time of depression could people about to starve load a few household goods into a wagon and go west. The historians are speaking truly of the horizontal frontier, the earth's surface over which the Americans in hordes could march or crawl, line after line, wave upon wave of them pressing westward or southward, until they came to the Pacific, the Mexican Gulf or the Rio Grande. That they shaped the character of the country and its destiny no one would dispute, no one would belittle the frontier as a factor in the making of America, and of all the factors it may have been that one most important if not controlling. The new peoples of the new states they erected have shot back into the original states of gentler, subtler, more seasoned culture the strong virus of a rude life drawn from deep fresh soils and forests of tall trees.

That a son of a Forty-niner came back from California to romp over the East, trample upon its habits and traditions of newspaper and magazine making and shake up the "Fleet Streets" of its cities North and South, and of the cities between the two oceans, is illustrative of the frontier in action. That the action may not be entirely graceful and may set up resentment and some disgust among the older folk in the metropolitan clubs is no matter.

There is a vertical frontier. If the historians do not ignore they usually underestimate it. It is the frontier to which the Hollanders turned centuries ago when their free lands were exhausted. When they came to the sea they built walls and took a part of it. They gave to the barebones earth a soil, and the richest cheeses are of Holland's products. The population of Europe has increased from 180,000,000 to 460,000,000 since 1800, but the European frontier had disappeared centuries before that. Italy with four times the area of South Carolina and twenty-three times its population, with a proportion of unproductive mountain land much greater than Carolina's, has just now reclaimed the Pontine Marshes and made them habitable after they had lain idle in malarial noisomeness twenty-five centuries.

Wherever is a piece of land out of which the most has not been made is the vertical frontier. It comprises much the greater part of the territory of the United States, much the greater parts even of the older states.

Once in Missouri were millions of acres of black lands and they had value only to buffalo and to the Indians who chased them. They were even slightly better lands perhaps in the year 1800 than they are now, but if pioneers paid fifty cents an acre for them they paid all they were worth. That they fetch $250 an acre in 1933 has nothing to do with the case. A Marylander and his family going to Missouri with patents in his pocket for a quarter section, 160 acres, of those lands would have been undesirable life insurance risks. Had insuring companies of the kind that we now have been operating in those days, the premiums they would have demanded of pioneers would have been prohibitive. That is by way of saying that the virgin lands, though they were given to the pioneers, scarcely had pecuniary value. Before they took on value in money thousands of men, women and children had to pay for them prematurely with their lives. Roads had to be laid out and constructed. Schools, churches, railroads, towns, had to be built. Until markets were accessible, life could scarcely be comfortable and had to be primitive. The lure of the valleys and the plains was irresistible, and they are right who say that their call to the spirit of adventure and romance as well as to the desire for wealth and independence caused the republic as we know it in the Twentieth century to take on flesh and robust strength.

It is the hasty conclusion of historians that the vertical frontier does not also and equally affect and alter the character of the nation—granting that the forty-eight states and the district of Columbia always shall be a "nation"—to which exception is taken. Let us compare the problems and experiences of New Yorkers or New Englanders migrating to Iowa one hundred years ago with those of others from the same Eastern section coming to Alabama or South Carolina in 1934.

The early settlers of Western territory moved by wagon or boat or afoot. With good luck and weather they traversed 1,000 miles in ninety or seventy days. They found a glorious soil, easily cultivated, richly productive in grains, vegetables, and fruits of the North temperate zone, and therefore in horses, cattle, meats, poultry, butter, milk, and cheese.

The lands had to be cleared. How much work the particular quarter section required before it was fit for the exceedingly simple life of the settler's family depended upon variants of climate, soil, geography. Two or three generations had to be born, to live and to die, before the land could have the schools, the colleges, the doctors, the hospitals, the libraries, the cities, the railroads, the highways, the complex and elaborate set up of mechanical appurtenances that are counted essential to "modern civilization." Without these, land that is as fertile as the valley of the Nile is no more valuable than would be a plantation in that famed region to one who could never see it or plant it or have communication with it.

So if the good lands of Iowa have a present market worth of $250 an acre, it has been given to them by the three or four generations that have fabricated the state and its communities. The individual owner alone has improved the farm, but its worth would have remained as nothing but for the century of cooperative effort by the people, the taxpayers. Always the soil was deep and of prodigal fertility, but who would buy an improved farm in Iowa if it were in the midst of a million acres of equally fertile lands without a good road leading through and out of them? Men and their hands are necessary to give value to land. Mr. Henry George was right about that.

If one comes out of New England or Illinois in 1933 to establish a home in the South, the cost is, when the risks, the hardships, the dangers, the decades of toil in the lonely if rich wildernesses are weighed and counted, no greater in money than it was to the pioneer family who received the land as a gift. If the immigrant coming to a Southern state expend the equivalent of $50 or $75 an acre on the land in the course of a generation, he will probably have at the end of the period a possession as valuable reckoned in money as is a farm of the same area in Iowa. For, it is to be remembered, the appurtenances of civilization, the roads, the cities, that are the product of community or cooperative effort, are already prepared, in the main complete.

The vertical frontier is wherever are lands to be acquired at low prices and susceptible to improvement at a cost not prohibitive. It may be twenty miles out of New York or Cleveland, it may be anywhere in the country, but it seems to me that until, throughout the United States, there shall be some approximation of development, in height and depth, it were error to say that the frontier had disappeared. Relatively, great districts have merely been traversed by the caravans, sometimes not much more affected than if pioneers had navigated the air above them.

In the school readers of fifty years ago was the story of the gold hunters whose diggings uncovered no precious metal and when, in despair, they acted upon the advice of some neighborhood sage and sowed wheat they harvested wealth richer than mines yielded. The American pioneers have sought only the richest, they have spurned the lands that would have entranced the French, Bavarian or Piedmontese peasants and have halted to till them only when the alternative was hunger.

It is admitted that the vertical frontier is wanting in the romance, the mystery, the call to adventure, of the older frontier, and those who seek it will be heedful of colder, harder, more commonplace, less sentimental and ambitious considerations. They must be men and women whose first concern is economic security, who are capable of appraising independence and freedom as treasure trove. Even these will hold back as long as they can close their eyes to it, for they are accustomed to the glamor, the gaiety, the swift change of light and scene, the stir and the thrill of the city, and to them those things are as the flesh-pots of Egypt. Yet there are some in the cities who will at last perceive that existence cannot be indefinitely prolonged by tightening one's belt, that when all is said living on a dole, by whatever name, is a form of slavery and a very low form at that. The Negro on the Southern plantation eighty years ago was conscious that what came from "ole Marster" was owing to him. There must have been a vague satisfaction in it, but it is questionable whether an intelligent person tramping the sidewalks of Detroit or Bridgeport can fully persuade himself that the hand-out from Uncle Sam is his by right however cringingly or bluster-ingly grateful for it he may be. The Negro had no right of free contract; neither has the organized laborer however expedient and necessary to his welfare organization may be. Who must accept alms or a dole must also have imagination if he can per-suade himself that he remains a free man albeit the almsgiver be the government, his country. When Americans, some of them, come to be children who take their pap from "Uncle Sam's" spoon that they may live, they are no longer freemen save by courtesy. Robbers are more dangerous to their fellow citizens than beggars are, but they may be more useful to their country—in time of peril.

The vertical frontier will not stir bold youth to action, there is in it nothing to quicken pulses, the vision of it is given only to the clear-headed realists, those capable of assaying "the glorious privilege of being independent." One farmer from two acres of his land paid the cost of his farming operations and gained a support for his family, and whether or not on his other acres he made a profit is an important but not paramount question. He was not of the unemployed, nor ever for a moment in fear of unemployment. He asked for and received no federal or state or county relief, he would have been insulted if it had been offered, yet the cottage and two acres are the barrier between him and the breadline, the flophouse—two acres in a region of hundreds of thousands, millions, of acres like it.

These things being true, is it not sheer nonsense to say that in the United States is no longer a frontier? It is everywhere, somewhere in every American state, and I am emphasizing the districts near me because I am most familiar with them. A farmer says that where he lives the conditions are "too easy," and that is explanatory in part of the backwardness of some of the most inviting parts of the United States that stretch almost across its territory and hundreds of miles in strips here and there to the north and south.

Twenty years ago Germany demanded "a place in the sun," or colonies for surplus population. In that country 62,348,782 people are occupying 180,976 square miles, approximately equal to the combined areas of Kentucky, Tennessee, Alabama and Mississippi. Japan with 64,447,724 inhabitants is smaller than California by about the size of New Jersey. The population of Japan has doubled in the last seventy years and Germany's has tremendously increased. Industrialization has had most to do with making the increase possible, but it may be set down that in those countries is no waste land, that their vertical frontiers have long ago been recognized and developed. If the Japanese in their archipelago had the lands that the Americans have in North America, they would have no pretext or incentive for seizing territory on the continent of Asia. The German population to the square mile is 360.7, the Japanese 433.3, and the American 41.3. That in countries where is not land sufficient to produce the food, clothing, fuel and other necessaries to comfortable existence are restiveness and danger of civil commotion is not difficult to believe, but that there should be complaint in a country that has in abundance what those lack is, at first glance, puzzling. Finally, one discovers the solution in the fact of a fictitious and artificial definition of what is necessary, in short, in that myth invented by the politicians and known as "The American standard of living." It is non-existent. There is no such standard.

A few years ago a study made by investigators in Columbia University revealed that Negroes who had come to Harlem from one of the coastal islands of the South and who were earning yearly about $1,100 were buying with it creature comforts and luxuries that cost their brothers back home about $400.

Two brothers, therefore, one in Harlem and the other in St. Helena, were living about equally well, and so a Chinese Mandarin and an English earl may maintain equal establishments and state at antipodal points of the globe—but it would be ridiculous to say that in either case the living standards were identical or similar. The colored man in Harlem once having gained a footing probably would not return to the island for twice or three times the material rewards offered, and that one now on the island would leave for Harlem by the next train if the chance of his finding a job were one in five. Diversity in ways of living may be and often are so great that no common denominator for the measurement of a standard can be had. Moreover, in the population are large groups widely differing in productive, or earning power and, for that matter, in capacity to live on the same plane though their material resources be approximately equal.

In any solution of the American problem the false exaggeration of urban values by ignorant masses is a mighty obstacle. Motoring in Virginia I picked up a husky and intelligent youth, a sailor hiking to the nearest port. He had come from Brooklyn. "Why don't you buy fifty acres of that land and be your own man?" I said. He had his answer pat, as if it had been drilled into him at school—"Not for me, the farmer's standard of living is the lowest in the United States." His standard was a good wage drawn by obsequious obedience to another man's orders. The farmer has paid a high price for the privilege of captaining his own affairs, and the eyes of most city workers are so scaled that they cannot envy him. But when the departed job does not come back and public "relief" fails, as it must fail, hungry men will seek new homes even as the sons of Jacob sought them.

How the utilization of the vertical frontier would react upon the country is interesting as speculation, though what we are chiefly concerned with is its effect on the congested districts and upon the fugitives from them—for fugitives they will be from hard times as were the blazers of the paths to the horizontal frontiers. It is the immediacy of the new movement and the necessity for it that demand inquiry now; in another century

Professor James Jackson Turner and James Truslow Adams may write of its larger influences.

There stands, or lolls rather, the state of Georgia; area 58,725 square miles; population, 1,836,974 whites, 1,071,125 Negroes, and other races 360; population to the square mile, 49.5. Its whites boast "Anglo-Saxon homogeneity," as do all of the Southern states. This "homogeneity" is in truth an affliction, a grandiose name for stagnant blood. The state virtually has received no new blood in two hundred years—since General James Edward Oglethorpe brought his colonists (many of them from the ranks of the unemployed) to it. The coming of 20,000 or 40,000 white families out of crowded urban districts to the lands of Georgia would renovate the commonwealth. It needs renovation. If the newcomers, Italians, Czechs, Irish, Germans, Yankees, Jews, Protestants, Roman Catholics, should prove too strong for the natives in fair economic competition, in time becoming dominant, so much the worse for the natives. Friction would be unlikely—the roominess of the state would prevent it, unless the immigration should be in torrents and not in a steady stream. The chances are that a weaker race, if one there be in Georgia, would flee before the peaceful invaders; that Negroes, if they are not so forceful as white men, would vanish before the advancing white hordes as the Indians vanished. To this time, in the South, has been so much room that bare subsistence has been the problem of no one, white or black, and the ease of living has made habits lazy and slothful. If 40,000 families or 160,000 immigrants came into rural Georgia in ten years it would be a revamped state and another 40,000 would follow in another ten years. Georgia is one of a dozen states of the South of like features and characteristics with room to spare, and in the states of the West the spaces are wider.

The vertical frontier would react upon the districts out of which came the new pioneers, in Fords, Chevrolets, and Plymouths, not prairie schooners, not less than the horizontal frontier influenced the colonies and states of the Atlantic seaboard.

Chicago, Milwaukee, New York, South Bend, Philadelphia,

Bridgeport, every industrial city, most of them lying east of the Mississippi and north of the Ohio and the Potomac, have been socially reconstituted in the last half century. With here and there an exception, like Charleston, S. C., Fredericksburg, Va., and Annapolis, Md., they bear distant resemblance to the old towns that Washington and William Henry Harrison knew. Immigrants came, until lately, in so great companies that the old towns were newly stratified. Italians in New York were so numerous that they were sufficient to themselves a long time, so were Czechs in Chicago, and assimilation was slow. It is now probable that when the new exodus from the cities shall begin it will be, in part, of companies of different nationalities and perhaps religions, to localities of their selection. I have in mind a county, 650 square miles, low hills, rivers, brooks, healthful, drained, within four hours of twenty cities and hundreds of towns. One may drive through it, thirty miles, over a hard road, and not meet a dozen cars. It would comfortably support four times its present population, and lands in parcels of hundreds and thousands of acres in it could be bought at prices of $10 an acre or less. Many a spot in it would be ideal for the new home of a thousand Slavs or Germans now two or three years out of employment and uncertain of the next meal. Of the fate in general of the metropolitan cities I shall speak again, but at least one benefit offsetting their losses of population would be that their stratification would soon be less distinct. The nationalistic layers would thin. A metropolis would no longer claim to be one of the greatest Italian as well as one of the greatest Jewish and German communities of the world. It is neither natural nor desirable that Chicago, Boston, or New York be thought of as other than greatly American.

When the millions shall scatter from the cities to the vertical frontier, to the sparsely settled districts and the low-priced lands, what will they do? For the moment let us think of them as farmers, albeit that is, to my mind, not to be their narrow, their exclusive destiny, for the vertical frontier is to refashion the farmer himself. The man long out of a job, the victim of prolonged depression and unable to plant cabbages in the streets, wants (there is emphasis on the verb "wants") food, shelter, clothing, warmth. Those are the necessaries; those the Indians had, those the Southern slaves were never without in the panics, of 1837 and 1857.

"But," one interrupts to say, "the present-day farmer sells his berries and fruits on the nearby markets and fifty or twenty new farmers would glut it. That is the trouble with the American farmer—over-production." What is the answer? It might be that the farmer would be compelled to give up his car and his radio. He might have to abandon some of his ambitions for his children. He would be in no peril of hunger, of perishing from cold or exposure. Those perils this day confront millions in the cities, and no man, however poor, unless sick, wounded, disabled and forgotten, dies of starvation or cold in that one fourth or third of the United States that is called the South. Dispatches this afternoon (October 13, 1933) tell of riotous strikers in New York shouting as they marched, "We want bread!" In any rural county the answer to them would be, "Go and get bread," and it is a rare American county where they cannot dig it out of the ground.

Not yet has the notion gained lodgement in the countryman's mind that it is some one else's business to provide him with a job, that an obligation rests on some employer or other to see that a mill or foundry runs and that he has work. That is an urban notion, and however vociferous and belligerent a worker may be in expressing it, confession of servitude and dependence lurks in it. When one upbraids another for remissness in not furnishing him with an occupation and wages, he is doing homage to that other, acknowledging himself that other's "man." Hodge may be a country lout, but where there is land, he can find and make his own job, and in the South he can be a black Negro, the son of a slave, and be free in a sense that no mere wage-earner in a great city, unless he has saved a competence, knows of.

Signs are plentiful that the present policy of the American government is that the United States live unto itself, that it be self-sufficient. That purpose was distinctly forecast if not declared by its right-about face in the World Economic Conference in respect of stabilizing an international currency. Curiously, while this national self-sufficiency, or "autarchy," is stressed, government's policy for the individual is exactly the opposite. The American citizen is told that his economic salvation turns upon the surrender of more of his personal freedom of action in trade and industry in a few weeks than he has been asked to give up in a century preceding. The New Deal is to be a new game in which everybody shall play partners, and the only antagonist is some monster that is postulated and personified as Poverty, or Hunger, or Destitution, or Depression. Yet, with our vast territory the American citizen, relatively, has far more room to turn about in than has his republic in the narrow world.

"Back to the land" for millions of Americans does not promise two cars to the family, but if it would not "put a chicken in every pot" it would be the fault of the family. Farm life certainly does not at present hold out the prospect of a fortune or of easy money, but it is the way out of the stifling crowd where men are gnashing their teeth at one another. The failure of "the full dinner pail" in town does not imply empty stomachs where turnips and cabbages grow, and the immediate want in America is turnips and cabbages.

Chickens, turnips, cabbages are not money, but they satisfy to a far degree. Mr. G. K. Chesterton has touched the seat of the world's diseases when he says that we confuse "good" with "goods," that we think so exclusively in terms of selling, or exchange, values that we have lost capacity to enjoy the "kindly fruits of the earth," and that "the notion of a man eating his own apples off his own apple-tree seems like a fairy tale . . . The complexity of commercial society has become intolerable, because that society is commercial and nothing else. The whole community is occupied with the idea, not of possessing things, but with the idea of passing them on. When the simple enthusiasts . . . say that Trade is Good, they mean that all the people who possess goods are perpetually parting with them."

Mr. Chesterton concludes: "And I for one do not believe that there is any way out of the modern tangle, except to increase the proportion of the people who are living according to the ancient simplicity." I agree with him.

CHRISTIANITY AND THE CRISIS

(1933)

"Christianity and the Crisis" was delivered before the 11th annual meeting of the Episcopal Diocese of Upper South Carolina at Anderson, S. C., January 17, 1933.

SCARCELY can one take up a magazine of serious bent without finding in it an attack on religion. Some of the articles are coarse, if clever, and they probably are the least effective. The tone of most of them is dignified, respectful, courteous, but the aggressiveness is not the less present and often they are written by scientists and philosophers of the widest fame and firmest standing among the intelligentsia. These same publications would not have dared admit the articles fifteen years ago. That they *are* admitted is evidence that readers are interested in them. Not many magazines, if any, are in the habit of offending considerable bodies of readers. They are printed to sell; if they are not read they are not sold; and if they are not sold they are not long printed. Nor am I censuring the publications—I believe in a free press as long as it is not indecent, obscene. What is indecent, obscene, must, ultimately, be defined and determined by the public. Press and public act, react, interact, upon each other, and if the press should try to lead and guide, it should be and usually is a jump or two ahead of the public. It is not so that the press either creates or moulds public opinion. The factors in that product are numerous, innumerable. The press is rather the reflection than the maker of it, important part though it have in the making. Notwithstanding its oracular manner of speaking, its "we-ness" as an English writer called it, infallibility would be the last of its claims, and that exactly is the claim that it would set up by rejection of all ideas out of harmony with those of editors.

Newspapers are, as yet, not anti-religious. They are written for the masses, and from this it is inferable that the masses are still far from being arrayed against the churches. Mark, I say "as yet," for I have in mind that usually the thought that prevails percolates from the top downward, that what the intelligentsia is saying today the populace is likely to say tomorrow or next year. Of this the populace is not aware, but in truth, it is all but helpless against operating brains. Advertising, or printed salesmanship, is the best illustration of that. You may not buy a new radio set before 1936, but it is not unlikely that you will buy it under compulsion that is being exerted now, and you may think you have bought of your free will when in reality you have been driven.

Nor are you to understand that these magazines, read by cultivated people, are partisanly against religion. On the contrary they print many religious articles, from the ablest pens available, and it is not said that the non-religionists have the advantage. Indeed, open-mindedness, fair-dealing, non-partisanship, is the distinguishing characteristic of the present-day publication of the better order, which is a way of saying that it finds that those things pay. Intolerance, fanaticism, common as they are, have been pretty well exorcised from the sophisticated and even the politicians appealing to them know better.

The non-religious writers often assume that revealed religion is of the past. They proceed to discuss problems of conduct without regard to it. Often they are nonchalant, sometimes cocksure. They dismiss the existence of organized religious bodies, the church, as the hull of a wrecked ship, not yet visibly broken but doomed to sink shortly, leaving no trace behind except the ripples of an old wife's tale. My business in large part has been most of the last forty-two years to write political editorials, and I have some vanity in recalling that as the editor of a country weekly I subscribed to the principal Republican party daily in the country. I doubt if then it had a dozen subscribers in the state. I wanted to know what was going on in the enemy's camp, and I mention this as a suggestion to you gentlemen of the clergy, for what it is worth. Would you hazard your orthodoxy? It may be so. You believe that "The truth will make you free," and if it be disaster come upon you and your orthodoxy be shattered, your God will still be merciful to the honest truth-seeker, or He is not the God that you have confessed.

There is a crisis. Religion is beset and beleaguered. But not for the first time. It always has been beset and beleaguered, and it may be that the present onset is not more threatening than others have been. One can harbor that hope, but it is no ground for taking a chance. All weapons, physical and intellectual, are modern. Wars are fought with gas bombs and tanks, not with javelins and bull's hide targes, nor yet with the implements of twenty years ago. The "chariots of Israel" went out of use many centuries ago—yet soldiers are fighting with something very like chariots nowadays. After all, what survives is the fight and the cause, and I say that Christ still has a cause.

We would be very silly to delude ourselves that the enemies of religion are gaining no ground, making no captives. Empty pews are not to be accounted for solely as the aftermath of war. Many pews are empty. If there be among young people a vast indifference, some of it may proceed from a vast if shallow unbelief. No one likes restraint. All of us fret under it. Were I young again it might well be that, after reading an intelligent article questioning the very existence of the things that I had held to be holy, I might seek in the aura of my resulting doubt an excuse to dismiss from mind the duties incident to my faith. Your average young man is not loath to find a defence for absenting himself from religious services. Nor is your adult. I speak as one not without authority in this matter, for I seek excuses and too often find them—without reading a magazine article. There are elderly people, or middle-aged, whose adherence to the church is explained by their cowardice. Some of them actually vaunt their scepticism. Some dare not omit to have their children baptised and to have members of their families given Christian burial. That the church does not deny its consolations to those who misuse its offices at least is evidence that it practices the gentleness and charity that it preaches.

All good men honor the honest doubter. It is the conforming, the cringing doubter subverting the church to the pursuit of the respectability that it is supposed to confer who clogs its wheels. That sin, too, has its Biblical precedent, as have all the sins. In very truth, most of modern sinners, the scoffers, the irreverent, are ignorant upstarts, illiterate sinners, to whom the holy Bible is the last of open books. They thrust aside the old restraints, not in truth that they are unbelievers but that they would dodge restraints. I certainly do not say that the miseries of the "hard times," the "depression," come from irreligion. I do not know anything about that. But I do say that had the people of South Carolina practiced the restraints that have been taught through the uncounted centuries, there would not have been the indulgence, the extravagance, the prodigality which were the prelude to the calamities and the tragedies of the times. They may be taught elsewhere, but they are all taught in the Bible with a wealth of apt and striking illustration that I, and I speak the mind of all journalists, believers or not, do not find in any other book. That book tells that "The fool has said in his heart there is no God," and I shall not discuss that. But I say, from my little store of worldly wisdom, that every competent journalist tells his juniors to search the Bible for the uses of his profession whether he look for God in it or not.

Nor am I here to say that all the old restraints are good. Diffidently, yet not without conviction, I declare that many of them ought to have been junked. Once as a little boy (a very little boy) I played mumble-the-peg on a Sunday afternoon, and was sorely conscience-stricken about it. I have arrived at the deliberate conclusion that that also may have been one of the occasions upon which my conscience was wrong, and there have come to be other performances that do not shock my hardened heart. This I do say, that the life of a good man, Christian or no Christian, demands restraint, demands sacrifice, and I am wanting in faith in the human heart that men will endure them without the help of God.

Your bishop has brought to speak to you tonight not merely a layman but a confirmed worldling, not an active church worker, and asking himself why he is here, he points you to your bishop, who if you ask him for the reasons of his appeal to me, cannot "with reasons answer you." I cannot but speak falteringly, and, I trust, with humility, yet there are things that seem to me plain. The assault on the church, as I have said, is not new, it has always gone on with rising and subsiding waves of violence since the church was born on Calvary. The cultivated and many of them conscientious men who marshal the discoveries of science and adhere to its methods, to the rejection of whatsoever they cannot demonstrate, leave us poor mortals on a trackless waste. They give us no code, they do not so much as chart the stars for our guidance. This sentence I quote: "The writers against religion, whilst they oppose every system, are wisely careful never to set up any of their own." It was written a century and a half ago, by no bishop, no preacher, but by a layman and statesman, Edmund Burke, and it is as true now as it was then. One penetrates the wilderness and wanders in it, of the writings of these clever men, and comes out of it stripped even of simple rules of conduct. As to those there is no agreement among them, no unity, only dissension, and conflict, and brilliant as the intellectual display may be, it does not illuminate the way; it is for average men and women, bafflement, anarchy, destruction, even for this world, though we disregard the next. Here in the brief span on this planet, "man cannot live by bread alone." In very truth, he does not so live, and without some spiritual impetus, some vision, some yearning and clutching, if blindly, at things beyond, he dies prematurely and his nations with their civilization die.

Do you thoughtful men and women dare allow your minds to run upon the miseries, the sorrows, the wrongs, the failures, the suicides, the disasters that befall your fellows, those about you, near you, within a radius of a hundred, of twenty, miles from your homes? What if you had carefully catalogued each morning, from your newspaper, for ten years, 3650 days, the record of human wreckage, would you dare read it? It might be dangerous to your sanity too much to dwell upon it, and, you might, if you believed in nothing beyond this life, ask, is it a life worth living, is it worth taking the chance, and why live it? What of your children?

Facing squarely the facts and figures that you would have gathered and collated from your newspaper, what chances have these children for what we call success and to avoid disaster? In savage or semi-civilized lands, destruction of children is not uncommon, and if parents can have no hope for them shall one say that this destruction is savagery? In these latter days, in the civilized lands, the destruction of children is avoidable. I shall not discuss birth control, disturbing churches and dividing them into hostile camps, further than to say it is a fact. That I suppose no one will dispute. If reflecting people dismiss the notion of God and future life, they are reduced to contemplation of the earthly life, and they may question their right to perpetuate the race. Is it quite fair that life be created if the chances be against its happiness? If cattle and hogs could think and were masters of their fate, they would not prolong the existence of their kind to provide supplies for slaughter houses. I say that among intelligent people this thing that is called birth control and is so widely talked of is a fact. And I leave the thought.

I cite you to a worldling, the most distinguished of all political correspondents, Count Henri de Blowitz, the Paris representative more than twenty years of the London *Times*. He had the entry to every circle, social and political, royalty included, in Europe, and once, using his mighty newspaper, he averted war between France and Germany. Laurence Oliphant, author and traveler, his early associate on the Parisian staff of *The Times*, had become convert in the United States to one of the crazy cults that are periodically rising and falling, usually the contrivance of some imposter or deranged person, and he attempted more than once to proselyte de Blowitz, a Roman Catholic. At last de Blowitz answered him:

"Excuse me, I think we ought to settle once and for all this question of proselytism which might cause difference between us. I cannot accept the views of your prophet, which are based on pride. He has proved to you that you are greater than other men because you have submitted to drive a dust-cart. I prefer the word of Christ, who taught us not to consider ourselves greater or better than other men, because we are dust ourselves. Humanity oscillates between atheism, which rejects reason, and reason, which bows to faith. Those who would substitute the everlasting harmony of the world by successive aggregations arising out of chaos in fulfilment of an unconscious and sublime order, claim a greater effort from me than those who ask me to believe in one God and in the doctrine of the Trinity. When I have admitted that God created the world, I have expressed a belief, certainly, which makes revealed religions appear infinitely less miraculous and a thousandfold more acceptable than the theory of spontaneous creation and automatic development. That from the midst of the people of God, trodden under the hoof of the pagan conqueror in the corrupt Graeco-Roman world, there should have arisen a prophet who, instead of hatred and revolution, preached charity, forgiveness, brotherly love and good-will toward all men, was itself a greater miracle than any of those attributed to Christ during his sojourn on earth. Unless you can teach me a religion which inculcates precepts more sublime than those of the divine philosopher of Nazareth, which your prophet does not do, leave me my faith without seeking to trouble it. You may make an unhappy man, but you will not make a disciple."

You would find it hard to frame in words a more rational answer for the faith that is in you than that of this man absorbed in world politics, diplomacy, and fashion, yet, however you accept it, you must find still another. That other must come out of your own heart, your own experience. "Sensible men are all of the same religion," Disraeli has one of his characters to say, and, asked what it was, to reply, "Sensible men never tell." I suppose none of us would reveal everything that lurks in the recesses of our minds and hearts, I suppose that none of us could if we would, yet those of us who stand here, and in other churches, confessing our God and his religion, arrayed in the forces of the Master, must be conscious of some link with them. Though it be feeble and flickering at times it is an existent and real faith unless we be knowing and wilful hypocrites. At this point one may pause to say that there is some small compensation for the attack on the church in that it lessens any gain to be had from hypocritical connection with it. It has been a long time since an enemy of the church found more support outside of it than he may find now.

I say then that a man's relation to God and the church is personal, he cannot be called upon to explain; if he say, "Seek and *ye* shall find," it is enough, or it should be for critics who are just and fair.

For this man, in this crisis, openly lifting up his face toward the Christian God and trying to keep step with the Christ, what is the obligation? As to that I offer you nothing that is newly informing. You have your Bible, your creed, your ordinances, your sacraments, your liturgy, your prescribed duties. They are comprehensive, they are enough if you give attention to a few of them not only to advance the cause of the church but to insure your increase in spiritual stature. They have been laid down by wiser men perhaps than any of us, they have endured the centuries. It may be that our very human interpretations of them are far from perfect, that in non-essentials some that seemed right two centuries ago or less seem erroneous now. In 1733 in South Carolina, when this church was the established church, many good men and women doubtless believed, with utmost sincerity, that taxation of members of other religious bodies for the support of the establishment was scriptural, holy, that denial of it was downright impious, yet to say as much now would be to make one's self ridiculous. So, in England, until about seventy-five years ago a statute, long disregarded, requiring attendance on service of the Church of England at least once a Sunday, disobedience of it being punishable as a misdemeanor, was still on the books unrepealed. Some people devoutly believed, I suppose, in its righteousness. Opinion has changed as to hundreds of rules of human conduct and some of those to which we are zealously attached now will be abandoned in other centuries, but they do not touch those basic things upon which the church is founded.

One hears another say flippantly, "Yes, I believe in the church, but I am opposed to foreign missions"—it is rather a common saying. Do you believe in them? You should be aware that you cannot reject the duty of supporting foreign missions without rejecting the church altogether, for is not your church the product of missionary labors and sacrifices? I suppose that the Romans of the Fifth century entertained scarcely a higher opinion of the savages in the British Isles than you entertain of those in the Congo, and I suppose too that Christian men and women by contributions of one kind or other made possible and practical the expedition of St. Augustine. He did not swim the English channel or fly across it, and I suppose that even if he "took no thought wherewithal he should be clothed," or fed, the cost of travel, relatively, was greater in his day than it is in yours. So, in South Carolina your church is a missionary product, and it is here now because some people, somewhere, some time, made sacrifices to place it here. If one say that other peoples, or races, are not worth saving, that Christianity has been carried as far as it ought to go, he has a precedent for it. The Pharisee furnished it when he thanked God that he was not as other men. Foreign missions are basic, the Christian church outside of Jerusalem and its environs was built by foreign missionaries.

If you ask me why I am an Episcopalian, I reply that I find in it the essentials common to all branches of the Christian church and that its ways, its forms, its government, address themselves to my preference, but that is not saying that these essentials are absent from other Christian bodies. Years ago the story was told me that the late Dr. James Woodrow, Presbyterian minister and a distinguished scientist, uncle of President Wilson, was, after a meeting of scientists, a guest on an excursion on the Hudson. The talk fell on the differences among Christians, and, though many Protestant denominations were represented, it was soon revealed that they had common ground for agreement. Then two or three of them were appointed to approach a Roman Catholic priest who was on the boat, and after brief discussion, one of them suggested that he believed in The Apostle's Creed. "Of course I do," was the answer, and complete Christian unity was realized by the whole party at least for that time and occasion. It is difficult for some of us to see why it does not last, why it is not permanent and universal but it cannot last if one presume to judge his brother in respect of the minutiae of human conduct. The Christian road is described as straight and narrow, but it is broad enough for men to travel without jostling one another.

It is a stony path and rugged. Let us not deceive ourselves that the Christian life does not demand sacrifices, much as some of us avoid them, dodge them. It is impossible to perform even a moderate part of the Christian duties without giving up pleasures, without subjecting ourselves to restraints. Many a man who appears to you or to me to take the church lightly, to be at best a formal and lazy churchman, would be dissolute and abandoned once he severed himself from it, and the cost of this restraint, this sacrifice, to him is not for us to measure. It may be that he seldom darkens the church's door, but it may be a door to turn him from others that he should not enter. This I fancy is the case especially with young people at this time when restraint of every kind is more keenly than in many years before resented. Some day will be discovery that whatever the maledictions, the scoffings, the proofs of contradictions and infirmities, the elaborate reasonings alleging unreason, no substitute for the church is offered, that without its vision "the people perish." The young men will wander back into the fold.

No, I cannot tell you how to be Christians. If I could I would be inventing for you some new and strange creed with its formularies. But I can tell you this: that the church, our church, is beset and beleaguered, that there is a crisis. It is a trite thing, but there is nothing else to say, it is for us to exert ourselves with the more valor and energy in the Church's defence, and to press on. I say it with a poignant sense of one unworthy to be heard, impelled to explain that I am here saying it because to have been absent and silent would have been to shirk another clear call to duty.

Fifty-six years ago, Alexander Graham Bell, a self-sacrificing teacher of the deaf in Washington, had invented the telephone.

Few believed in his claims for it. After much solicitation he induced the managers of the Centennial Exposition in Philadelphia to permit him to give a demonstration of it on the grounds. He rigged his crude apparatus and stretched a line a few hundred yards, from one building to another. Dom Pedro, the emperor of Brazil, was the guest of honor that day. He was handed the receiver and he placed it to his ear. "My God, it speaks!" he exclaimed, dropping the instrument. He did not understand. He might have died without understanding. A scientist may die and never understand, and one not a scientist may believe that God speaks.

On the night before Christmas, in the quiet of two o'clock, I heard voices. They were voices of Chicago, of Montana, of Pittsburgh, of Winnipeg, speaking good wishes and "Merry Christmas" to friends in Labrador, at Baffin's Bay, in Alaska, lands frozen from the rest of the world. In Charleston, South Carolina, I heard the voices, in the quiet night, cheery, happy, heartening voices. I believe they were heard in the frozen lands. They tell me so, and they tell me the words I heard were spoken in far cities. They tell me that men skilled in the electrical arts made this possible by their inventions. I do not understand, but I do not deny it. I have read that the little maid, Jeanne D'Arc, heard voices. I do not deny it.

I understood what the voices said. They were Christmas messages. I know that the scientists did not invent Christmas.

THE SOUTH AND PASSIVE RESISTANCE

(1934)

One of the very first, if not *the* first, Southern editors to take issue with the objective of the Roosevelt administration and its influence on the Southern states, William Watts Ball did not hesitate to offer bold and original suggestions to the people of his native state. He comprehended the fact that the plight of the South and the pressures exerted against it called for extraordinary measures if the South were to preserve its integrity.

THE Southern states struggling to get out of the "depression" might make a little progress by passive resistance. Why should Gandhi and his Indians have a monopoly of it? I say the "Southern states" but I shall write in the main of South Carolina—I know something of it, and it is representative of them. The diversities among them are considerable but minor. Their larger problems are identical.

Were South Carolina to refuse to elect two senators and six representatives to the Congress, its loss would be negligible. There might be positive gain from it, and in saying this I have no reference to the eight statesmen now in service, for they are as capable as any eight likely to be elected. The state would proceed as usual to carry on government, electing governors, legislators, judges, sheriffs, mayors and the like. The federal government would send judges, marshals, revenue collectors as usual and they would perform their duties. Our people would be without a voice in Washington, and if federal officers, presuming upon it, should indulge in outrageous tyranny the South Carolinians would find a way to temper it.

The Southern states are getting nothing out of Washington beyond protection from foreign invasion. Puerto Rico gets that. Free trade among the states would continue whether a state had congressmen or not.

By withdrawing congressmen a state would not withdraw from the Union. It would express dissatisfaction with unfair treatment; it would dramatize its protest. These Southern congressmen are causing confusion, clouding the facts. They are begging for handouts and snatching a few. The people back home are deceived. They think their representatives are dredging pearl oysters for them in Washington. Not only are they deceived, they are corrupted. Once they were independent, self-reliant, upstanding. Now when they send a man to Washington they send him to beg, and when he "brings home the bacon" they exult. They do not discover that it is no more than a bit of skin, that they are getting an ounce while the pounds go to some place like Chicago. As for the congressman, he holds up the appropriation for the post office building, the bit of skin, and between it and the eyes of his constituents he holds a magnifying glass. He megaphones about it on the stump. It is his nature to do that and his interest—it reelects him.

The subjugation of the Southern people was not at Appomattox, in 1865. Resistance came to an end with the administration of the lovable Mr. McKinley and the Spanish-American war, when he spoke kindly to Confederate veterans and gave some of them commissions. The talk of "force bills" died away. After Colonel Roosevelt's two or three paroxysmal manifestations of Harvard College virtue, no more appointments of Negroes to office were made. The doors of the spider's parlor were flung wide and the flies strolled in, thinking they were home again. When the Congress was dividing swag, politely they pleaded for a slice, or as Senator Tillman put it rudely, "If there is going to be any stealing, I want my share for my state." Seemingly it never occurred to one of them that he was not getting his share. Sometimes one landed a few thousand dollars for the sufferers from a freshet or drought and there was a great gloating. Now the subjugation of the South is a thing accomplished. There is no spirit left in us—we are all beggars, and poor as Job's turkey.

Most of the factories are in the North and they cannot sell as much as they can make. That is the immediately visible cause of the American depression, whether or not deeper causes underlie.

If a plant in Pittsburgh was built and equipped at a cost of $5,000,000 to turn out 1,000 engines a year and it can sell but 500, nothing is left to do save to close down half the plant. The stockholders lose on an investment of $2,500,000 and the operatives who drew fat wages during the Coolidge-Hoover boom are out of jobs now. That is the condition in the automobile, the rubber tire, the radio factories, in a thousand kinds of factories, big and little.

Over-development explains unemployment and depression in the United States. Everyone knows it; no one denies it now. The industrialists in the North misjudged the ability of the country to buy, to consume, to absorb. They had the prescience of the business leaders of Punktown, population 5,000, who erected an eight story hotel. The prescience of Punktowners is not a shade inferior to that of Wall Street, and that revelation may be a dividend from the depression. Big Business built too far and too fast.

In the South conditions are exactly opposite to those in the North. The South is undeveloped. Cotton is its principal crop and the average year's production between 1920 and 1930 was less than between 1910 and 1920. In South Carolina the industry second to agriculture is the manufacture of cotton goods. That has had little expansion in the last decade, and the spindles added in the South have for the most part replaced those abandoned in the North. Northern mills have been moved to the South, attracted by cheap labor. Cheap labor does not make a country wealthy, but the South is blamed for not paying high wages in an industry so impoverished that it flees from a region that can afford wages only slightly higher and in which the severe climate raises the cost of living.

The aggregate wealth of ten Southern states, not including Texas with its area of five big states, is less than the wealth of New York and not much greater than that of Pennsylvania. Of course the per capita wealth in these states is at the bottom among the forty-eight. Investigation would show that the equity of the Southern people in Southern possessions is pitifully reduced when the Southern municipal, railroad, and industrial bonds and stocks held by Northern residents are subtracted. The South's largest city, New Orleans, is sixteenth in population among those of the country.

Is the cause of this wretched showing to be found in the poverty of natural resources? To describe a land stretching from the western border of Texas to Chesapeake Bay as poor would call for temerity. Are the people inferior? The whites are generally of the early English, Irish, and Scottish stocks—if they are inferior to Northerners it must be to the later comers of other than Anglo-Saxon ancestry. Is it the presence of the Negroes, the continuing "blight of slavery"? The Negroes have been free sixty-seven years—they had about an even start with the Japanese dating from the time their empire began to be "westernized." If after two thirds of a century the Negroes are to be the explanation of the South's material backwardness, a defense of their sudden emancipation and enfranchisement should be offered with it. Is the South suffering from the effects of the Confederate war itself? It ended five years before the Franco-Prussian war began, and surely France had recovered from that conflict as early as 1914.

These Southern states are conquered and tributary provinces. That is the explanation. The exploitations of them began with the enactment of protective tariffs more than a century ago and after the military conquest of the sixties it became impudent and ruthless. A Southern farmer cannot have sugar in his coffee without paying more than double the normal price for it in cotton. In Marion County, South Carolina, is a farmer who started life (many years ago) with nothing. Now he has a store, he has two crops of cotton unsold, he owes no money, and he operates a forty-five horse plantation, which implies the possession of some thousands of acres of land and an annual production of two hundred or three hundred bales of cotton besides thousands of pounds of tobacco. He is generous and helpful to his neighbors and he continues to prosper despite the depression. He has exceptional ability and managerial talent. Ah, if he can do this, why may not others, on the same lands, under the same skies? What becomes of the contention that the Southern farmer is down-trodden, oppressed, robbed?

On this man's plantation are forty-odd families. They are Negroes. Including their cabins and perhaps an acre or two about them rent free their annual wage is the equivalent of $300 or $350. That may be a little more than coolies earn, but such a population does not and cannot create a prosperous state. Divide the total population of the plantation, say two hundred and ten, allowing ten for the planter's and the foreman's families, into its annual production, and you have the answer to South Carolina's low per capita wealth. "Pay higher wages, so that these people would have greater buying power?" Would that raise the price of a bale of cotton, now $30, to $50? Would that reduce the price of plows, tractors, a thousand articles that these Negroes as well as the master must have if they are to work and live? They are "protected" articles.

Were this farmer and his fellows in the South to raise the wage scale, they would plunge into bankruptcy. They accommo-date themselves to cruel circumstances imposed upon them by the national legislature—and, here and there, one of them thrives because he is exceptionally able and provident, because it is a thriving and lavish land that he lives in, still a frontier with its greater part uncultivated and for sale at the buyer's price.

Not the tariffs alone, though they are the chief factor, have kept the South poor. Sixty years the people paid their quota of federal taxes and out of them their share of pensions to soldiers were paid. No soldiers of the South received pensions. Where a dollar was spent grudgingly on a Southern military or naval post, or on a public building, ten dollars or fifty were spent elsewhere. In the South were no cities of a million people worthy of a fifteen million dollar public building. How could there be? Towns do not distend to great cities in tributary provinces.

Negro labor is the basic labor of the South. It is a curious circumstance that fiscal policies and laws of the republic bear hardest on those people that the republic, or part of it, glories in having liberated from slavery—and nobody cares. The poor white people are borne down by them too, but some of them escape. They are more agile, resourceful—they operate filling stations or drive buses; they segregate themselves in factory villages.

"I have been against the bonus, but I am coming around to favor it. We've got to pay the taxes anyway, the damn government is going to spend money, we'd better get back what little of it we can." The man who said this to me the other day wanted no bonus, needed none. He is a prosperous business man (one of the rare exceptions). He lives in a city and has an income of $15,000 or $20,000 a year. He is no politician and was an officer in the A. E. F. in the World War. What he said, revealing a state of mind, has prompted this article.

After Appomattox the South fought on, its spirt undaunted. It had to fight, for reasons that need not be recalled. It sent to Washington Lamar, Ben Hill, Henry M. Turner, the Culbersons, Morgan, Hampton and hundreds like them because there were trenches to be held. Such men could not be in Congress without contributing something to the fibre and form of the nation. Their presence as well as the presence of George F. Edmunds, George F. Hoar, Thomas Brackett Reed, Allen G. Thurman, Walter Q. Gresham, helped to strengthen the character of the Republic.

Then came security to the South, of a kind. No longer was there a menace to the civilization essential to the operation of a Northern owned factory or power plant within its borders. There was no relaxation of the inexorable laws that "wrung the rascal counters from the hard hands" of a people of whom the great majority, white and black, were ground to peasantry.

A full generation later the South subjugated, spiritually conquered and abject at last, became a mendicant. Its stronger men turned to business and left public affairs to the management of persons of aptitude and taste for herding the rabble in primaries. Fortunately, a few honest men and gentlemen still look on office-getting and office-holding as respectable, and they are decidedly useful in emergencies.

The legislative policies of the Republic have syphoned wealth from the South to enrich other sections, and the whole Republic has paid a price for it. The price is the creation of a great group of states sightless of the Republic as a whole, indifferent to its national character, dwarfed in aspiration, niggardly in statecraft. It has even come to pass that a Southern state can sell itself to the Republican party for an impost duty on sugar without arousing resentment or comment.

I do not complain that in fifty-one of the last sixty-seven years the South has had no voice in national affairs. Right or wrong, its important men have accepted the fate of the Democratic party in the belief that it was necessary to the integrity of their civilization. Even Louisiana has made that concession to common decency. Nor do I complain that the paltry local federal offices have been given to aliens, immigrants from other states, or to persons who accepted them at cost of being regarded as the favored agents of a power unsympathetic and foreign. In the last two decades service has not suffered on account of them; in personnel these officers have been respectable and not inefficient. I point to the Southern states converted into an area of diseased tissue by economic policies. It is a large part of the body of your republic. Drained of its life's blood, shall it not be undernourished and anaemic? Is it the South's fault that it has looked to Northern charity to save it from hookworm? Had it been given a chance it would have extirpated hookworm for itself. Who has a right to lift eyes in pious deprecation that it is a prolific breeding ground for religious bigotry, that too often it is represented on the Republic's stage by a "freckled whelp of Sycorax."

Do I over-draw the picture? Is this mere tirade? Native "uplifters" of the New South will say with fine indignation that it is, and reforming strangers who come among us to expose the naked miseries of the poor, white and black, on the farms, and of the whites in Southern factories, will say the picture is true. These visitors might remember that somebody had to build the palaces they left behind them. They could have found the cause of a standard of living low in the South before they boarded their Pullman trains. Meantime, a town in New Jersey seriously considers deporting its recently acquired Negro citizenry to the South from which it came!

Why do the Southern states send representatives and senators to Congress? One of them has elected a woman to be Senator. No one can object because she is a woman. She is a lady, an excellent lady, long familiar with the ways and manners of Congress. Doubtless she is decidedly superior in attainments and intelligence to the level of her fellow citizens. She can be relied upon to vote with her party associates and, because she is a lady, she may have some special courtesies of which her constituents will be the beneficiaries. Has anyone imagination sufficiently elastic to fancy that she will count in debate and in counsel or that she is sent to the Senate to represent a tributary and conquered province, to draw the salary provided for a senator lest there be no taker of it, and to keep a sharp look out for the rural mail carriers of her great commonwealth.

This good woman will bear favorable comparison with most of her Southern colleagues. She is the political product of the same motives and considerations that they are. She will conduct herself with greater dignity and decorum than is habitual to most of them and her ingenousness rightly will be less suspect.

Obviously, passive resistance illustrated by voluntary withdrawal of representation in Congress and in federal government by the Southern states is a grotesque suggestion. I am aware that the proposal of surrendering a salary is treasonable. We Southerners expect to get much from the Roosevelt administration. That, in fact, is why we voted for him, or one of the good reasons. Nevertheless, there is cunning if not sagacity in the philosophy of the Mahatma. Imitation of it might bring the South to its senses and it would hardly fare worse by giving the experiment a trial. Besides, it might bring the plight of the South to the attention of the country, and that would be substantial gain.

CALL IT BY ITS NAME
(1935)

William Watts Ball, graduate of the old South Carolina College and one-time Dean of the School of Journalism at the University of South Carolina, gave this paper as the concluding address before the South Carolina conference on public affairs at Columbia, S.C., June 27, 1935.

PARAPHRASING the English statesman I am astonished at my own audacity in facing this or any other audience to speak on "public affairs" in these times. To discuss a subject without a sense of infallibility is to discuss it handicapped. In that sense I am wanting. If one never can be sure he is right how can he go ahead? Whatever I shall say to you may be all wrong and foolish, and no one knows that quite so well as I do. I shall speak to you as if the world, or my world, did not come to an end about twenty-eight months ago. I used to think that two and two made four, that the multiplication table was reliable, that a straight line was the shortest distance between two points and that the minus sign had a meaning. Of none of these things, more especially the minus sign, am I sure now, and from that reflection I derive the satisfaction of believing that I am still in my senses.

If I talk about government it must be with the suggestion that my notions of it have not been barred by the statutes of limitations, and I cannot talk to you intelligibly except upon the postulate that they have not been. So I set out by saying, or opining rather, that, politically, judgment day has not come in the United States or in South Carolina, and I envy those who KNOW the contrary.

One business of the government of the United States is to defend the states against foreign enemies. That notion I think survives. Most of you agree with me in it, although some worthy people are addling it.

A second is that it should keep the peace within the republic, as between the states, or within a state upon proof of its impotency to do so.

A third is, or was, to maintain free trade among the states. In practice this was nullified more than a century ago by Henry Clay's "American System," the protective tariffs. It transformed government into an agency whereby a South Carolinian is virtually compelled to buy a saw made in Pennsylvania and to pay twenty pounds of cotton for it though it is worth only ten pounds of cotton in a market wherein both saws and cotton are sold; the world market, Mr. Calhoun called it, which is our market. That is the negation of free trade among the states. We Southerners have got to sell a great part of our basic products in the world market at world market prices, or not sell them at all. Southern farmers can be subsidized, they are at the moment subsidized, but the compulsion upon them to buy within the states remains. Long ago free trade among the states became a delusion, a snare—so long ago that the sensibilities of many of our people have become indurated and they are not aware of it.

That is the kind of government, for defense, for maintenance of the peace and free trade among the states, that the makers of the constitution framed. Loosely we call it a "democracy," which it never was and was never designed to be. It was and is a government by states. They, not the people, elect presidents. A state with a smaller population than Charleston county has two senators, a vote in the Electoral College for each, and New York with its 12,500,000 has no more. The six New England states with little more than half the population have six times the weight in the Senate that New York has, and no state can lose this senatorial representation without its own consent though the constitution be rewritten. "Government by the people shall not perish from the earth" was Mr. Lincoln's fine rhetorical flourish, but we have never had it in this country, and I don't think we have ever wanted it. The Constitution prescribes ways for its amendment, for its replacement by another constitution, but it seems plain to me that the provision about senators makes the rebuilding of the Constitution and reordering of the government practically impossible except by revolution.

This man-made Constitution is no more to be worshipped than a totem pole. It has been twisted and man-handled. The nine amendments adopted since the Twelfth had better never have been placed in it. The Thirteenth, abolishing slavery, merely recorded a fact, and the Fourteenth and Fifteenth, more nearly affecting us, were adopted when the Southern states were conquered provinces and so treated; instinctively we rebel against them and nullify the spirit of them, in-so-far as they relate to the Negroes, and other states assent. The Constitution undoubtedly is frayed and outworn in spots, but amendment usually is patch-work, leading to confusion and contradiction, and I for one doubt if a new constitution can or should be made, certainly not until the social constitution shall greatly change, until we shall be a united, assimilated, amalgamated people as well as United States.

The Americans are not a united people and it is nonsense to say that they are. The million and three quarters Mississippians, and the 7,000,000 New Yorkers, of the city, would join again as they have joined to resist a foreign foe, but they have little in common. For discussion's sake, not that I believe it, let us assume that Mississippi is backward, fifty years behind New York. Identical industrial regulations of wages, hours of labor, cannot be imposed by law on these two peoples without injustice to one or the other. Time and space are translatable. The traffic laws of Columbia would be ridiculous in Hankow. If Hankow is not modern, surely its streets should be widened before Columbia's ordinances should be forced upon it. In a thousand ways the Americans differ. They differ within the states, but the states are units small enough for regulation, small enough for the inhabitants to know and understand one another.

Parts of the United States are living this day in different centuries—just as London and Delhi are different in geography, topography, climate, religion, history, racial origins. Their countless varieties of habit and thinking are the equivalent of differences in time, and if "fifty years of Europe" is better than "a cycle of Cathay" we Americans, so-called, had better not dodge the truth that in our nearly 3,000,000 square miles are all sorts and conditions of Europes and Cathays.

In cultural values, Mississippi is not inferior to New York City, but I really don't think that the Mississippians could be trusted to legislate for the metropolis. Therefore, when the representatives of the two communities gather to legislate for themselves and the rest of the country the only safety lies in confining the legislation to general and simple principles. That is what the Founding Fathers intended, and in no other way can collisions be avoided. I am prepared to admit that no other way can collisions be avoided. I am prepared to admit that London's degree of domination over Delhi is probably good for Delhi, but whether domination by New York of Mississippi would be good for it or not, I don't expect the Mississippians to agree to it without a fight.

Abraham Lincoln's slogan, "Save the Union," saved it, marshalled the boys in sufficient numbers, but, the truth is, that war in its motive and essence was a war of commercial conquest. We might have another war of conquest within the Republic, in which case one or another slogan might work, but we shall not have a war to save the Union. Michigan and Wisconsin no more would send armies to prevent the Pacific States from seceding than South Carolina and Georgia would offer their boys as cannon fodder to hold New England states within it if they should again pass the Hartford resolutions. H. G. Wells lately has written of improved communication and transportation knitting the parts of the world and of the peoples within countries together. He pronounces it the change of overshadowing importance in this century of monstrous change, and I agree with him, but to that knitting are two sides. In the family life communication always has been close and it is reason enough that as the family enlarges its members cannot comfortably live under the same roof. They communicate too easily. I have no doubt that the daughters-in-law of Noah made life unlivable in the ark as soon as the storm passed (personally I have no daughter-in-law), and a country has no business with other roof than the firmament studded with stars.

The frantic effort in this country is to put a roof over it and regulate its inhabitants as a household. That is the meaning of the New Deal. It can't be done, it shouldn't be done. The country is too big, too diverse, and here let me say that I am not making a secession speech, I am making the opposite. I want the Union, the federated Union, preserved, and the only rational prescription to that end is the plan of the Founding Fathers in its purity. Their plan may decay, it may fall apart like the One Horse Shay, but the time for it has not come. Germany, Italy, Russia, are absolutisms. The first two are small countries, of about the size of four or two Georgias, densely settled, so they can be controlled from a center, a capital. In less than forty-eight hours an army corps can be sent to any part of them. Russia, on the other hand, twice the size of the United States, has never tasted freedom. Half its population were serfs longer than our Negroes were slaves, and with slavery they are still content, having good reason perhaps to hold the new slavery of Stalin better than the old of the czars. The truth remains that in the three countries absolutism rests on force, the army, and once Stalin, Hitler, Mussolini lose their grip on the army, the people will off with their heads. You can't regulate a people under the rafters of a house-government without force, more than you can regulate six daughters-in-law in the same establishment. If you can't have force, the army, the only recourse is the cottage system, separate houses scattered over the plantation.

In the United States can be no force, no army, to coerce its various peoples. The thing has been tried once, here in the South, and in ten years it failed. The conquerors in the long run no more than the conquered would stand for it, so government in due time gave up the bad and nasty job. The Americans have tasted freedom, drunk deeper drafts of it than any other people save the British, and, say what you will, they are still very British, thank God. I like the British for their "barbaric virtues," and as I pass

I say in parenthesis that there can be no sort of alliance between them and our folks too strong to displease me.

I digress to say that in the fine city where I live the most interesting single object is the marble statue of William Pitt, later Earl of Chatham, in Washington Square. The statesman is clad in the robes of a Roman senator, and the right arm is gone; it was shot off by a British cannon ball fired from James Island in the siege of Charleston in 1780.

The inscription reads: "In grateful memory of his services to his country in general and to America in particular, the Commons House of Assembly of South Carolina unanimously voted this statute of William Pitt, Esq., who gloriously exerted himself in defending the freedom of Americans, the true sons of England, by promoting a repeal of the Stamp Act in the year 1766. Time shall sooner destroy this mark of their esteem than erase from their minds their just sense of his patriotic virtues."

Rawlins Lowndes, distinguished among the earliest Democrats of the colony and state, introduced the resolution and wrote the inscription. Mark you the words—"*Americans, the true sons of England!*" The political bands that held these "sons of England" to the British Crown were soon to be sundered, it would be foolish to suggest that they can be rewelded, but the sundering was not of the soul of the peoples. Surely we South Carolinians, we Southerners, who are the same in blood and have been all the years since 1783, are still in spirit "the true sons of England," and when we shall not be true to the essential political principles of individual liberty of Pitt, Fox, and Conway, and of those Irishmen, Burke and Sheridan, and their associates in the Eighteenth century, we shall not be true to ourselves.

We can have no dictator in the United States for the ample reason that not one could have the army. If one declared himself dictator in Pittsburgh, another would mount his horse in Dallas to resist and another army would spring from the soil and follow him. So we might see a "man on horseback" in Seattle and Detroit, Atlanta, and Bangor, each with his army, but we shall see no man bestride the United States like a Colossus.

We can have in the United States a temporary dictatorship based on money, if there be enough of it and five thousand millions is a great deal in one man's hands, more probably than ever another has in time of peace in any land. Fortunately it cannot buy and consolidate legions in and from half a dozen groups of states, but in one or two political campaigns it can have influence insidious and tremendous. It can act upon the country as a mild and pleasant anaesthetic. I think upon the after effects. It will leave the people weakened and soft. It is silly to talk of "recovery" brought on by opiates. We shall not march through the wilderness as long as we are fed on manna from Washington. The ligaments of the Union will degenerate from it. If, for example, we shall resort to currency inflation by way of repudiating obligations after the burden of debt shall seem intolerable, different sections will be differently affected, with consequential danger of splittings—secessions, if you are not afraid of the word. With inflation come, the man on the land can still fill his belly, but there may be no husks, much the less bacon, for the man in the street where are no swine.

Here we fetch up at the new American cleavage and peril. It is between the urban and the rural districts. In New York City are seven million people of whom about three million are, or were, workers in factories. The steam age built the great city. London was a town of a million when Dickens began to write; he found half a million in New York on his first visit. Paris and Berlin were towns of the numbers of Rochester and Toledo. The factory shed was erected around the stationary engine and the people had to dwell close to the factory or the railroad station. The cities were built by the centripetal force of the engines of the time. Now the engines are in reverse. The thousand horse power of the engine is distributable in a thousand units by wires over thousands of square miles. The motor carries the people on their own schedules in every direction and the necessity or excuse for manufacturing goods on one hundred thousand dollars an acre land has vanished. Many a shirt factory in the deep country of the South is taking jobs from Philadelphians and New Yorkers.

The over-built urban structure is the seat of the American

economic disease. If a city of half a million remove itself from Chicago, real estate values will crack and with them the financial and municipal structure. How can New York meet its annual city budget of $550,000,000 if it cannot hold its population and how can it hold population if the jobs are gone not to come back? Wages paid for public works may save the situation for a time, but when that work ceases the last state of the city is worse than the first. The federal government's real purpose at this time is to save the American city, and the resources of the country are being diverted to it. I set it down as being axiomatic, if there be any axioms in these times, that if the cities cannot support themselves upon their own tax revenues the revenues of the rural districts must be drawn upon. There is no other source. By rural district I mean any region that is not preponderantly industrial, and that includes all the Southern states. They can support comfortably four times their present population and would if they had to—as the French, the Italians, or the Danes do. What the Government is sending in gifts to the rural regions is sent to keep them quiet, to keep them fooled. The allocations for rural housing, soil erosion, the Tennessee Valley and the like seem to have the solution of the urban problem in view, but they are overwhelmingly contradicted by the greater gifts to the cities. One hears hints of outbreaks of violence, of civil commotion, and they may be well grounded. In the Carolinas, the whole South, never was a period when the people were more able and more resolute to preserve order. Here and there may be a brawl, even a little riot, but we shall have no uprising that our own people will not put down.

The Government is by its nature unproductive. Its business is to keep the peace so that production by men will be possible and it lives by taking tolls or taxes. From this our government is departing. It is itself entering into production and taxing the people prodigiously to maintain itself a corporation managing industries and commerce. A few years ago the only federal government that we came into association with was in the persons of postmasters, R.F.D. carriers, a few revenue collectors and occasionally a federal judge. A federal soldier in uniform was a novel sight in Columbia's streets as late as 1915. In 1935 every man and woman in this audience owes about $240 as a share of the national debt and so does every child, white and black. Heavy as your state and municipal debts are, too heavy for your health and happiness, the per capita, including the self-liquidating highway debt, is about $110. The federal tax collectors are at your heels. Washington is a devil fish with tentacles stretching to every one of you and taking your money.

What is going on—let us call it by its name—is Revolution. It may be necessary, it may be good, but it is Revolution. Violence and terror are not essential ingredients of revolutions. Germany and Italy have had them with negligible bloodshed since the World War. The British Reform Bill of 1832 was a revolution.

Revolutions, they say, never turn back. They do not perhaps once they have succeeded. The present one in this country is not completed. As yet it is an attempt. A few weeks ago it suffered a mighty reverse at the hands of the Supreme Court. The attempt goes on, insidious and persistent. Unless it shall be halted, the United States in a little while will be no more like the Republic that it was as late as January, 1929, than like a monarchy or a republic of the soviets, which is not saying that it will be like either of those. It is saying only that it will be utterly unlike itself, its old and historic self of free, self-assertive and self-sustaining states.

It may be a better United States, or more accurately, United State. I do not think so; I oppose the Revolution, but it may be that I am an ingrained and ingrowing reactionary with a mind shut to the new lights. All that I ask is that you face the fact of the Revolution now attempted and call it by its name. If you like it, embrace it. You may serve your country and mankind by helping to destroy the old republic and the old South Carolina. The old form of government under which I was born and lived half a century in some knowledge of its character may be worm-eaten and decayed beyond the hope of health, but I would have you to recognize the attempt to dismantle and remove it and to call it by its name, however the leaders of the Revolution do not yet dare to do so.

OF CHIEFS AND STAFFERS
(1938)

"Of Chiefs and Staffers" is a portrait of persons, places, and customs in the newspaper world now vanished. The essay points to the fact that the journalism of our time need not be ruled by men of mechanized mind.

ONE of a thousand good stories of the late Yates Snowden, newspaper man, historian and poet of South Carolina, was of a North Carolina notable named Shockoe Jones who flourished in the 1850's. He got his paper and pen and began, "Having nothing else to do this afternoon I concluded to sit down and write a history of North Carolina." So, this Saturday night, after reading the discussion between Mr. Oswald Garrison Villard and Mr. Wilbur Forrest at the Institute of Public Relations in Williamstown, it occurs to me to expound journalism.

One may except to Mr. Forrest's saying that "the working journalist has been miserably underpaid a great many years." He is getting at least double his pay of 1890, the year that I, a college bred ignoramus, set out as owner, editor, and guild, of a country weekly. In South Carolina the Charleston *News and Courier* was then the one daily newspaper that could afford a decent press service. Its first and greatest editor, Francis Warrington Dawson, had been murdered the year before. James Calvin Hemphill had succeeded him. Carlisle McKinley who wrote *An Appeal to Pharoah*, a book on the race question that for a time stirred the country and had it guessing the authorship, poet as well, was his associate. Narciso Gonzales, first editor and a founder of *The State*, Columbia, Matthew F. Tighe, later chief of Hearst's Washington bureau, and Snowden, whom I have mentioned, were of the staff. So was Willie Gonzales, who was to be Wilson's Minister to Cuba and Ambassador to Peru, and is now editor of *The State*. Roswell T. Logan and John A. Moroso, telegraph and city editor, were not so well known in other states but measured with them in talents. The *News and Courier* has never had a staff comparable in brilliance with the men who worked with Dawson when the newspaper was scarcely a third its present size, and in number its writers are about the same now as then. Henry Grady and Evan P. Howell were running the Atlanta *Constitution*, and their helpers were Joel Chandler Harris, Frank Stanton (columnist and rhymester, little remembered but at one time quoted in London as well as throughout the United States) and a dozen other clever men. They were making that newspaper famous. The Atlanta *Journal* was coming on at a great pace, and J. P. Caldwell, of princely intellect and wit, about that time, was training men like Avery and McNeill, on the Charlotte *Observer*.

What were these men paid? Editors received from $50 to $75 a week, and $25 to $30 was tip top for desk men. Fifteen or twenty was the stipend of a seasoned reporter. Before the "gay nineties" ended I was sleeping in a hall bedroom and trudging the streets of Philadelphia, doing hack work for the clean and scintillant Philadelphia *Press*, (Dr. Talcott Williams and Ralph D. Payne, whom I did not know, were of the staff), and every Saturday $12 was in my pay envelope. I am drawing dividends on those months in Philadelphia; they made me a reporter, of a sort, and I'm proud of that. "Why are you always interested in reporters and not at all in editors?" one asked Mr. Joseph Pulitzer. "A reporter is always a hope and an editor is always a disappointment," was the answer. (I don't think Frank Cobb was a disappointment, even to Mr. Pulitzer.) If one could only be a reporter again—but it takes legs as well as head.

Of my Philadelphia cronies—we knew the places where a small steak could be had for twenty cents and the word was passed when a new one opened—was a youth of New York, a good fellow, a gentleman, one of the three best educated men that I have personally known. He could speak three or four languages, and the story was that he was familiar with Sanskrit, or it may have been Arabic. He used to make me seriously ashamed with his knowledge of the history of South Carolina. Eight dollars was in his weekly pay envelope, and I don't think

he would have ever been a reporter. Albert Payson Terhune tells
of him in his reminiscences.

Tramping those streets (the office rule was that we could ride
in a street car and turn in the fare in weekly expense accounts if
the assignment called for a walk of at least seven blocks) the
thought would come to me that if a reporter could have a carriage
and horses or even a buggy, covering assignments in the Fair-
mount Park or the Kensington district would be right pleasant.
(You see I had luxurious Southern ideas and it was the horse and
buggy age.)

One day I saw a crowd collected at Tenth and Chestnut streets
and I strolled across Chestnut to it. It was in October, 1898. The
thing of interest was a "horseless carriage," the first that ever I
saw, a delivery van which a shopkeeper was using to advertise his
business. Now reporters and desk men of my acquaintance have
horseless carriages, and they pay as much for them and their up-
keep as a two horse rig would have cost me in 1898.

Far be it from me to say that newspaper men, or other men
(and women), are paid enough, but in Charleston a cub reporter
is paid as much at the start as a cub bank clerk, and his wage is
raised as rapidly to the point of a teller's or assistant cashier's
salary. There the chances are that he will stop a long time, perhaps wear out, but bank workers also stop and wear out.

In the field that I am familiar with, two or three states, the
newspapers do not attract the keen and able lads that they did in
my youth. They enlist some, but not nearly so many, and this
saying is not the wandering of an old-timer's memory. Between
1865 and 1900 were many more talented men, both in country
and daily journalism in South Carolina (I could name them),
than are in the state now. In the 'nineties the exceptionally bright
men began to disappear. Some fled to the great cities, and their
places have not often been filled.

There are skilled workmen, safe, sane fellows, industrious,
careful, reliable, and not too many of them. When I tired, and I
did shortly, of a country newspaper (though I made a good living from it in the depression of 1893 and had a royal good time at
the World's Fair), $12 a week would have brought me to the

News and Courier, but in those days a vacancy occurred once in three or five years. In the last ten years have been scores of vacancies on this same newspaper, and, despite shoals of applicants from the schools of journalism and from other newspapers, at least one in three that we have taken on has been a misfit. Others have gone to other newspapers or businesses. The graduate of a medical school works years in a hospital before he begins to earn. The young lawyer half starves for years, or often chases ambulances, or runs for the legislature, which may be worse. The newspaper publisher (I am not a publisher or shareholder in a newspaper) takes far greater chances with cubs than hospitals take with their cubs and sinks many a dollar in duds.

Some time ago an interesting woman called at my office and introduced herself as a director for three or four states of the "Writers' Project," "The American Guide Book," and she said: "I know you are not in sympathy with the New Deal and the WPA, but I want your advice and help. In one of the states of my district the work is lagging and we need an editorial supervisor—we can pay $166 a month for at least three months. I want you to recommend a man."

"What you are looking for," I said, "is a fairly diligent and honest man, a reliable person, reasonably accurate, who has a little scholarship, has had some editorial and executive experience and who won't get drunk?"

"You have described him exactly," said the lady.

"Well, you shan't have him if I can catch him first, I'm combing the woods for him at this very moment!" It so happened that three of our men had lately left us to begin a project of their own, and their places had not been filled.

To be sure, the country over-runs with newspaper men, trained and raw, so the applications that come to me nearly every week, from Minnesota, Texas, Oregon, prove. Why do they wish to come to Charleston—they with their excellent recommendations—as excellent as a congressman presents for a constituent who has influence back home? Do they speak and write our language? Are they acquainted with Bull Swamp township where we have subscribers who have notions and habits of their very own? If I have a quality of usefulness to our newspaper it is that I know my people, my "territory." It is my only specialty. I need helpers who know them, and I want to know those helpers, their sympathies, their backgrounds. What is it to me that a man is underwritten by a "guild" in Milwaukee if his tongue, or his typewriter betrayeth him as not of Charleston's Fifth Ward or Horry County, South Carolina? No, I refrain from betting my employer's money on a recommended expert if I can find a likely colt from one of our own stock farms; I'm taking fewer chances.

One time there was a flourishing newspaper—the incident is within my recollection—in a Southern city. It had been built from the ground by a parcel of bright boys who were pinching middle age. They knew their newspaper and their town, and they knew one another. They seemed unmethodical, they looked lazy, perhaps slovenly, but day by day they got results and scooped the country roundabout. The newspaper passed into a new hand, who imported a managing editor from Chicago or from Mars, paid him grandly (for those days), and he spread "efficiency" all over the shop—aye, to the point that hard-bitten veterans of the craft pulled off their hats in his presence and made reports to him on printed forms. They were foolish journalistic virgins, over-confident in their prowess, and, though they had no guild, they rebelled and set up a rival newspaper. It failed. Of course it failed, and the ground those men stood on was sold from under their feet. It was bitter experience for them, and costly to the mother newspaper of prestige and power to the sum of not less than $100,000. It was bad business loaded with misfortune to two sides—and still I hold that the owner of that older newspaper had a right to be a fool with his money.

In another Southern city a capitalist who was cursed in his heart with a cause (this too is within my recollection), set up a newspaper and hired a staff of forceful and ambitious young men downstairs and upstairs. As is the almost invariable rule, the new journal in an occupied field two or three years lost money, in spite of the cause ably defended, but it was beginning to see the dawn, or so the business office believed. Then one day came the order from the stubborn owner that next day the newspaper would not be published, and never again it was. Reporters, printers, editors, pressmen, were jobless, and, if they swore mightily, there was no disputing that the capitalist was chipping in from his private bank account every Saturday night to balance the weekly budget.

In both these cases the owner was right. It is always admissible for owners to blow themselves into kingdom come, and if they came into their kingdoms by indirection it is another story and irrelevant. "Freedom of the press?" There is none without authority of the individual, and the alternative (there is none besides) is ownership, in Albert Jay Nock's phrase, by "our enemy the state." The ideal is the combination of editor and owner in one person, as was common in an older and smaller day. The better word were *idyllic*, for mass production, God save us, infects journalism, strengthens it, and sickens it at the same time.

The right of a railroad or a public utility company to own a newspaper is beyond question, and if it be aboveboard it is honorable. It is only the masked newspaper that is dangerous.

The last word must rest with the owners. It is beyond gainsay. Usually the owner, if not himself an editor, delegates authority to an editor. I have held that authority many years, on more than one newspaper. Once I set out on a legislative campaign involving taxation of certain interests without consulting the owner. He approved it. Long afterward, when we had won our contention, I learned, not from him, that a group of irate advertisers had boycotted the newspaper and withdrawn business to the amount of $5,000. That owner was the late Ambrose Gonzales, of *The State*. He did not tell me of the boycott, and, what is more, if any man connected with the advertising department had told me of it with the object of halting my effort, "Mr. Ambrose," as we called him, would have kicked that man out of his office.

To write of one's self is not enjoyable or instructive unless to present a case history; so, for this paper let me be so considered. In forty-seven years I have never had a contract, oral or written, with an employer and have never thought of asking for one. Once I was fired. I resented it and with reason, but the bitter medicine made me stronger. Never as reporter, city editor or editor was I asked to falsify a fact. Always my chiefs were my friends and stood by me. Of course I have not written everything that came into my head. I have not followed every impulse or seized the newspaper of which I am a trustee for my employer to express convictions opposed to his. I know the policy of the newspaper, the opinions of the owner, and if I was not in sympathy with them, I abased myself when I became his employe. Anyway, he assumes the "hazards of the trade." I do not choose to walk the floor the night before a payroll is to be met (that is why I am an employe), and surely it is not his obligation to provide me with the instrument upon which to improvise compositions which, however they might delight me, would be to him extravaganzas.

There is no absolute freedom of the press or anything else, and the device of private ownership, despotic ownership if you like, that may be sometimes hard and cruel, is the single escape from the slavery of the state. Control divided between a guild and the owner is inconceivable without the guild's protection by the state, and the guild's control unacquired by purchase or creation can be protected only by a measure of confiscation enforced by the state. Newspapers are competitive. They are racers. The owner is the rider. It were as well to dope the steed as to take the bit from the staff's bridle.

If newspaper workers (I am not conceding it) are underpaid, their quarrel is not with the owners. They are competing with superior talents, with the Bob Quillens, the Emily Posts, the Grantland Rices, the E. C. Segars, and the like. They are not many, but they are enough to go around. Quillen works for us for a song, so do a dozen or two others; and, unhappy as it may be, it is the fact that somebody's brains invented the syndicates (I hate them), and they sell to newspapers at wholesale prices. For that reason the clever men do not throng the newspaper's doors as they did fifty years ago. Some of the men I have mentioned would have been gobbled by the syndicates were they living now. Thus, distinction has departed from most newspapers; shining individuality is lacking often in the gazettes even of the great towns; and owners are under the same compulsion that makers of motor vehicles are to produce on an assembly line.

Consequently, the sane, the average, the mechanized mind fills the newspaper offices and infects its spirit. In time it may exorcise the spirit or drive out the devil. On its face this is argument for the Newspaper Guild, or union. If journalists are mechanics, why should they not organize as other mechanics do?

It is poor argument. In the other unions many a mechanic a little above the level of his fellows in mind or strength, wittingly or not and not always from motives altruistic, sacrifices himself. It is the unwillingness to sacrifice that cleaves labor into the craft and industrial unions, the American Federation and the C.I.O. Mr. Green's men, of more skilled companies, will not allow themselves to be jellied with labor's mass, nor finally will Mr. Lewis's United Steel workers take pot luck with the Southern cotton pickers.

Despite the abominable standardization of the newspapers there is wider diversity among their writing and newsgathering mechanics than among most other craftsmen. To digress a moment, the reporter cannot be stripped of a dangerous individuality. A politician may with a measure of safety mistreat an editor, but let him beware of wrong doing to a reporter. The boy can bide his time and, if he be no dumb ass, his time will come. Many a politician has been laid low by a shaft not at random sent and has well deserved it for an affront to a lad which he has long forgotten. No one, not even his editor, can tell what is under a young reporter's hide, and sometimes it is the courage, strength and cunning of a wolf.

The argument is bad because of its assumption that the standardization and mass production of newspapers have come to stay. That is the faulty assumption of most reformers, or radicals, whether Russian Bolsheviks or American New Dealers. The horse and buggy age, after all, was short-lived; the chariot, the ox-cart, the caravan ages were before it. Integration of cities, on the grand scale, came with steam; electric power, aided by vehicles running on their own schedules and everybody's right of way may, I am sure *will*, in part disintegrate them. Despite that so many "readers" are now picture-lookers, organs of opinion are still popular. All children like pretty colors in pictures, most men are Peter Pan-ish, but the most purchased periodical in America has a positive and sometimes a scarcely concealed partisan policy.

So it will come to this: if in a city the readers shall not know that the owner of a newspaper is speaking, they will ask, "Who is?" Divided or mixed responsibility is too subtle for them to understand—for you or me to understand. When the great newspaper shall sound to the ears of the people a confusion of voices, they will turn to smaller voices. The voices will multiply. The Guildsmen will turn executives to supply the demand. The Newspaper Guild will work its own cure, eating out the spongy foundation on which it builds.

The neglected opportunity of the day is the weekly, the country, newspaper. A hundred, or fifty, years ago its influence was tremendous. Thinking men wrote for it, and thinking men read it. The last half century has been for it a period of decay. It has degenerated into the side issue of a job printing office of the small town or village containing the personal, the "society," news of the neighborhoods. To be sure, it cannot compete with big dailies in gathering and distributing news or in printing features, but it is not perceived that the very bigness of the dailies is their undoing as stimulants to thinking, as reflectors of thought. Does anyone dispute that the average editorial page of the daily is inane, apparently the product of mental eunuchs? Even when the editorials are entertaining and strong they are lost in thirty or fifty pages. I remember when the Springfield *Republican*, with a circulation of 30,000, was quoted from the Atlantic to the Pacific. So was the Portland *Oregonian*. Who quotes them now? They are not written to be quoted; there would be no business in it if they were. But I deny that the appetite for food-thought has been killed by the sport writers and makers of comic strips.

The time has come that the weekly published in a town and county capable of supporting it in decency will yield a decent livelihood to two men, a business man and an editor. (So, for the thoughtful, honest, straight-speaking weekly may be a place in the ward or neighborhood within the metropolitan city.) Now, in most cases, the editor is most commonly boss printer and business man. Consequently, he is a journalistic derelict at middle age. In the town are at least two or three lawyers, clergymen, teachers, respected for the possession of a little scholarship and ability to express themselves. Does the inquiring visitor to the town ask for the editor as a ranking thinker and informed authority? I trow not, however I protect myself (I may visit some of these towns) from decayed vegetables by remarking that there are exceptions.

Nor am I summoning from the vast deep such spirits as the William Allen White who has made his daily gazette, in a town of 7,000 or 9,000 souls, nationally famous. Nor do I summon the spirit of Disraeli's Rigby to write "slashing articles" for a party. I am calling for men who think of themselves as journalists and are not ashamed of that good word for which there is no other in the English language to sharply define them. They are, or should be, students in at least the degree of the lawyer who prepares his brief with the care to command the attention of the high court. They would take their work seriously; they would not be slurrers; not only would they be informed, but they would not be malpracticers on the mother tongue as are some of the latest brood of weekly magazines appealing to the quack clientele with success that I hope will pass with other quackeries.

It will be said that the daily journals monopolizing the publication of the world's and the state's news and its gathering will make subject the rural and village editor's mind, that it will unconsciously reflect their coloring. It is not so. There are too many colors. The specialist is urban, but the grasp of the ruralist is broader. Always it has been—even in the time when the country-man's radius of movement was thirty instead of three thousand miles. Everybody flits about considerably nowadays. May I boast? Well, I do, that the first newspaper that ever I subscribed and paid for with my own earned money was the New York *Tribune* when about twenty-three years from the time that I was born, in a carpetbagger's administration in South Carolina, I hated it with a capacity that I lost three or four decades ago. I knew, or felt at any rate, something of "my side," and the *Trib-*

une kept me from being entirely infatuated. Now, every literate man reads both sides, for they are flung at him, and every intelligent man with a world's almanac and an encyclopaedia can see clean through New York or Chicago if he have eyes in his head.

In the United States should be 2,000 of the newspapers of the kind I have described. There may be 200, but they are not in my ken. If their editorial pages were not brilliant they would be as interesting as those of nine in ten of the dailies now are. They would be infinitely more interesting, in their curtilages, or the six hundred square miles where their readers live. For they would be written by free hands with their own pens. Men who go afishing without saying "By your leave." Men not anhungered for public office—that hunger is the bane of country editors in the South—independent men, "cadets of Gascoigne," don't-give-a-damn-men, cursed if you please with the traditions of their fathers come down to them from Cedric the Saxon and that Williams who struck the glove that Fluellyn wore in his cap. Withal, disciplined men, faithful, welded to the office, the "shop," wherein Madam Duty presides. Hear Sir Walter, old, not well, striving, fighting, to pay his debts, confiding to his diary: "After all, I have fagged through six pages—and my head aches—my eyes ache—my back aches—so does my breast—and I am sure my heart aches, and what can Duty ask more?" A little later in that same diary Sir Walter conferred with Madam Duty, wrote of her as "a d—d old bitch," but he stuck by her and did her bidding till he died.

"Mendicant friars" Thomas Carlyle called editors and had a wholesome respect for them. Perhaps they should be friars, or monks; newspapers carried on by monks taking the vow of celibacy would be interesting. Anyway they should be not petticoat bound to spouse or mistress, but they need not be mendicants. The time has passed for that, and the independent journalist should and can be independent of debt much as he may scorn money-bags. In America is a place for him. Thousands of places yawn for him—him who knows his Shakespeare, his Lawrence Sterne, his *Spectator*, his John Elia, and his own people, his neighbors, their needs and their natures.

The metropolitan journals would go on as usual, the camera-men purveying to the picture-lookers, the mechanic minds capitu-lating to the guild-bunds, with meal tickets insured by their union cards and no man objecting to the voluntary servitude that is to their taste and fancy.

The soul of a journalist inhabited a body that lived in a tub. The conqueror came to him asking, "What can I do for you?"

"Get out of my sunshine!"

IMPROVEMENT IN RACIAL RELATIONS IN SOUTH CAROLINA: THE CAUSE

(1940)

This paper deals with the problem of crime and inter-racial relations in the Southern states in the years prior to World War II. It was published in *The South Atlantic Quarterly* (October, 1940), Vol. XXXIX.

THE announcement that for the year ending May 3, 1940, had been no lynching in the United States was hailed everywhere with satisfaction, and as a cause of the happy improvement the exertions of a society or commission on "inter-racial relations" in the South were praised with emphasis and, I say, with ignorant exaggeration.

With no intent to belittle the worthy efforts of the men and women of the society, I say that among the factors causing the decrease in lynching in the South has been the very great decline of "inter-racial relations."

Steadily and, of late years, rapidly, the relations between the white and black races in the South have diminished, the separation in living, in the industries, therefore in association or contacts, has widened and hardened. Other factors, of which I shall speak, have been important in reducing inter-racial crimes, but the separation, the movement of the races from each other, has been the chief among them. Before proceeding I shall explain that I am writing from memory and observation covering a period of at least sixty years, from the time I was ten or eleven years old, or earlier, and that I write of my South Carolina as representative of the Southern states. What I shall say is subject to discount according to the reader's pleasure or judgment.

The twelve years following Appomattox were a time of disorder and turbulence, or semi-warfare in the South, and it did not end suddenly with the return of white man's rule in this state. "Reconstruction," the rights and wrongs of which need not be here discussed, inflamed the two races, the one against the other. Murders, lynchings, riots, arson and other crimes of violence were common in South Carolina in that time, and the crimes were not the monopoly of whites or blacks. Once, as many as eight or nine Negroes who had murdered a one-armed Confederate soldier were taken from a jail and lynched, by the old Ku Klux Klan, and once, in the village where I was then a baby, in 1870, a riot started and nine or ten Negroes and a white "carpetbagger" were killed in an area of 700 square miles—this was six years before Reconstruction ended. In two riots, in Charleston county, in 1876, white men were victims.

Brutal murders were sometimes committed by white men, and by Negroes too. The waylaying and shooting in the dark of a white man by Negroes was sometimes followed by secret murders by white men in revenge. All that is an old story and historians have carefully collected and recorded its facts.

When the white men came into power in South Carolina, in April, 1877, the resentments kindled in Reconstruction did not die in a year or wholly vanish in three or four decades. Among the whites were a few selfish, gross and cruel persons—and the white race was dominant again. Lynching and murders of Negroes increased, greatly for a time. The crime of rape infuriated the whites, and sometimes, not often, on flimsy evidence, a Negro was hanged. In some cases white men of standing, in rural districts, approved lynchings and participated in them. Still, the first lynching that I, a nine year old, heard of was of a white man, the owner of a farm, who had cruelly murdered a white girl of the mountains after assaulting her. This was in a county of preponderant white population, and within four years of that lynching two white men in that county were tried, convicted and hanged for the murder of Negroes, after their convictions had been affirmed by the highest court. That county, Spartanburg, and those executions were exceptional, one concedes.

A few weeks ago a writer of fiction, a Southerner, had a short story in a magazine the gist of which was that a good Negro was murdered by a planter for no other reason than that the Negro desired to improve his condition, to become a property owner. That could have happened in South Carolina fifty years ago. It might happen in Georgia or other Southern state now, I do not know, but not in South Carolina. In the days that such infamous crimes were occasional in South Carolina, not less cruel murders of white men by Negroes were sometimes done, and I note an habitual if not studied effort of writers for a press that champions Negro causes to forget that there have been Negro slayers of white persons. I think they were at least as numerous as the white slayers of Negroes half a century ago and afterward.

In the eighties and nineties, when the resentment lingered from Reconstruction was also fear among the whites. In 1880 the Negroes in South Carolina were 604,332, the whites 391,105, and ten years thereafter the Negroes were 688,934 to 462,008 whites. There was many a neighborhood in the "deep country" where the Negroes were ten or twenty to one white person.

It was an unsettled and violent period that hung over from Reconstruction, and it was not rare that white men of prominence, lawyers some of them, toted pistols and shot one another in the street or in the court house of the village.

Meantime, in those bloody years, the kindly relations between tens of thousands of decent Negroes and their white folks (they were not destroyed altogether even in Reconstruction) survived.

Now for the changes. Slowly they came to be noticeable after 1900. The decade preceding had been full of violence, of lynchings and homicides. Many of the slayings were political, to which Negroes were not party. It was the decade of the angry division of the white Democrats, the followers of B. R. Tillman and his opponents. The state liquor selling system ("dispensary") was set up, and liquor constables and bootleggers sometimes "shot it out."

In the last forty years, the homicide rate has continued high, but with steadily declining frequency white men have killed Negroes and Negroes have seldom killed whites. "Shooting scrapes" between white men of social or professional standing have not been half a dozen in the period. The slaying of Narciso Gonzales, editor of *The State*, Columbia, a brave gentleman, who, by the way, exposed his life more than once in warfare against lynchings and lynchers, by the then lieutenant governor, in 1903, was one of the last tragedies in which the parties were prominent. The pistol carrying by men calling themselves gentlemen came to an end.

Homicides to which only Negroes are party are numerous every year and the reformers of distant states profoundly concerned for Negro welfare do not discover that intra-Negro slaughter by Negroes takes twenty or fifty times as many Negro lives as ever lynchings took. There is far too much homicide among whites, but it is for the most part confined to persons that one does not "meet at the club."

Fifty years ago white tenant farmers in South Carolina numbered 12,918, and the white farm owners 38, 353. The great expansion of the textile industry was between 1895 and 1905. In 1890 the male adults in cotton mills were about 2,500. In fifteen years they were 20,000, and they are now about 40,000. The landless farmers took refuge from labor competition with the Negroes on farms and plantations. They now live in villages, owned by the textile companies, from which Negroes are excluded. The Negroes do not work within the cotton mills. The associations of white and Negro laborers in the cotton, corn and tobacco fields have been greatly diminished. White women no longer prepare noonday meals for cotton pickers, white and black; and whites and Negroes, men and women, have nearly ceased to plow and "chop" cotton in the fields together.

In towns and cities of South Carolina no "segregation" laws and ordinances were passed, but long ago the Negroes, of their own will, began to flock together. In Columbia they owned as late as 1910 a church on the corner where the postoffice now stands, across a street from the State House Yard, and they sold it, as they did a few residences in the heart of the white district which had been acquired during Reconstruction. I helped a colored servant who was and is my friend to buy a house in Columbia, in a colored quarter of course, and later when I offered to

help the same man to buy a house in Charleston in a block inhabited by whites and blacks he would not hear of it; he wanted
to be with his own people. After the Confederate war Negroes
gained possession of many houses of impoverished white families
in "down town" Charleston. In the last thirty years nearly all of
them have moved to Negro districts, the down town houses have
been reconditioned, and white people inhabit them.

In his annual report to the diocesan convention of South Carolina last April Bishop Harold Thomas of the Protestant Episcopal
church said that a reclamation, or slum clearance, project for
whites, of the federal government, was scattering the Negro
population of a Charleston city district and that half the congregation of one of the oldest churches for Negroes in South Carolina, built nearly a century ago by white slaveowners, was being
compelled now to find homes elsewhere and were leaving the
church without a sufficient congregation to support it. This
brick church was not necessary to the housing project, but unless
government would pay a price for it that would erect a building
elsewhere, the bishop said, the outlook was that the church would
not survive. What government has done about it I have not heard.
The federal government in its housing projects in South Carolina
is rigidly segregating the races, whatever the Supreme Court may
have said about the ordinances of St. Louis and other cities some
years ago, and to this I am certainly not objecting.

I was twenty-six years old (1895) before I saw a white barber
in South Carolina, and not until after the World war did I see
white waitresses in South Carolina hotels and restaurants. One
sees them now. As a boy and young man in my village I not
often saw a white carpenter, cabinet maker, bricklayer or blacksmith. The Negro artisans are now, relatively, few. The garage
mechanic has taken the place of the blacksmith and is a white
man. This taking over of skilled trades by whites is one explanation of Negro migration to Northern cities.

Negroes are not barred by rule from industries. One finds
them in the sawmills. In one city of South Carolina are furniture
factories, and in one of them that I lately visited 30 per centum of
835 workers were Negroes—but, mark, this was a mill in which

only men worked. White women work in textile mills. In the furniture factories has been no race friction.

The gradual and seemingly hard exclusion of Negroes from the skilled trades is not caused by prejudice in the South more than in the North. Employers prefer whites to Negroes when they are to be had at the same wages. I am not discussing the right and wrong of it: I state the fact.

Negro migration on a large scale began in this state in the decade 1910-1920. In 1910 the Negro majority was 156,682 in a population of 1,515,400 and in ten years it dropped to 46,181. In 1930 the white majority was 150,359, in a population 1,-738,765 the whites having made the astonishing gain of 307,041 in twenty years. In the 1920-1930 decade infestation of cotton fields by boll worms drove Negroes from the lands and demand for labor in the North at wages better than they had dreamed of lured them. Those causes do not sufficiently account for the migration. It goes on. The present census will reveal it, unless signs and prognostications are estray. South Carolina is now a white state by 200,000, possibly 250,000, and federal policies that restrict agricultural acreage are accelerating this gain. I like those policies: they are of the few federal policies of which I am enamoured. To me, an elderly citizen, living without Negroes would be a hardship, but I am not protesting against the division of the Negro problem or its transfer to Northern cities. It may be axiomatic to say that, other things equal, the reduction of numbers of Negroes to whites tends to reduce "inter-racial" relations.

In those bad days when lynching was common was also a kinder relation between some of the whites and blacks than now exists. A respectable white man usually had Negroes who were his friends, or dependents, who came to him in trouble. Often the Negroes had been family slaves or were their sons, and I could name lawyers of the 'nineties who never failed to defend "their Negroes" if they were indicted in criminal courts. That relationship has almost disappeared. Between men under fifty and their Negro employees, the dealings now are "strictly business." The dealings are fair, but there is no longer sentiment in them. If a white man give to Negroes, unless to a blind street beggar, it is likely through the Associated Charities, or the Red Cross. The generation of whites that has succeeded to the Confederate veterans and their wives has not the understanding of Negroes that they had, and it is probably not desired by either race.

So, I repeat, that well meant and praiseworthy as are the works of inter-racial committees, admirable as is their denunciation of lynching and effort to prevent it, the steady decline of inter-racial relations has done what they could never have done. Their accomplished results have been in inverse ratio to their good intentions, and it detracts nothing from the good thereof.

Other factors in reducing lynching to a minimum (I am not saying that there will never be another of the savage, cowardly crimes in South Carolina) have been better policing of rural districts, to which paved roads, automobiles, telephones and radio have immensely contributed. A few months ago, this year, a Negro armed with a gun and "behaving strangely" was arrested in Saluda, the court house village of Saluda county. An hour or two later news of the finding of the dead bodies of two women, one a Negro and the other white, reached the village, and suspicion instantly pointed to the Negro in jail. No demonstration followed; there was no talk of hanging him. The officers of the law took no chances; in an hour and a half the man was safe in the penitentiary, in Columbia, forty-five miles distant over a cement road. He has confessed that he killed his wife and his landlord's wife and is awaiting trial. Twenty years ago those murders would have been swiftly and unlawfully avenged. South Carolina now has a small force of rural policemen and also highway, or traffic, officers.

There has been no lynching in a town of 10,000 or more inhabitants in South Carolina in a century, if ever, and the last "race riot" in the state occurred forty-two years ago.

The white man lynched in 1878, or 1879, mentioned earlier in this article, was taken from the jail in Spartanburg, then a village of 2,500 persons. About forty-five years later Spartanburg had become a city of 12,000 or 15,000 and had, besides a new and strong county jail, a gallant sheriff named Vernon White. A white woman of a textile community accused a Negro of the "usual crime," and he was promptly arrested. That night a mob of 1,500 demanded the prisoner. He was not surrendered. The mob dynamited the jail's outer gate. The sheriff stepped forward his rifle in hand, and warned the mob that they might overpower him and get the man but that he and his deputies would kill the first twenty men that stepped across a line in front of the jail's door. The mob milled. No man crossed the line, and the mob disappeared. A few weeks later prominent white men got an inkling that the accuser of the man was not a normal person. They investigated, and the prosecuting officer, the late Abner Hill, who told me the story, was convinced of the man's innocence. The man was tried and acquitted, principally on the testimony of the prosecuting witness—the court as well as the jury approving.

About 1914 a Negro was accused of the "crime against woman" in Fairfield county, was arrested and was carried to the penitentiary for safe-keeping. The sheriff and a deputy brought him back to Winnsboro, the county village, for trial, and as they were entering the court house the husband of the accuser shot the sheriff dead. Within the court room of that court house is a mural monument to "Ed" Hood, the martyred sheriff.

Generally, not always, a prisoner has been safe from lynching once he was in jail. The weak or cowardly sheriffs and jailers have been the exceptions. Detection and arrest of lynchers has been difficult, virtually impossible. The crime was never prevented by punishment of the criminals, the lynchers, but prevention, which is policing, is effective. If in a great city race-friction occur, a truckload of policemen armed with tear gas bombs, perhaps machine guns, arrives in three minutes, a crowd of 5,000 is cowed and "moved on." I hazard the opinion that were the policing in New York not infinitely better than it was outside of a city in South Carolina until recent years, there would be race riots and lynchings in Harlem once a week until one or the other race were run out of that mixed community.

To omit saying that the Southern Negroes have notably improved in habits since they were set free would be less than fair. In the decade after 1865 when everybody was poor, stealing by former slaves was (Reconstruction scarcely discouraged it) common. Pilfering by servants was expected, and perhaps many cooks saw nothing wrong in it. So Negro men robbed hen roosts and melon patches. I have had, in three or four Southern towns, twenty five or thirty Negro domestics and I remember but two who would steal. Other servants warned against one of them, to protect themselves from suspicion, and she was dismissed. As for the drivers of my automobile, my family has been as safe with them as my mother and her sisters were with "Big George" the carriage driver seventy-five years ago.

Most of the Negroes can read and write, in a manner, but I am not sure that immense improvement has followed the acquisition of that facility. Indeed, the spread of literacy among the whites, (white illiteracy was common in South Carolina thirty years ago) has not yet ennobled that race. The Negroes are cleaner than they used to be, they dress better, they are more self-respecting, but they are not acquiring homes as fast as they acquire cars. (Nor are the white people.)

Incomparably more serious than lynching, let me stress, is Negro homicide. In the rougher Negro districts of cities it is far too common and ought to have attention from intra-racial committees. Crimes of violence in Do as You Choose Alley, (Don't you like the name?), Charleston, S. C., deserve attention of white and colored reformers too much engrossed with contemplation of white men's offences against "the race."

I would not be interpreted that there is no assertion of white supremacy in the South. It is more dangerous for a Negro than for a white man to shoot a policeman. (It is not often done.) The commanding fact is that separation of the races grows. White men do not object to Negro advance; they are increasingly willing to give them their share of the public revenues for schools and hospitals, but, unconsciously perhaps, they draw apart from the Negroes and the Negroes draw apart from them. If the races meet on terms approaching equality it is apt to be a meeting of the baser representatives of both.

As for the courts, the disposition of judges to deal toward them has always been fair, indeed, generous. The judges have in mind their shortcomings, their lack of advantages. In the great majority of cases the white juries are of the same disposition, but there are exceptional cases. The emphasis of the professional writers is on the exceptions, and many of them like to forget that ever a Negro committed a crime against a white man or woman.

In South Carolina inter-racial crime moves toward the vanishing point because of the decline of inter-racial relations.

A STATEMENT OF BELIEF
(1945)

"A Statement of Belief" was delivered before a Negro group at Morris Brown A. M. E. church, Charleston, S. C., February 2, 1945.

WHAT I say to you to-night is no more than repetition of what has been said in the *News and Courier* time and again since its editorial policy has been under my direction.

Under the constitutions and laws in the United States and the states the people are American citizens and entitled to equal and exact justice; therefore every person qualified by the laws to vote is entitled to protection in registration and voting. Intimidation, fraud, corruption of every kind ought to be punished, without discrimination as to race, color, or creed.

To insure honest and free elections the ballot should be secret. This especially is essential to the protection of the poorer and weaker people. An employe should not be exposed to domination by his employer. Therefore, he should be allowed to go into a booth where he would be "alone with his conscience and his God," and mark the candidates of his choice, as is provided by law in many states. Public officers are chosen in elections regulated by law. Primaries are not elections. They are a device for the nomination of candidates, as conventions are. The right of political parties to choose candidates by conventions, instead of primaries, cannot be questioned. No sanctity surrounds the primary system, and at one time in South Carolina, in Charleston until 1890, officers were nominated by conventions.

Every person, without discrimination as to race, color or creed, should be paid equal wages or salaries for equal service.

The right of an employer to hire whom he wishes is as good a right as is that of an employe to choose whom he shall work for.

As to this seems to be some difference of opinion. I hold that I am deprived of freedom if any person or society of persons shall tell me that I must select a white cook in preference to a colored cook. If I wish to employ, as I do, a colored barber to trim my hair, that is my business, and so it is nobody's business but mine if I employ a white man to drive my car, which I have never done. I hold that no organization of labor has a better right to monopolize a certain service than has a body of share-holders, a corporation, to monopolize the manufacture and sale of a certain kind of goods. The right of laborers to organize unions cannot be denied, and I believe that unions are advisable and valuable. I am a laborer, an employe, owning no part in the company for which I work; I belong to no union and I deny that anybody has a right to compel me to join a union.

In the use of the word democracy, which literally means government by the people, is confusion. One meaning of it is a political party and is usually spelled with a capital "D." The other, with a small "d" means government by all the people. In the United States has never been pure and unlimited democracy. Presidents are elected by states. New York has 130 times as many voters as Nevada has but only 15 times as many votes in the electoral college that chooses the president and the vice-president. So, Wyoming, with a population about equal to that of Charleston and Colleton counties together has the same strength in the United States senate, two senators, that New York with 14 million people has. We cannot have democracy in this country without wiping out the old constitution and starting over again with states stripped of their powers.

The acute racial issue in this country, at present, seems to be as to how far shall be racial separation. Whether one believes in this separation, or not, it is a fact and it will continue. I am sure that not many responsible leaders in either race desire a breakdown of all barriers and a general admixture of the two. Men can and do gather and organize in separate groups. There are white, as well as colored groups which I could not enter if I wished to do so. If the hour strikes when you can not refuse entrance to your club, or to your home to persons whom you do not want, you will cease to be free. The whole question is one of degree—how far shall the separation go. Shall races be separated in railroad cars and buses? There are ruffians in both races. Wrongs are done to Negroes in buses and the wrong-doers should be sent to jail. Would there be less friction, less ruffianism, were the two races occupying seats together than there is now? You can ponder that. Whether the white or the colored people shall sit in the front part of the car would be a matter of indifference to me, but I am convinced that disorder would be increased were they sitting together in all parts of the bus. Mark, I am saying that were there no ruffians in either race, no problem would arise. Self-respecting white men have not been lynchers. As far back as I can remember and that is 70 years, they have been struggling to suppress lynching. In South Carolina no man has been lynched since 1930. In that year two Negroes were lynched in the northern part of the state. Whatever we may say about race separation, or, if one like the term "jimcrowism," the fact of separation will continue. However colored children may go to school with white children in the North, a Charlestonian visiting in New York City will scarcely have any contact with colored persons, although in Harlem, a segregated district, are nearly half as many Negroes as live in the whole state of South Carolina. In New York City are about 500,000 colored people, and by the last census the white number in this state was 814,000. Of the 13 million colored people in the United States 4½ million in round numbers live in the North and nearly all of them live in 12 or 14 great cities. One may find in Orangeburg, town of 8,000, or in Laurens where I was raised, colored men running a business, and no one objects. Often white people patronize them. One will not see similar establishments in towns of 8,000 or 50,000 in Iowa or in New York. The really great race separation in the United States is in the rural, that is the farm and small town and city, districts of the North and West. No law prevents a colored man from working on a dairy farm in Wisconsin but one seeking a job on such a farm would meet a cold reception. The evidence, the proof of what I here say is that the millions of colored people who have migrated to the North in the last 25 or

30 years have gone to the great cities. Most of them have been farmers in the South but they are not welcomed on Northern farms.

To talk about repeal of poll-tax as a requirement for voting is, so far as this state is concerned, waste of time. Of a little more than one million adults in South Carolina more than half are not subject to poll-tax. No woman is required to pay it and no man past 60. It would be nonsense to say that any able-bodied person, white or colored, who is in his right mind, is unable to spare a dollar a year to pay a poll-tax. Of 625,000 white grownups only two in five voted in the primaries last year and only one in six in the general election.

Were attempt made to force admission of colored people into white primaries in South Carolina, the result, I think, would be destruction of the primary system and return to nominations by conventions. That might be a good thing. No law can prevent 25 or 50 white persons meeting in my lodge-room or in my house where they would decide upon candidates and if 1500 such meetings should be held which would elect delegates to county conventions, that would be the convention system. You can have conventions in your lodge rooms and homes. The objection to mixed primaries is that they would give us too much democracy. There is too much democracy in the white primary. To be sure there are numbers of colored people as capable and willing to cast an honest and intelligent ballot, as, for example, I am, but I fear that the number of colored people who could be improperly influenced is decidedly larger than in the white population. Were these added to the element of ignorance, the element whose emotions are easily aroused so that they become the prey of demagogues in the white population, the conditions would be chaotic. They are bad enough now.

With this I come to the second and more important part of this address. The ballot will never make you or any other people rich or independent, but soon or late independence, much the less riches, will give any people the ballot.

What are your opportunities in South Carolina? You are in a state of two million inhabitants, 19 million acres, or 54 persons to the square mile. The underlying cause of the horrible war in which we are engaged is land hunger. The great countries of Europe, except Russia, have from 250 to 700 to the square mile. Your opportunity in South Carolina is to go out and possess the land. It is the promised land for every man who will work, sacrifice, and save. I tell you that those who do not take and occupy this land and make the most of it here in South Carolina will be driven out of it, by newcomers, by immigrants.